641.563
L175
2015

FOND DU LAC PUBLIC LIBRARY

WITHDRAWN

P9-CDM-139

DEC 1 5 2014

the wellness kitchen

the wellness kitchen

FRESH, FLAVORFUL RECIPES FOR A HEALTHIER YOU

Paulette Lambert, RD, CDE

Avon, Massachusetts

Copyright © 2015 by Westlake Wellbeing Properties, LLC.
All rights reserved.
This book, or parts thereof, may not be reproduced in any form without permission from the publisher;
exceptions are made for brief excerpts used in published reviews.

Published by
Adams Media, a division of F+W Media, Inc.
57 Littlefield Street, Avon, MA 02322. U.S.A.
www.adamsmedia.com

ISBN 10: 1-4405-7441-3
ISBN 13: 978-1-4405-7441-2
eISBN 10: 1-4405-7442-1
eISBN 13: 978-1-4405-7442-9

Printed in the United States of America.

10   9   8   7   6   5   4   3   2   1

Library of Congress Cataloging-in-Publication Data

Lambert, Paulette.
  The Wellness Kitchen / Paulette Lambert, RD, CDE.
      pages cm
  Includes index.
  ISBN 978-1-4405-7441-2 (pb) -- ISBN 1-4405-7441-3 (pb) -- ISBN 978-1-4405-7442-9 (ebook) -- ISBN
1-4405-7442-1 (ebook)
  1. Cooking. 2. Health. I. Wellness Kitchen. II. Title.
  TX714.L3377 2014
  641.5--dc23

                    2014026447

Many of the designations used by manufacturers and sellers to distinguish their products are claimed as trademarks. Where those designations appear in this book and F+W Media, Inc. was aware of a trademark claim, the designations have been printed with initial capital letters.

Always follow safety and commonsense cooking protocol while using kitchen utensils, operating ovens and stoves, and handling uncooked food. If children are assisting in the preparation of any recipe, they should always be supervised by an adult.

The information in this book should not be used for diagnosing or treating any health problem. Not all diet and exercise plans suit everyone. You should always consult a trained medical professional before starting a diet, taking any form of medication, or embarking on any fitness or weight-training program. The author and publisher disclaim any liability arising directly or indirectly from the use of this book.

Interior photos by Harper Smith Photography, Daydreamer Productions.
Cover design by Frank Rivera.
Cover photos by Harper Smith Photography, Daydreamer Productions and © Bogdan Ionescu/123RF.

This book is available at quantity discounts for bulk purchases.
For information, please call 1-800-289-0963.

Contents

Poultry

Tofu

Chapter 6: Vegetables

Acknowledgments

I am forever grateful to every person who has contributed to this book. Many may not even know how they influenced me in a way that has enabled me to take on this project. Every patient interaction and every food experience I have had over the years has given me a portion of the insight needed for such an undertaking.

A special thanks to:

Mr. David H Murdock, whose vision inspired, bringing California Health & Longevity Institute and the Wellness Kitchen to fruition.

The Four Seasons Hotel Westlake Village, for allowing me the opportunity and support to develop a truly amazing program that was a longtime dream come true.

Becky Leehey, Executive Director at California Health & Longevity Institute, and the entire CHLI team who all touched the book along the way.

Our guests in the Wellness Kitchen in the past years who, through their enthusiasm and quest for a healthier lifestyle, have inspired me to create recipes that are truly delicious, easy, and quick.

My Wellness Kitchen chef and manager, David Kinville, who has never ceased to amaze me in his rapid transition from chef to wellness chef extraordinaire. He has provided me with endless support and many days of testing, tasting, and tweaking hundreds of recipes. His humor, energy, perseverance, and patience—and the knowledge that he always has my back—made this project doable and successful.

Our kitchen support staff, Gaby and Joanna, for the endless tasks that made running the Wellness Kitchen and producing a book possible.

The behind-the-scenes team that was the glue that held this project together and to whom I am forever indebted: Allison Kross reviewed and formatted hundreds of recipes and provided positive support each step of the way. Sara Scott and Kameron Nesen, whose organizational skills are amazing, made sure this book actually got done on time. Harper Smith, whose eye for finding beauty in everyday life is truly amazing, captured the essence of my recipes in the most beautiful photographs. Andrew Mina Hanna provided creative supporting photography. Shelby Taylor and Allie Web helped create the vision of what this book could be. Annetta Hanna and Carly Watters enthusiastically helped plan and organize the concept of the book and helped pave the way to find a publisher.

To everyone at Adams Media who believes in the message of this book along with the recipes: I could not be more honored that you have invited me to be part of your cookbook tradition.

To my family and friends who have encouraged and inspired me: The countless, memorable meals were the origin of this book. You have been supportive for years as I honed my cooking skills and my profession as well. To my son, Chase, who has been subject to endless experimental meals: Your honesty is why the food in this book is delicious. And to David, my partner in all: Thank you for always being game and supportive of any food adventure I take us on.

To everyone who helped make this happen, I send a sincere heartfelt thank-you.

Preface

As the Director of Nutrition for California Health & Longevity Institute and creator of its Wellness Kitchen, I am always surprised that most people believe it is difficult and time-consuming to eat healthily and live well. I hope the time spent delving into this book convinces you that making a few easy changes in the kitchen for optimal health and wellness can be just as quick as buying lower-quality foods, and that the dishes you make can still be delicious! My objective is to make you healthy with as little work as possible, and to have you blissfully enjoying every tantalizing bite of my healthy, nutritious food. All it takes is a dash of thought, a touch of organization, a smattering of basic skills, and, of course, fresh ingredients.

All of us at California Health & Longevity Institute's Wellness Kitchen love good food and good health. It's not just a nine-to-five occupation; it's our lives. When developing recipes for the Wellness Kitchen, taste is the first priority, but we use our professional training to tweak just about any part of a dish to make it healthy. I truly hope that this book will prove to you and your family that healthy food can be great-tasting food, too! The great benefit, of course, will be more energy, a slimmer body, and peace of mind knowing that you are engaging in a way of eating that promotes health and longevity.

If you're a novice cook, you'll find step-by-step instructions that are not intimidating or difficult. It makes our day when a guest who clearly is a novice smiles broadly and states, "I can do this!" I have designed all of the recipes with the simplest instructions possible and using basic cooking techniques. If you're a seasoned cook who has spent your fair share of hours in the kitchen, this book will add to your skill repertoire and suggest ways to revise older, unhealthier recipes with newer, healthier cooking techniques. It's often an "Ah-ha!" moment in the Wellness Kitchen when experienced cooks find out they can sauté with much less oil than they ever thought!

Over my career, I have spent much of my time in the kitchen devising ways to simplify the process of delivering a healthy, delicious meal. I know what it means to have little time; I have been a working mom. Even though I consider myself a "foodie," I've never had much patience for tedious kitchen tasks. Between work, driving my son to soccer practice, and finding time to hit the hiking trail, I always looked for ways to be more efficient and timely. In my opinion and experience, fast food can be real food, and healthy, if you know how to do it. Watch for the tips given throughout the book—they will help broaden your skills in food preparation and nutrition. These tips will help you plan ahead, work faster, and cut down the amount of time you spend in the kitchen. (For those who need help with specific medical concerns, such as heart disease, please see the General Nutrition Guidelines chapter in Part 1 of the book for more specific, in-depth information on eating for health and specific disease prevention.)

Knowledge is power, but the power of practice is much more important. You must cook great food over and over again, until it becomes second nature, until it becomes habit. Practice various recipes until you find them easy and then move on to others. Perform these new cooking skills until they come naturally, even if it means that you start out with something as simple as a natural peanut butter and banana sandwich on whole-grain bread versus opting for processed food. Make a habit of eating new foods that are not processed, such as "whole-grain only" carbohydrates, natural peanut butter with no added sugars, fish, and fresh vegetables. Believe it or not, you can develop a taste for these ingredients, and studies tell us that you can change your food preferences if you take the time to work at it. I cannot believe how many men come into the Wellness Kitchen adamantly opposed to consuming any vegetables, only to ask for seconds of the cauliflower soup with truffle oil. You can change your attitude about what you eat, and the way you eat it, one meal at a time. You can master this!

I hope you enjoy my seasonal selections as well. I think that you'll find the Cedar-Grilled Salmon with Fresh Herbs (Chapter 5), with its hint of smokiness, absolutely delectable, and the Couscous and Arugula Salad with Fresh Basil Dressing (Chapter 3) outright addictive—and that once you've tasted any of our silky, puréed soups, you'll be craving vegetables in a way you never thought you could. The best outcome would be that you eat healthily because it tastes so good and it's easy to do. And better yet, it's guilt-free!

Bon appétit—and to your health,

Paulette

Part 1
For Your Health

What Is the Wellness Kitchen?

The Wellness Kitchen is a real place, an open, light-filled teaching kitchen and dining room that, as part of California Health & Longevity Institute, is set in the lush gardens of the Four Seasons Hotel Westlake Village in Los Angeles. There, as small groups of people gather in classes to cook, chat, and enjoy the meals they have prepared, I share what is, to most of them, an entirely new way to approach food and health.

By the end of their visit, participants have created and tasted a number of dishes, and they have learned how to prepare meals that are truly healthy and downright delicious. I don't call what I do cooking classes—they are more like culinary experiences where people get a chance to rediscover the pleasures of fresh ingredients, simple recipes, and glorious tastes. And yet when this approach to cooking and eating is applied to everyday life, the results have proven to be transformative.

Over the course of my thirty-two-year career as a registered dietitian, I have created healthy recipes and easy meal plans that have helped thousands of people regain their health and lose literally hundreds of pounds, one simple, scrumptious dish at a time. If you have watched past seasons of ABC's *Extreme Makeover: Weight Loss Edition*, you have seen me teach the show's participants, all of whom are at least 100 pounds overweight, how to cook and eat from the Wellness Kitchen.

It has been tremendously rewarding to see these folks regain normal lives after spending years trapped by diet-related illnesses, massive weight, and unhealthy lifestyles. Their radical transformation is based on the same insights, techniques, and recipes that I share with all of our guests at the Wellness Kitchen—and now with you, in this book.

Some take my classes to learn how to make healthy dishes that their families will enjoy. Others come to gain new insights to help them prevent, manage, or reverse chronic and debilitating diseases, including heart disease, hypertension, type 2 diabetes, and some types of cancer. Many of them come simply because they want to make better food and have more fun in the kitchen.

A few of my students are highly experienced cooks; many barely know how to handle a knife. But luckily, nothing is complicated at the Wellness Kitchen. There are no difficult recipes, no strict regimens, no forbidden food groups. What we do have is a plan that works. If you want to cook and eat for genuine pleasure, maximum health, and optimal body weight, you can learn to do so at the Wellness Kitchen.

Too many people today are overwhelmed by the prospect of substituting healthy choices for all the cheap, fast, and unhealthy foods that fill grocery store shelves and restaurant menus. But no matter where you are starting from, you can follow the Wellness Kitchen's recipes. And just about anyone will gain energy, normalize their glucose levels, and improve their blood pressure by following the 21-Day Food Plan of modest, sustainable changes. That is because everything in this book reflects the evidence-based best practices that have been established by medical and nutritional research.

Despite all the diet fads and contradictory "breakthroughs" that are hyped online, on TV, or in bookstores, medical researchers are in agreement about a number of guidelines for healthy nutrition. Rigorous studies conducted over decades all point to the importance of a balanced, plant-based diet, with small amounts of meat, if desired. In addition, they've clearly demonstrated that the standard American diet is, at best, making us fat and prone to diseases. At worst, it's killing us. (You'll read more about this in the next pages.)

As a trained nutritionist and chef, I am committed to showing people how to cook and eat well for both health and pleasure. I have spent thousands of hours chopping, mixing, and sautéing alongside regular folks with average to nonexistent cooking skills. I know what most people can produce with a knife and pan—and what they'll be happy to dive into with a knife and fork. So I have developed hundreds of quick, tasty, family-friendly recipes, with step-by-step directions and easy-to-find ingredients.

This is a simple way to cook. No matter where you're starting from, you'll find that you can follow my recipes. Even better, you'll discover that the food you prepare is fresh, flavorful, and absolutely delicious. That's the Wellness Kitchen approach to a healthy diet!

The Case for Change

Today, we have a much greater understanding of anti-aging techniques and chronic disease prevention than ever before. Nutrition, the cornerstone of a healthy lifestyle, is a "magic pill" that can offer life-altering benefits. Many chronic diseases are preventable, treatable, or at least deferrable with good nutrition.

A 2012 study by the Commonwealth Fund showed that the United States is no healthier than twelve other developed countries that spend less on health care. We are meeting neither the human body's potential for quality of life nor its potential for longevity. According to the Centers for Disease Control, 68 percent of the U.S. population is overweight: of that, 34 percent of the population is considered obese, while one-third of children nationwide are either overweight or obese. Heart disease is the number-one killer of both men and women, 80 percent of which is preventable with lifestyle changes. It is predicted that one-third of the U.S. population will have type 2 diabetes by 2020, yet the disease is 90 percent preventable. One out of two men and one out of three women will have cancer in their lifetime, yet it can be 65 percent preventable with lifestyle changes.

What we need is health care reform, but not just the financial kind. As a country, we need to change the actual way we live our lives, down to the very food on our plate. We can no longer think of healthy eating as a lifestyle choice—we must consider it a necessity.

How We Got Here

The situation is clear: Americans are getting sicker and sicker from our poor food choices. We got to this point when the availability and intake of cheap, poor-quality food dramatically increased. In the early 1970s, the American food industry changed. Industrialized farming of corn and soy brought hydrogenated soybean and corn oil and high-fructose corn syrup to the food industry. This allowed for greater advances in processing food, giving it a long shelf life and the taste of sugar and fat that humans can't resist. The soft drink industry boomed thanks to the cheap source of sugar. Medical academia wrongly pointed fingers at fat alone as being responsible for heart disease, which fueled a whole new industry of fat-free or low-fat processed foods that were high in sugar. The downside: none of these foods were healthy.

For a few generations now, we have been increasingly less likely to prepare our own food. No longer do we have to make pizza from scratch; we can heat up a frozen pie, or grab one from the nearest chain pizzeria. Prior to these revolutions in food production, which transformed the way Americans choose and prepare food, the concern was simply about getting enough food to eat. While in many parts of the world people lack enough food of any kind, Americans are faced with a different issue: too much poor-quality food.

To say I am disappointed in and angry with the government and its collusion with the food industry is a gross understatement. We hear chatter in Washington about government-imposed regulations, possible taxes on junk food, even government regulations on portion sizing; but all of those propositions would take years to come to fruition. The food industry is making token efforts to reform, but these are simply not enough—and none of it is transforming fast enough to head off the disaster we are facing individually and as a nation.

What Can We Do? Cook!

So, what is the solution to this grim situation?

1. Eat less processed food.
2. Consume proper portion sizes.
3. Cook your food yourself!

Think of this three-step plan as the solution to the health care crisis. Sounds so simple, yet many of us still struggle.

Before 1970, almost everyone cooked. It was what you did; it was not an option. You learned how to cook from your mother, or had to teach yourself. With the onset of processed foods, we no longer had to cook, which has resulted in diminished abilities and skills in the kitchen. Today, Americans cook about 50 percent less often than we did before 1970. We can even approximate the obesity rates and overall health of a culture when we know how many minutes its members spend in the kitchen each day; the less time spent in the kitchen, the more obesity and chronic disease there will be.

We need to go back to cooking, but this time with more thought and efficiency. We need to incorporate all of what modern science, technology, and medicine offer us and put it on the dinner plate, one delicious meal at a time—and in a short time! Modern science and medicine, with long-term studies, have proven that a plant-based diet promotes health and longevity. Technology has made it easier to eat healthily in many cases: We can purchase flash-frozen vegetables and fruits that are as high in nutrients as fresh—maybe higher in some cases—and that can be prepared in a few minutes in the microwave. The produce sections of markets are filled with pre-prepped and washed produce in antibacterial packaging that makes fixing a salad as easy as opening the package and pouring it into a bowl.

The time for action is now, and I am going to help you, one step at a time. With the strategies in this book and a willingness to participate in the process of change, you'll find you look and feel better. My experience in the Wellness Kitchen, with thousands of guests, has shown me that many of us are motivated but aren't quite sure what to do or how to get the ball rolling toward healthy living. This book is designed to help you begin to make these kinds of changes. The Wellness Kitchen plan is not extreme; it doesn't eliminate entire food groups, and it's not a crash-and-burn diet. This book is a training manual for sustainable improvement that will inspire you to change your eating forever.

How to Use This Book

First and foremost, this is not a diet book with specific diet restrictions, fads, or diet concepts of the moment. What I present to you is the latest scientific knowledge regarding nutrition and health, expertise in interpreting that knowledge in practical terms, and years of experience creating healthy meals. I offer no recipes requiring elaborate techniques and hours in the kitchen to prepare, or exotic, hard-to-find ingredients. Instead you will find a guide for healthy living that is within reach, whether or not you can cook. Since good nutrition is the cornerstone of good health, I have included sections on chronic disease prevention and treatment along with specific menus for

breakfast, lunch, snacks, and dinners for those who desire weight loss.

I would like to think of this book as a practical healthy-eating guide that you can use every day you cook, the go-to guide when the question "What's to eat?" comes up in your home. I designed this book so that you can cook from it every day, even holidays and special occasions, knowing that it's all healthy and yet wonderful food. I tell you what I know both in terms of clinical nutrition and culinary arts, melding it together so you can be confident that when you cook with these recipes, you are providing yourself and your family with healthy and delicious food. When your kids, or even grownups, clamor for Italian food, you can be certain that our Turkey Meatballs al Forno (Chapter 5) or our Chicken Parmesan with Basic Tomato Sauce (Chapter 5) served with shredded zucchini will make everyone happy and promote good health, too. It's the kind of quick and easy cooking that makes healthy eating realistic for all of us. The focus of this book is on bringing a nutritious, plant-based diet to life with vibrant recipes such as Miso Grilled Salmon with Bok Choy (Chapter 5) or Perfect Roasted Chicken with Broccoli Rabe and Potatoes (Chapter 5), which you can prepare easily and in a short amount of time. We have even included desserts that are "less bad" for you that make use of wonderful seasonal fruits such as Balsamic Roasted Strawberries (Chapter 8) to top lite ice cream. Along with the recipes, I have included tips, shortcuts, and nutrition pointers to help increase your culinary skills and understanding of nutrition. In addition, basic recipes with variations will help you become an intuitive cook. By learning a fundamental technique with one recipe, you can change a few ingredients and have another great recipe. We become better cooks when we develop knowledge about a technique and then use it different ways. A Chicken Sauté (Chapter 5) can have a variety of lite sauces, giving us three different chicken dishes—Piccata, Marsala, and Dijon. Roasted Green Beans with Pine Nuts (see Roasted Vegetables in Chapter 6) uses the same technique as roasted broccoli, carrots, and many other wonderful vegetables. I hope that the book's practical information and tips will upgrade your cooking abilities and your understanding of the concepts of good nutrition.

Pantry Basics for a Healthy Diet

In this section, you'll find a list of widely available products that make great replacements for the less wholesome equivalents you may be buying. I've also included the criteria for the right margarine, the best choices for your morning cereal, and a list of common spices that will improve not only the taste of your cooking but your health as well. Try these foods for a while until they become your new norm. Your taste buds will adjust to these healthier options, usually within three weeks.

Cold Cereals

Choose cereals with 5 or more grams of fiber and less than 10 grams of sugar per serving. Here are some options:

- Fiber One
- All Bran Buds, 51% fiber
- Kashi cereals, such as Good Friends, Heart to Heart, GOLEAN, Autumn Wheat, Island Vanilla
- Bran flakes
- Plain shredded wheat with bran

Hot Cereals

- Oatmeal, plain old-fashioned or quick-cooking
- Oat bran
- McCann's Quick & Easy Steel-Cut Irish Oatmeal
- McCann's Instant Steel-Cut Irish Oatmeal (microwavable)
- Kashi Heart to Heart

Breads

Choose bread products with 3 or more grams of fiber per serving. These types are good choices:

- Rye
- 100% whole-grain (not simply 100% whole wheat)
- Whole-wheat sourdough

- Whole-grain high-fiber English muffins
- Corn tortillas
- La Tortilla Factory Low Carb, High Fiber tortillas (various flavors) or other low-carb, high-fiber tortillas
- Whole-grain pita bread
- Oroweat Double Fiber Bread and English muffins
- Thomas Double Fiber Honey Wheat and Multi-Grain Fiber Goodness English muffins

Pasta
- Barilla Plus, high-protein, high-fiber pastas
- Whole-wheat pasta

Other Grains
- Brown rice
- Whole-grain couscous
- Near East Lentil Pilaf
- Quick-cooking brown rice
- Barley
- Farro
- Quinoa
- Lentils

Crackers and Snacks
- Reduced Fat Triscuits
- Ak-Mak crackers
- RyKrisp
- Kashi TLC crackers
- Kavli crispbread
- Wasa crispbread
- Reduced Fat Wheat Thins
- Genisoy Soy Crisps
- Fat-free graham crackers
- Orville Redenbacher or Pop Secret mini, lite popcorn bags
- Tostitos Baked! tortilla chips

Mayonnaise and Salad Dressings
- Lite mayonnaise
- Olive oil mayonnaise
- Newman's Own Lighten Up! salad dressings, any variety
- Girard's Light Caesar and Champagne
- Follow Your Heart low-fat dressings
- Flavored vinegars, balsamic or champagne

Margarines and Oils
Choose options that have no trans fat and less than 2 grams of saturated fat.

- Brummel & Brown
- Promise Light
- Smart Balance Omega-3 or Light, soft tub-style margarine
- I Can't Believe It's Not Butter!
- Extra-virgin olive oil
- PAM organic olive oil or canola oil cooking spray

Nuts and Nut Butters
- Unsalted nuts, such as almonds, peanuts, walnuts, pecans, pistachios
- Emerald 100-calorie nut packs
- Seeds, such as pumpkin, sesame, and sunflower
- Natural, no-sugar-added peanut butter (it will likely have oil on top in the jar)
- Natural soy, almond, or sunflower seed butter

Dairy or Dairy Substitutes
Choose organic dairy products when possible (they're antibiotic- and hormone-free).

- Nonfat or 1% milk
- Nonfat lite yogurt, with less than 20 grams total carbs per serving
- Nonfat or low-fat cottage cheese
- Nonfat Greek yogurt, with less than 20 grams total carbs and 120 calories per serving

- Fat-free half-and-half
- Organic soymilk
- Silk, EdenSoy, WestSoy, or 8th Continent organic soymilk
- Soy creamer
- Almond milk (An important note: almond milk is low in protein, so look for protein-fortified options. Soymilk contains the same protein content that cow's milk does, 8 grams per 8 oz. serving, equivalent to 1 oz. of complete protein.)
- Alpine Lace provolone, mozzarella, Parmesan, feta, or low-fat cheeses with less than 6 grams of fat per oz.
- Laughing Cow reduced-fat cheese wedges
- Laughing Cow Mini Babybel Bonbel Light Cheese
- Lite string cheese
- Reduced-fat Mexican blend shredded cheese
- Daiya soy cheese

Meats
- Hormone-free, antibiotic-free chicken breast or ground turkey
- Grass-fed lean ground beef
- Nitrate-free deli turkey or chicken
- Wild or farmed fish (from the United States, Canada, or Northern European countries such as Norway or Scotland)

Dry Goods
- Sardines
- Foil-pouch or canned wild salmon
- Pomi tomatoes (avoid cans of tomatoes that contain BHP)

Soups—Reduced Sodium
Choose fat-free, low-sodium versions.

- Progresso Heart Healthy and Light soups, any variety
- Campbell's Healthy Request soups, any variety
- Amy's Organic Light in Sodium soups, any variety
- Chicken, beef, or vegetable broth, organic, reduced sodium, and fat-free
- Health Valley soups, any variety

Proteins
- Canned beans, organic, such as garbanzo, kidney, black, cannellini
- Canned or foil-pouch wild salmon
- Canned or foil-pouch light (less mercury than the white) tuna

Fruits and Vegetables
- Boxed diced tomatoes
- Sun-dried tomatoes, not in oil
- Marinara or tomato-based pasta sauce

Frozen Foods
- Boca or MorningStar Farms soy-based veggie burgers
- Frozen unsweetened fruit, any variety, organic if possible
- Frozen vegetables without sauce, any variety
- Birds Eye Steamfresh vegetable packs
- Frozen edamame beans
- Wild-caught peeled and deveined large shrimp
- Frozen organic precooked brown rice
- Frozen grain products, such as brown rice, barley, etc.
- Sweet potato fries (to bake)
- Dreyer's or Edy's Slow Churned fat-free frozen yogurt
- Frozen chopped herb cubes, basil, cilantro, parsley

Frozen Entrées

Choose options with less than 10 grams total fat, less than 4 grams saturated fat, and less than 800 milligrams sodium.

- Healthy Choice
- Lean Cuisine, Honestly Good
- Weight Watchers
- Amy's
- Gardein

Condiments and Seasonings

- Kosher or sea salt
- Ground black pepper
- Honey
- Pure maple syrup
- Dijon mustard
- Chopped garlic
- Chopped ginger
- Dried herbs and spices, oregano, basil, thyme, nutmeg, cinnamon, etc.

Desserts

Limit amounts for weight management.

- Dreyer's or Edy's Slow Churned lite ice cream or frozen yogurt
- Healthy Choice low-fat Fudge Bars
- Frozen yogurt or sorbet under 120 calories per serving
- Skinny Cow Fudge Bar

Drinks

- Flavored waters with no added sugar
- Flavored sport drinks, with no more than 10 calories per 8-oz. serving
- Diet sodas (avoid cola drinks for bone health)

Going Organic

Most of us recognize the importance of buying food that doesn't contain potentially harmful pesticides, antibiotics, or other additives. Looking for organic generally implies that you're buying a cleaner, healthier option. But what does organic actually mean? Though farming practices vary, organic plants are generally grown without the use of pesticides or industrial fertilizers, and organically raised animals are not routinely treated with antibiotics or growth hormones. Organic foods typically contain no genetically modified organisms (GMOs).

Many of us favor the kinder, "gentler to the planet" way of organic farming; one can assume that what is good for the health of the planet would be better for humans as well. That premise alone makes a sound argument for going organic.

But in many matters, a black-and-white way of looking at something may not be the best practice for the majority of us. While we can make assumptions that organic food is better, it's best to look at the hard evidence compiled to date to determine the real benefit to our health. There are hundreds of studies on the differences between conventional and organic food production. The most recent consensus, based on 250 individual studies published in the *Annals of Internal Medicine* in 2012, is that organic produce reduces exposure to pesticide residue about 30 percent overall. Pesticide residue is a bigger concern with some fruits and vegetables than others. Conventionally farmed meat, chicken,

pork, and dairy were 33 percent more likely to harbor antibiotic-resistant bacteria, which is becoming a growing concern of the medical community in terms of public health as well as individual health.

So what is the bottom line? If you can afford organic food, buy it. However, if you are comparing prices and cringing as many of us do, you may be wondering what your options are. How can you improve the quality of your food if all organic isn't affordable or available?

First and foremost, increase your overall produce intake, regardless of whether you can eat organic or not. The health benefits are so significant that it outweighs the risk more times than not.

Buying Organic, the Smart Way

For produce, it's wise to buy organic for the "dirty dozen." These are twelve fruits and veggies that contain the most pesticide residues when tested by the not-for-profit Environmental Working Group (*www.ewg.org*). The dirty dozen includes:

1. peaches
2. apples
3. sweet bell peppers
4. celery
5. nectarines
6. strawberries
7. cherries
8. lettuce

9. imported grapes
10. pears
11. spinach
12. potatoes

If you cannot buy the "dirty dozen" produce organic, be sure to wash, rinse well, and peel, whenever possible, to lower the risk of contamination.

Many experts recommend buying organic meats, chicken, dairy, and eggs. If organic meats are over your budget, look for labels that state "growth hormone free" and "antibiotic free"—you can find these options in most major markets nowadays. While the meat may not be totally organic, it does have a lower risk of hormone and antibiotic contamination.

Shop large warehouse and discount markets that are now promoting their own brands of organic foods. Prices are much lower because of much larger production quantities, and these brands often include many products priced just a little higher than conventionally produced food.

Organic baby food is recommended if possible. Very young children do not have the physical ability to get rid of contaminants like adults do. Buy organic baby food at the supermarket or make your own from organic foods.

Not all food has to be organic to be safe and environmentally friendly. The risk of pesticide contamination is around 80 percent in foreign produce but only 20 percent in U.S. produce.

The Environmental Protection Agency (EPA) has developed detailed science policies describing the methods it uses to quantify pesticide dietary risks. The Dietary Risk Index (DRI) is based on these methods and on the EPA's evaluation of pesticide toxicity. The Organic Center (*www.organic-center.org*) has put together a list in which produce is scored with a DRI number from the EPA's data (lower numbers mean fewer pesticides):

Fruit	Score
Peach	100 (highest pesticide load)
Apple	93
Sweet Bell Pepper	83
Celery	82
Nectarine	81
Strawberries	80
Cherries	73
Kale	69
Lettuce	67
Grapes—Imported	66
Carrot	63
Pear	63
Collard Greens	60
Spinach	58
Potato	56
Green Beans	53
Summer Squash	53
Pepper	51
Cucumber	50
Raspberries	46
Grapes—Domestic	44
Plum	44
Orange	44
Cauliflower	39
Tangerine	37
Mushrooms	36
Banana	34
Winter Squash	34
Cantaloupe	33
Cranberries	33
Honeydew Melon	30
Grapefruit	29
Sweet Potato	29
Tomato	29
Broccoli	28
Watermelon	26
Papaya	20
Eggplant	20
Cabbage	17
Kiwi	13
Sweet Peas—Frozen	10
Asparagus	10
Mango	9

Fruit	Score
Pineapple	7
Sweet Corn—Frozen	2
Avocado	1
Onion	1 (lowest pesticide load)

The EPA regulations have no impact on foreign imports, so one of the ways to ensure you're eating food with less potential for contamination is to avoid foreign produce as much as possible. This means buying more locally grown, seasonal produce. Food grown close to where you live is always the best choice, and food grown in the United States is a much better choice than imported, especially when concerned about contamination. In the off season, try using U.S.-grown frozen fruits and vegetables to supplement what is seasonal versus buying imported off-season produce.

Since expense is the major barrier to an organic diet, I think spending food dollars wisely and buying better-quality food should be a priority. But paying twice as much for organic broccoli when the DRI is only 28, or for bananas with a DRI of 38 (and you peel them anyway), is probably not the best way to prioritize food dollars. In my household, I make it a priority to buy organic milk and yogurt, as well as organic or hormone- and antibiotic-free meat and chicken; but I buy less of those items than most Americans do. Industrial production of livestock has allowed us to eat larger portions of animal protein than we need for good health and weight management. My philosophy is to buy better quality, but buy less: 1 pound of animal protein is enough for three adults/teens, or two adults and two young children. Another way to not break the bank at the meat counter is to serve animal protein less often. Not only does eating vegetarian meals improve your health and save your wallet, it also helps save the environment by using fewer resources in production, i.e., less feed and water. Being a total vegetarian may not be appealing to many of us, but being a "flexitarian," one who consumes a diet with both cuisines, really is a deal for both your health and your budget.

Guidelines for Washing Produce

Whether you buy organic or not, it's important to clean your produce before you eat it. This might seem obvious, but many people skip this step, or don't do a complete job. Here are some tips for making sure your food is clean and ready to eat.

- Firm fruits or veggies: Hold under warm, running water for 10 to 15 seconds, scrubbing with your hands or, better yet, a produce brush.
- Fragile fruits, such as berries: Place in a colander and gently tumble the fruit as you rinse.
- Salad greens: Wash in cold, running water to maintain crispness.
- Potatoes and other "underground" veggies: Scrub vigorously with a brush.
- Melons or citrus fruits you cut, such as lemons: Scrub the outer rind with warm, soapy water so the knife won't drag surface bacteria into the fruit.

(Source: Penn State University, College of Agricultural Sciences)

General Nutrition Guidelines

In thirty-plus years of guiding thousands of clients through nutrition changes, I understand how overwhelming the process can seem. We often think we are resistant to change when, in fact, we make many changes all the time, from where we purchase our gas to how we use our tech-toys. We experiment, we have positive experiences, and we get excited about new ideas and directions. If something does not work one way, we try it another way. We overcome one obstacle at a time, and that is exactly how I want you to use this book. Don't worry about overhauling your entire diet in one day. In fact, eating to prevent or treat a disease can start with something as simple as eating two pieces of fruit a day and moving forward from there! Making a change in your nutritional intake is about:

- Ensuring better health
- Picking up new skills for healthier food preparation
- Adopting a new way of thinking about food
- Taking personal responsibility!

While each chronic disease does have specific recommendations for prevention or treatment, a healthy diet boosts your overall well-being. No matter what age or state of health you're in, eating healthier foods helps all your body's systems—including immune, digestive, and muscular—function at optimal levels.

Nutrition Basics

I often get asked, "Aren't I too old to start eating healthy?" No! It's never too late to benefit, but obviously the younger you start, the better. All ages benefit from eating a healthier diet, whether it's for prevention or treatment. Each chronic disease has target strategies that address that particular disease but, again, a healthy diet is the same basic diet for everyone, no matter what the disease or the age.

Daily Nutritional Guidelines

Here's a summary of the latest research on what constitutes a healthy diet. This basic plan can prevent or treat many chronic diseases, and can add years of quality life and wellness.

Fruits and Vegetables

A rule of thumb is to eat 7 to 10 servings of fruits or vegetables per day. One serving equals ½ cup cooked, or 1 cup raw, including dark salad greens (not iceberg lettuce). Mother Nature color-coded most vegetables and fruits; the brighter and more vibrant the colors, the higher the antioxidant level. Our plates should be a rainbow of colors; not only does that look more appealing, it's better for you!

Whole-Grain Carbohydrates

Carbohydrates that are high in fiber, such as whole-grain breads, brown rice, barley, oats, lentils, beans, and ancient grains such as quinoa, are best. They need to be consumed in the right quantities for age and activity (see Meal Plans for specific amounts based on your caloric needs). Aim for a diet that is low in refined carbohydrates such as white bread, refined cereals, white rice, and white pasta.

Sugar

You definitely want to limit your sugar intake. This includes any white sugar, corn syrup, honey, agave, maple syrup, and any other sweetener with calories and the potential to increase inflammation. Recommended amounts are no more than 25 grams a day of added sugar for men and women. Added sugar means not what is naturally in fruits and vegetables but those added either by processing or in food preparation. Four grams of sugar is equal to one teaspoon of sugar. So, for example, one 12-oz. soda has 40 grams of sugar, which means 10 teaspoons of added sugar! Remember, sugar is added to many processed foods, so get used to reading labels!

Another important point to remember is that sugar is sugar, even if it's in a "natural" state. Honey, agave, and maple syrup are often touted as better for you, but the truth is that they contain the same nutrient content and cause the same cellular damage in large amounts as white table sugar or high-fructose corn syrup. The amount of antioxidants present in sugars in the "natural" state is so minimal that it would take pounds of natural sugars a day to really make a difference in your antioxidant intake. There are much healthier ways to get more antioxidants into your diet. While there is natural sugar present in vegetables and fruits, the fructose level, the damaging part of all sugars, is relatively small compared to sugars added to processed foods.

Fruits and vegetables are packed with nutrients, vitamins, minerals, antioxidants, and fiber that slows down the metabolism of those natural sugars, causing much less inflammation than those added to processed foods.

Healthy Fats

Fats such as olive oil, canola oil, grape seed oil, nuts, nut butters, seeds, and avocado are optimal, considered to be healthy fats, helping to decrease inflammation in the body. Everyone's intake should be low in hydrogenated and partially hydrogenated vegetable oils, trans fats, and saturated fats that are considered to be unhealthy fats, increasing the inflammation in the body that is the base of chronic disease. Recommended saturated fat intake is no more than 16 grams per day for men and 10 grams per day for women and children. While trans fat has been removed from the majority of processed foods (though it's still found in large amounts in movie popcorn, among other things), hydrogenated and partially hydrogenated fats are used in oils designed for deep-fat frying, commercial baked goods, snack foods, and coffee creamers.

Animal Protein

Men need no more than 10–12 ounces per day and women and children no more than 6–8 ounces per day of animal protein. The more you consume, the higher your saturated fat intake is, even in fish and chicken. Physical activity generally does not impact your protein needs, not unless you are an elite professional athlete—so even if you're getting a lot of exercise, you don't need to eat more animal protein.

Limit Red Meat

Twice per week is plenty, not only because of its saturated fat, but also because of the higher cancer risk from the red meat pigment itself.

Increase Fish

Three meals per week is ideal. If that seems like a lot, remember to include fish in your lunches as well as dinners—for example, fish tacos, sushi, and salmon salad.

Vegetable Protein

Three to five of your meals each week should be high in, or made up of, vegetarian proteins, such as beans, lentils, nuts, nut butters, or soy.

Eat Clean

When you can, consume organic poultry, free of antibodies and hormones; organic dairy; and grass-fed beef. Consume more vegetable protein meals to balance out the increased cost of the higher-quality animal proteins.

Sodium

The recommended sodium intake is 2,300 milligrams per day. Most added salt is found in processed foods and condiments, so limit sauces such as salad dressing, mustard, barbecue sauce, etc. to 1–2 tablespoons per meal. Focus on eating real, fresh foods that are less processed. Instead of using salt, flavor your food with lots of herbs and spices, as they are full of antioxidants to prevent chronic disease. For example, fresh herbs such as basil, cilantro, and parsley are generally higher in antioxidants per gram than most vegetables and fruits, so adding handfuls to your food not only improves flavor but gives you a large health boost as well. (Try adding these herbs to your daily smoothie or check out our Green Rice recipe in Chapter 7.)

Eating to Manage and Reverse Chronic Disease

A chronic disease is a long-lasting condition that can be controlled but not always cured. Common chronic diseases include:

- Heart disease
- Hypertension
- Diabetes
- Cancer
- Alzheimer's disease

Chronic diseases also:

- Take place over a long period of time
- Cause premature aging and death
- Negatively affect quality of life and life expectancy

What Causes Premature Chronic Disease?

The human body does have a life span—but for most of us it should be into the late 80s or longer, even as long as 100 for many of us! Because of poor lifestyle choices, we are experiencing chronic diseases much earlier in our lives than we should, shortening our life expectancy and diminishing our quality of life sooner than biologically expected.

Our immune system protects us during short-term bouts of ill health; it's how the body heals itself from illness and trauma. Chronic, long-term inflammation, however, harms rather than heals, because the immune system attack never stops. When the immune system is triggered at a low level (because of irritants such as extra body fat or environmental toxins), it disengages the shutoff button, resulting in an endless trickle of immune cells that interfere with the body's healthy tissue.

Poor lifestyle choices can increase inflammation in the following ways:

- Smoking not only causes damage to the lungs themselves, but causes an inflammatory response throughout the cardiovascular system.
- Multiple studies show that consistent and moderate exercise decreases inflammation. If you're not exercising, you're increasing your risk for inflammation.
- Gum disease is also associated with coronary heart disease. Gum disease can cause inflammation in the body. Bacteria from gum disease enters the bloodstream and can harm organs and increase overall inflammation in the body.
- Large waist circumference (over 35 inches for women, over 40 inches for men) is associated with inflammation because of the metabolic disturbance and insulin resistance that result from a large amount of abdominal body fat.

These factors increase risk of coronary heart disease, type 2 diabetes, and breast cancer.

- A diet high in processed foods and low in fruits and vegetables is high in unhealthy fats and sugars, which cause metabolic changes that increase overall inflammation. A diet low in fruits and vegetables does not have the antioxidants, fiber, and other nutrients needed to prevent inflammation.
- Excess body weight and obesity increases hormones that are proinflammatory.
- Environmental contamination—such as smoke, additives in food, or chemical exposure—can increase your body's levels of inflammation, leading to poor overall health. Taking control of your diet and introducing healthy foods can help reduce these types of inflammation.

Heart Disease

How Does Inflammation Cause Heart Disease?

Inflammation influences the formation of artery-blocking clots, and it can trigger the immune system to form plaque in artery walls. Bad cholesterol (low-density lipoprotein, or LDL) filtrates into the artery wall, causing a blisterlike formation and the release of proteins called cytokines that lead to inflammation. The cytokines make the arterial wall sticky, which causes the immune system cells to be activated. To contain the damage, the body triggers an inflammatory response. The immune system cells engulf the fat particles, forming a plaque that builds up in the artery walls. In this inflammation process, the plaques can rupture, causing a clot to form, resulting in a heart attack.

The Goals of a Heart-Healthy Diet
- Reduce inflammation and clotting.

- Stabilize plaques so they do not rupture.
- "Shrink" existing plaques and improve blood flow.

Targeted Strategies That Make a Difference
- Decrease body fat; lose weight if needed.
- Consume less animal protein at meals to decrease saturated fat. Men should eat no more than 10 oz. per day, women no more than 8 oz. per day. Add vegetable protein, beans, nuts, nut butter, or soy, up to 5 meals or more per week.
- Eat fish or seafood 3 times per week or more.
- Consume 7–10 servings of fruit and vegetables per day.
- Eliminate hydrogenated or partially hydrogenated fats and trans fats, and limit saturated fat to 16 grams per day for men, 10 grams per day for women and children—including that found in animal protein.
- Use healthy fats, such as olive oil, canola oil, grape seed oil, trans-fat-free oils, low-saturated-fat margarine, nuts, or avocado.
- Limit added sugars to no more than 25 grams per day.
- Change carbohydrate servings to whole-grain breads, high-fiber cereals, oats, and ancient grains.
- Take vitamin D and omega-3 supplements (1000 IU of vitamin D and 1000 mg of fish oil for omega-3) if you're not eating fish three times per week.

Hypertension

How Does Inflammation Cause Hypertension?

High blood pressure, also called hypertension, results in abnormal vascular changes that increase the pressure of the flow of blood through arteries, damaging the cardiovascular system and leading to a heart attack or stroke. It is not clear whether inflammation triggers hypertension or hypertension causes an increase in inflammation, but either way inflammation increases risk of a heart attack or stroke. Hypertension, along with elevated C-Reactive Protein (CRP) levels (found through a blood test that indicates inflammation), makes the risk of a heart attack or stroke eight times higher.

The Goal of an Anti-Hypertension Diet

- Decrease blood pressure to safe levels through lower intake of sodium and sugar, and weight loss.

Targeted Strategies That Make a Difference

- Decrease body weight if necessary. Even losing 5–15 pounds can help to decrease blood pressure.
- Consume 7–10 servings of fruit and vegetables per day. The minerals and ions in produce help your kidneys regulate fluid, which also helps decrease blood pressure.
- Decrease sodium in your diet to less than 2300 mg per day.
- Decrease added sugar to less than 25 grams per day.
- Increase fiber to 30–40 grams per day by consuming whole grains and a high intake of fruit and vegetables.
- Increase cardiovascular exercise, beginning with walking 30 minutes per day.

Diabetes

How Does Inflammation Cause Diabetes?

Extra body fat produces inflammation that blocks insulin's ability to work, causing insulin resistance, which can result in diabetes.

The Goal of a Diabetes-Preventive Diet

- Increase insulin sensitivity by achieving ideal body weight.
- Control timing and quantity of carbohydrate-heavy foods to avoid high glycemic load (eating too many carbs at any given time can cause blood sugars to spike higher than normal if insulin is not working properly, or if you are deficient in insulin. Even moderately high glucose levels cause micro-vascular damage).

Targeted Strategies That Make a Difference

- Monitoring the quantity of carbohydrate foods you consume is of the utmost importance. Control the amount of carbohydrate food consumed at one time, for example; limit grains and starches to 1 cup per meal (with no bread), or 2 pieces of bread, not both.
- Consume a snack of fruit between meals to lower glycemic load at mealtimes.
- Timing counts; distribute carbohydrates evenly throughout the day. Avoid skipping breakfast or lunch and then overconsuming later in the day, which leads to a high glycemic load.
- Eat 3 meals with 1–2 snacks. Snacks allow for spreading out of carbohydrate foods, which lowers the glycemic load. Meals and snacks should be at least 2 hours apart.

- Avoid highly refined, "white" carbohydrates; consume mostly whole grains that are higher in fiber and take longer to digest, therefore not elevating glucose levels as much.
- Lose weight; 10–15 pounds can make the difference in insulin's ability to work.

Cancer

How Does Inflammation Cause Cancer?

Inflammation is the gateway to cancer. High body fat increases risk by inappropriately increasing cell growth. Inflammation also causes an abnormal amount of free radical formation. Even though free radicals are needed to kill viruses and bacteria, too many can damage healthy cells.

The Goals of an Anti-Cancer Diet

- Increase intake of antioxidants to help protect cells from free radical damage.
- Decrease body fat, which causes high-risk hormone changes that promote cell growth.
- Decrease exposure to environmental contaminants.

Targeted Strategies That Make a Difference

- Decrease body fat; even a 10–15 percent weight loss lowers risk!
- Consume 7–10 servings of fruits/vegetables for protective antioxidants.
- Eat clean (with fewer preservatives, less contamination); avoid sodium nitrates, antibiotics, and hormones in protein foods and dairy.
- Consume high-fiber carbohydrates such as double fiber breads, ancient grains, whole-grain cereals.

Alzheimer's Disease

How Does Inflammation Cause Alzheimer's Disease?

The role of inflammation in Alzheimer's disease is not totally clear. Current research points to inflammation in the brain playing a role, caused primarily by the inflammatory amyloid-beta protein (which causes damaging plaques in brain tissue).

The Goals of a Brain-Healthy Diet

- Reduce inflammation.
- Increase insulin sensitivity so the brain has increasing ability to fuel brain cells with needed glucose.
- Increase blood flow to the brain.

Targeted Strategies That Make a Difference

- Increase intake of omega-3s in your diet; consume cold-water fish, salmon, sardines, and tuna, nuts, and seeds. Eat healthy fats high in omega-3s, such as olive oil, nut oils, and canola oil.
- Consume 7–10 serving of fruits and vegetables per day to increase protective antioxidants.
- Eliminate processed foods as much as possible, especially those with inflammation-producing effects, such as hydrogenated fats and nitrates.
- Decrease added sugars (to improve insulin resistance) to no more than 25 grams per day. Increase intake of whole-grain carbohydrate foods, which also make insulin more effective in controlling blood sugars.

The Art and Science of Weight Loss

If you've ever tried to lose weight, you know that it's not easy. You need some understanding of your behavior, knowledge of the science of weight loss and calorie intake, and some creative problem-solving skills in order to be successful. Even though it's difficult, you *can* achieve sustainable weight loss. Not the usual "few pounds lost and more gained back" kind of weight loss, but permanent weight loss that improves health and well-being.

To be successful at weight loss, you must:

1. **Forget about fads, pills, and diet schemes.** Give up the idea that there is a magic bullet out there that will make this happen quickly and easily—it just does not exist or someone would have found it by now! Losing weight is a process that occurs over time and with much work. While people occasionally obtain short-term success from a crash diet, more times than not, the lose-weight-fast diets fail in the long run. They could even actually do more harm than good, putting you in even more peril from new health problems.

2. **Prioritize your health.** When you decide that being healthy will be one of the most important things in your life, you can lose weight. Your health needs to be the highest priority and requires total focus, but that does not mean that you must ignore other things such as work and family responsibilities. However, your weight loss needs to be first and foremost in your life. (This is where being a creative problem solver comes in.)

3. **Accept the science.** That means accept the reality of weight loss: You have to consume less and burn more in order to lose weight. Learning what you have to eat and how much you have to move is the first step in being successful.

4. **Engage in habit change.** Work on changing bad habits into healthy ones, one step at a time. There are no shortcuts here. Science tells us that it takes approximately 66 days of focus and effort to change a habit. It's important to prioritize what habits need immediate attention to help you lose weight. For example, if you drink two sugar-laden sodas per day, which can cause a 30-pound weight gain in a single year, that should be a priority to change. If you do not eat a good volume of fruit or vegetables, make that a priority. Unless you eat plenty of produce, you'll be too hungry and look for carbohydrates and protein to fill you up. If cookies out of the vending machine are a daily afternoon routine, eat an apple each afternoon instead. If your willpower and control are in limited supply, it can help to learn techniques that will aid you in changing your habits (check out *The Power of Habit* by Charles Duhigg for lots of good ideas).

Focus on habit change, not the actual weight loss. When your habits change, weight loss will occur. Work on substituting good habits for bad ones, one step at a time.

5. **Be honest with yourself.** Instead of saying "I just can't lose weight," be truthful about your actions. Are you *really* doing what you are supposed to do?

6. **Make sure you are medically fit**, so you'll know that no physical issues can hinder your weight loss efforts. After that, ask yourself, How accurate and consistent am I with my food intake and exercise? If you're having trouble keeping track of everything, look for an app to help you monitor intake and output. Also, use a kitchen scale and measuring cups to be sure your portion sizes are correct.

7. **Have realistic expectations.** We think that if we walk 30 minutes three times a week, we should be able to eat what we want and still lose weight. For most of us with less than 50 pounds to lose, 2–8 pounds a month is a realistic weight loss goal. We often get discouraged because we buy into the hype of losing large amounts of weight quickly and do not want to accept the truth that it takes time.

Overcoming Poor Eating Habits

If you're trying to lose weight, see if you engage in any of the following bad food habits. Recognizing these pitfalls is important—knowing you have a bad habit is the first step to changing it. If you have any of these bad habits, you're not alone. These common problems plague millions of us!

Eating Large Portions

What it looks like: You eat too much food. The food itself may even be healthy, but it's just too large a portion, therefore more calories than you need. Overeating is a common problem with

protein and carbohydrate foods. An extra cup of pasta can cost you 20 pounds per year in weight gain.

The solution: Weigh and measure the right portion sizes of carbohydrate and protein foods for you for a few days to establish correct visual perception. (The 21-Day Food Plan gives you a guide to correct amounts as well.) Adding more vegetables to meals does not add appreciable calories but will help keep you full.

Eating Constantly

What it looks like: You do not miss a meal, which is a good thing, but you are eating way too often. You snack constantly, so even if you choose healthy foods it adds up to excess calorie intake. You feel you need something in your mouth constantly.

The solution: Adults need to eat every 5 hours, so for most of us that means 3 meals with 1–2 snacks. It's helpful to assign a time for meals and snacks and then stick to it. If you get an urge to snack at the "wrong" time, find another replacement activity that does not involve eating anything—not even chewing gum, since it reinforces the act of eating. Playing a video game on your phone for a few minutes or putting a coat of clear nail polish on are activities that do not reinforce eating and help occupy you for a short time just as the constant snacking did. It is also helpful in the beginning to make yourself wait an extra 15 minutes for your designated snack to get you more comfortable not responding to the urge to eat. After not responding for a period of time, the urge lessens, which means you are on the road to breaking the bad habit of eating constantly.

Unbalanced Food Group Intake

What it looks like: You have a tendency to consume too much of one food group and do not have the right balance at mealtimes. For example, you will have a large portion of a particular food group, but nothing else, so you need a large amount of that one food in order to be satisfied. By having the right amount of protein, carbohydrates, vegetables, and fruit at each meal you are able to fill up on some of the lower-calorie foods and can get more "mileage" from a meal that helps you control your appetite. If you only eat carbohydrates at a meal, you will be hungry in a few hours, and if you only eat protein at a meal, you have to consume a large quantity of a high-calorie food to be satisfied. The more balanced a meal is, the better for appetite control.

The solution: Make sure each meal has protein, healthy carbohydrates (grain), and/or a fruit and vegetable. More balanced meals mean being less hungry over a period of time and more satisfied between meals.

"Biological Binging"

What it looks like: You go long periods of time without food, often eating very little during the day. This increases the appetite so that when you finally do eat, it's almost impossible not to overeat. A starve/binge pattern results from erratic eating that is associated with getting overly hungry. Feeling and being out of control with food volume is a biological response to not having adequate nutrition throughout the day.

The solution: Make sure your calorie intake is somewhat "even" throughout the day. Make your breakfast, lunch, afternoon snack, and dinner calories similar in quantity, versus consuming only one-quarter of your calorie needs all day and then consuming the remaining calories during the last 2–3 hours of the day. Also, remember that most of us only need one snack per day. Going more than 5 hours without adequate nutrition makes it very difficult to maintain control at your next meal. Plan your meals during the day and take a snack for the late afternoon to help you stay in control in the latter part of the day.

Emotional Binging

What it looks like: Food has become the way to cope with life's everyday stresses or particularly difficult situations. The more you use food to "calm" down, the less you use other coping skills, and over a period of time, food becomes the main coping skill. Often, emotional eating starts out with a difficult situation to cope with, such as a family illness or difficulty with a new boss, but it can become habitual after a time. You know you are an emotional eater when you have the need to eat when you become unhappy or anxious.

The solution: You may be able to break this habit by using the same techniques outlined in solutions for constant eating. If you are going through a difficult situation and are feeling anxiety or depression that drives you to eat, try to do another relaxing activity instead of eating. If you feel you have chronic depression or anxiety that makes you binge frequently for a long period of time, seek professional help. Therapy can be a helpful tool in learning to cope in a healthier way than eating.

Eating Too Many Treats

What it looks like: Your food choices are healthy and your portions check out right for you, but you are consuming way too many "treats," which increases the average daily calorie intake. A couple of glasses of wine nightly or two of scoops of ice cream nightly after dinner is all it takes to have a 30–40-pound weight issue.

The solution: Limit your "indulgence" to 500–700 calories per week, saving it for the weekends or special events. It is helpful to track "indulgence" calories you are consuming each week. If you crave sugary treats, limit your indulgence to one to two times per week, and not on two consecutive days, so as not to overstimulate a "sweet tooth." Remember, one bite of sweet is generally 50 calories, and those bites need to be counted in your calorie intake.

21-Day Food Plan for Health and Weight Loss

When you embark on a plan to improve your diet, it can help to have an exact outline of what to eat for the first few weeks. This section provides details of what and how much to eat each day to achieve or maintain ideal weight. You'll feel better and perhaps lose weight—in as little as three weeks!

More times than not, when a patient comes to the medical-nutrition office for an individualized nutrition consultation, what they really want and need is a food plan that tells them what to eat and when. It takes the guesswork out of trying to figure it out yourself, and more importantly, it can teach you about the patterns of healthy eating. It's not just about *what* you eat, but *how much*, something many of us struggle with.

The average caloric needs of most American adults are less than many would like to think. The 2000 calories per day that is often cited is an average and used to make comparing labels easier. The calorie needs reflected in my plan are more accurate for achieving and sustaining a healthy weight.

- **Women** generally need 1400–1600 calories with moderate exercise (4–5 hours per week) to *maintain* the weight range of 115–135 pounds.

- **Men** with moderate exercise need 2000–2200 calories to *maintain* the weight range of 165–185 pounds.

Again, these numbers are an average for healthy weight. Those who have physically active jobs, do high levels of exercise, or are taller and therefore can weigh more will need more.

Most of us suffer from "portion distortion" syndrome. We don't realize that we're often eating much more than a realistic serving size. If you're overweight, take a hard look at your portion sizes. With the average restaurant meal adding up to 1500–2000 calories, it's easy to see where the extra weight is coming from.

Three Weeks of Healthy Eating

In the following pages, you'll find a three-week daily meal plan that will help you feel better and lose weight. Use this plan as a foundation, then find your appropriate calorie-specific menu at the back of the book for exact portion sizes for each meal or snack.

This Wellness Kitchen meal plan:

- Is plant-based (meaning that it puts more vegetables and fruit on your plate than anything else)

- Follows recommendations for chronic disease prevention
- Promotes longevity

Calories are evenly distributed throughout the day (the number of calories in your Breakfast and Lunch are similar to afternoon Snack and Dinner). Eating even amounts creates a steady flow of energy and a lower glycemic load, a factor that not only helps decrease body fat production but also lowers risk of diabetes.

I have included sample menus at the back of the book for 1300, 1500, 1800, and 2000 calories. Most women will need to be between 1300–1500 calories per day *for weight loss* and most men between 1800–2000 calories. You will know you have chosen the right food plan for you if you lose weight slowly and steadily. Reasonable, healthy weight loss for the moderately overweight (10–25 pounds) is 2–5 pounds per month; for the more overweight (30–40 pounds plus), it is 5–8 pounds per month.

All the recipes are healthy, meaning they have less fat and sugar than traditional recipes. Even so, it is important to follow your designated portions at each meal to ensure success at weight loss. Eating the correct portions for three straight weeks will help you teach your body how much food it really needs, and make that type of eating a habit.

Calories for each meal are also provided to give you flexibility when dining out. Recipes that are included in this book are called out in capital letters in both the Food Plan and the Calorie Menus for easy reference. The amount of protein, carbohydrate, vegetable, fruit, and fat are given on your Calorie Menus to help you learn how to count each food.

Remember, it's meant to be a way of life, not a diet. Enjoy your meals of delicious food!

WEEK 1

Day 1: Monday

Breakfast	APPLE-CINNAMON OATMEAL, nonfat Greek yogurt
Lunch	Sliced turkey on whole-grain bread with lettuce, tomato, and mustard, lots of carrot sticks, and 1 piece fruit
Snack	1 piece fruit with 1 oz. low-fat cheese
Dinner	CHICKEN PICCATA, BARLEY WITH HERBS, ROASTED CARROTS AND CUMIN, mixed green salad with balsamic dressing

Day 2: Tuesday

Breakfast	BLUEBERRY BANANA BRAN MUFFIN, cottage cheese, and BALSAMIC ROASTED STRAWBERRIES
Lunch	TOFU EGG SALAD on whole-grain bread with lettuce, tomato, and fruit
Snack	12 almonds, 1 piece of fresh fruit
Dinner	TURKEY MEATBALLS AL FORNO, whole-grain or high-protein spaghetti, and GRILLED VEGETABLES WITH FETA VINAIGRETTE

Day 3: Wednesday

Breakfast	High-fiber English muffin with almond butter, banana, and honey
Lunch	ROASTED TOMATO SOUP WITH PARMESAN CROSTINI, TABOULEH SALAD WITH GRILLED VEGETABLES, and fresh fruit
Snack	1 piece of fresh fruit, nonfat Greek yogurt
Dinner	ROASTED CHICKEN, HONEY-ROASTED ROOT VEGETABLES, SPINACH SALAD WITH WHEAT BERRIES AND FETA

Day 4: Thursday

Breakfast	FRUIT SMOOTHIE and whole-grain toast
Lunch	Hummus on whole-grain pita with cucumber, tomato, lettuce, and fresh fruit
Snack	8 walnut halves, 1 apple
Dinner	CRISPY FISH STICKS WITH HOMEMADE BREAD CRUMBS, LIME- GLAZED ROASTED YAMS, and steamed broccoli with lemon

Day 5: Friday

Breakfast	High-fiber cereal, Greek yogurt or 8 oz. nonfat milk, and berries
Lunch	Tuna salad on whole-grain bread with lettuce, tomato, and fresh fruit
Snack	1 oz. string cheese, 1 piece fresh fruit
Dinner	SPINACH-STUFFED TURKEY MEATLOAF, garlic roasted potatoes, and ORANGE-GLAZED CARROTS

Day 6: Saturday

Breakfast	Vegetable omelet, whole-grain toast, and mixed fruit
Lunch	Bean and cheese burrito and fresh fruit
Snack	1 mini bag of lite popcorn, 1 piece of fresh fruit
Dinner	GRILLED MARGHERITA PIZZA WITH ARUGULA and mixed green salad with kidney beans

Day 7: Sunday

Breakfast	SPINACH FRITTATA WITH SUN-DRIED TOMATOES AND FETA, high-fiber English muffin, and fresh fruit
Lunch	Salmon salad on whole-grain bread with lettuce, tomato, and fresh fruit
Snack	100-calorie snack package or 12 whole almonds, 1 piece fresh fruit
Dinner	SOUTHWEST TURKEY CHILI, HOMEMADE CORN BREAD, and mixed green salad

WEEK 2

Day 8: Monday

Breakfast	Nonfat Greek yogurt with BREAKFAST GRA-NOLA, 1 cup berries
Lunch	Soft tacos, corn tortillas, grilled fish or chicken, salsa, and fruit
Snack	6 low-fat, high-fiber crackers with 1 oz. low-fat cheese
Dinner	BBQ SHRIMP, GREEN RICE, ROASTED CARROTS WITH CUMIN, broccoli slaw

Day 9: Tuesday

Breakfast	SPICED QUINOA BREAKFAST PORRIDGE
Lunch	ASIAN CHICKEN SALAD, 1 apple
Snack	12 almonds and 1 piece of fresh fruit
Dinner	ITALIAN CHICKEN SOUP WITH FARO AND PESTO, whole-grain roll, ARUGULA SALAD WITH APPLES AND MINT

Day 10: Wednesday

Breakfast	English muffin with peanut butter, banana, and honey
Lunch	PURÉED CAULIFLOWER SOUP, grilled chicken and provolone sandwich with pesto and tomato, 1 piece fruit
Snack	1 mini bag of lite popcorn and 1 piece of fresh fruit
Dinner	HONEY-MUSTARD SALMON WITH SPIN-ACH AND LENTILS, ORANGE-GLAZED CAR-ROTS, mixed baby greens with lite lemon vinaigrette

Day 11: Thursday

Breakfast	FRUIT SMOOTHIE and whole-grain toast
Lunch	SPICY GARBANZO DIP with whole-grain pita chips, cucumbers and cherry tomatoes, mixed fruit
Snack	8 walnut halves and 1 apple
Dinner	ASIAN FLANK STEAK WITH SWEET SLAW, LIME-GLAZED ROASTED YAMS, green beans

Day 12: Friday

Breakfast	High-fiber cereal, Greek yogurt or 8 oz. nonfat milk, and berries
Lunch	Tuna or salmon salad on whole-grain bread with lettuce, tomato, and fresh fruit
Snack	1 oz. string cheese and 1 piece of fresh fruit
Dinner	PULLED TURKEY SANDWICH WITH CRANBERRY BBQ SAUCE, whole-grain bun and CHIPOTLE CILANTRO SLAW, spinach salad with lite lemon vinaigrette

Day 13: Saturday

Breakfast	Breakfast sandwich, natural applesauce
Lunch	CURRIED SQUASH AND LENTIL SOUP, HOME-MADE CORN BREAD, mixed greens with bal-samic vinaigrette, 1 apple
Snack	1 mini bag of lite popcorn and 1 piece of fresh fruit
Dinner	QUINOA CHILI RELLENOS, Caesar salad

Day 14: Sunday

Breakfast	ZUCCHINI FRITTATA WITH TOMATOES AND CHEESE, whole-grain toast, and fresh fruit
Lunch	Tuna salad on whole-grain bread with let-tuce, tomato, and fresh fruit
Snack	100-calorie snack package or 12 whole almonds and 1 piece fresh fruit
Dinner	WHITE LASAGNA WITH TURKEY SAUSAGE, ROASTED GREEN BEANS WITH PINE NUTS, chopped salad with lite balsamic vinaigrette

WEEK 3

Day 15: Monday

Breakfast	FRUIT SMOOTHIE, wheat toast with trans-fat-free margarine
Lunch	HUMMUS WITH BAKED PITA CHIPS, raw vegetables, 1 orange
Snack	6 low-fat high-fiber crackers with 1 oz. low-fat cheese
Dinner	CHICKEN PARMESAN WITH BASIC TOMATO SAUCE, whole-grain or high-protein spaghetti, ROASTED ASPARAGUS WITH LEMON, mixed green salad with lite balsamic vinaigrette

Day 16: Tuesday

Breakfast	Omelet with tomato and spinach, whole-grain English muffin, berries
Lunch	PURÉED GINGER CARROT SOUP, ARUGULA SALAD WITH APPLES AND MINT, ROASTED CHICKEN, whole-grain crackers
Snack	12 almonds and 1 piece of fresh fruit
Dinner	FISH IN PARCHMENT WITH THAI SAUCE AND VEGETABLES, brown rice, butter leaf salad with edamame and shiitake

Day 17: Wednesday

Breakfast	English muffin with almond butter, banana, and honey
Lunch	Black bean and rice bowl, herbed harissa sauce, salad with lite dressing, 1 fruit
Snack	1 mini bag of lite popcorn and 1 piece of fresh fruit
Dinner	BEEF IN RED WINE SAUCE, CELERY ROOT AND POTATO MASH, salad with lite apple cider vinaigrette

Day 18: Thursday

Breakfast	APPLE-CINNAMON OATMEAL with vanilla Greek yogurt
Lunch	ROASTED TOMATO SOUP WITH PARMESAN CROSTINI, grilled chicken sandwich with honey mustard on whole-grain bread, 1 fruit
Snack	8 walnut halves and 1 apple
Dinner	LINGUINE WITH SHRIMP AND ASPARAGUS, ROASTED CARROTS AND CUMIN, salad with lite balsamic dressing

Day 19: Friday

Breakfast	High-fiber cereal, Greek yogurt, and berries
Lunch	Bean and cheese burrito with shredded lettuce, tomato, and salsa, 1 piece fruit
Snack	1 oz. string cheese and 1 piece of fresh fruit
Dinner	FRENCH CHICKEN IN A POT, mashed Yukon gold potatoes, HONEY-ROASTED ROOT VEGETABLES, baby greens with lite lemon vinaigrette

Day 20: Saturday

Breakfast	BREAKFAST FRITTATA, natural applesauce
Lunch	Soft tacos with corn tortillas, grilled chicken or fish, salsa, 1 fruit
Snack	1 mini bag of lite popcorn and 1 piece of fresh fruit
Dinner	ZUCCHINI BASIL SOUP, GRILLED SALMON WITH BALSAMIC GLAZE, GRILLED VEGETABLES WITH FETA VINAIGRETTE, whole-grain rustic bread

Day 21: Sunday

Breakfast	Breakfast sandwich on whole-grain English muffin, mixed fruit
Lunch	Pizza with vegetable toppings, mixed green salad with lite Italian vinaigrette, 1 fruit
Snack	100-calorie snack package or 12 whole almonds and 1 piece fresh fruit
Dinner	CHICKEN TORTILLA SOUP, salad with lite honey-lime vinaigrette

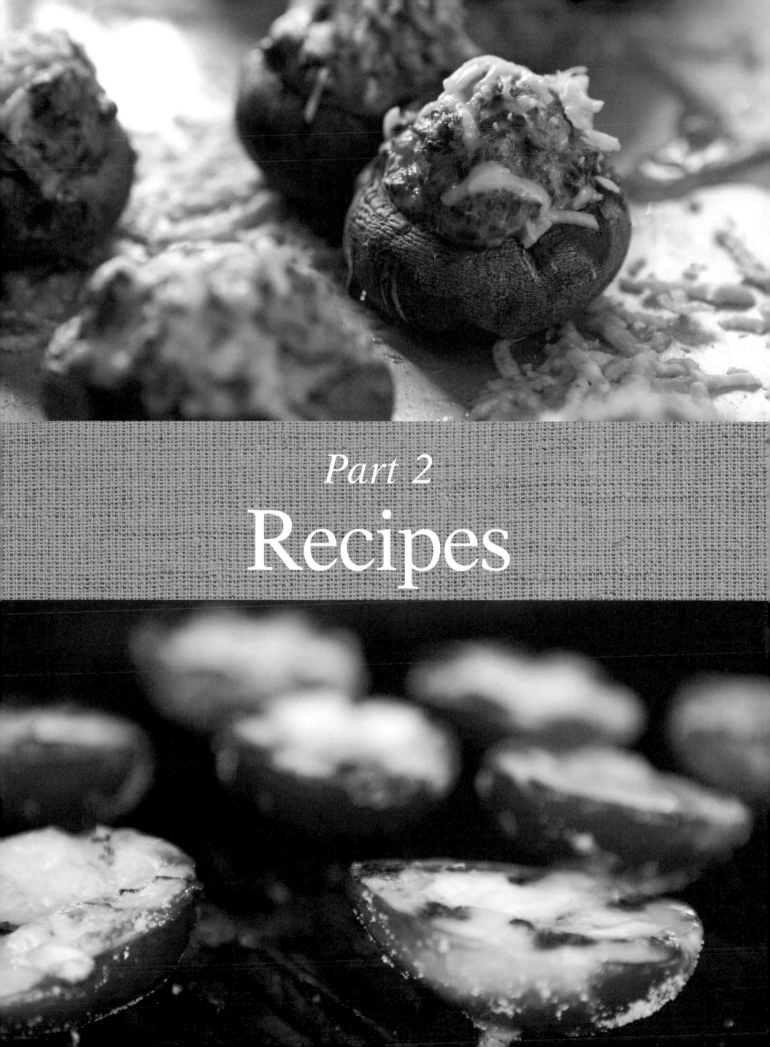

Part 2

Recipes

Chapter 1

Breakfast

I know that the typical "rush out the door" type of morning means that many people eat an unhealthy breakfast—or no breakfast at all. As a nutritionist I just can't condone this, as I have witnessed the damage it has done to my clients over the years. I know that breakfast needs to be simple. To answer some objections you may be forming: No, it does not have to be eaten the minute you wake up; no, it doesn't have to be a large amount of food; and no, it doesn't require a large time investment. Still, everyone needs to eat something healthy in the morning.

Why am I adamant about this issue? Skipping breakfast is just too detrimental to your health and well-being. When you awake in the morning, you have not fueled your body for many hours, so you need some food intake to fuel your day. If you skip it, you end up eating more at other meals, which means eating more food in a shorter amount of time. The better you can evenly spread out your needed calorie intake, the lower the glycemic load in the body. This is one of the most important anti-aging and diabetes-prevention strategies: not overeating at any one time. Think about it: If those who skip breakfast did not eat more later, everyone who skipped breakfast would be in a perpetual weight loss mode . . . and most often that is not the case! Eating breakfast ensures adequate energy production and even improves your cognitive ability. You'll make better food choices the rest of the day and manage your weight more successfully.

Few of us have time to sit down to a leisurely breakfast, except maybe on the weekend. A healthy breakfast should have some whole-grain carbohydrate and protein, which help blunt your appetite and keep you full until lunchtime. A simple meal of a piece of whole-grain bread, natural nut butter, and sliced banana is one of the best breakfasts that you can eat. A quick, creamy Fruit Smoothie can have all the nutrition you need, can be made in just a few minutes, and is easy to take on the run. You can make the high-fiber Blueberry Banana Bran Muffins in advance, freeze them, then thaw overnight or reheat quickly to take out the door. Throw my delicious Apple-Cinnamon Oatmeal in the microwave and you'll have a bowl ready in minutes. I also have included some delicious choices for when you have more time for that leisurely breakfast. No matter what you choose, these breakfast ideas will get your morning off to a great start.

FRUIT SMOOTHIES

Fruit smoothies are cold, refreshing, and a great source of nutrients for breakfast, or before or after exercise. It's best to use frozen fruit; it's less expensive when out of season, offers great variety, has the same nutrition as fresh fruit, and lets you skip the ice cubes. (Freeze any bananas that are getting too ripe in a ziptop bag to use in smoothies.) If you need to lower your cholesterol, add a couple of tablespoons of oat bran or ground flaxseed. This smoothie is an excellent source of antioxidants and calcium, too. Great for breakfast or an afternoon snack, it's filling and satisfies a sweet tooth!

1 cup frozen fruit: berries, peaches, or tropical mix
1 banana
8 ounces nonfat Greek yogurt
¼ cup nonfat milk, soymilk, or almond milk

Place all ingredients in a blender or food processor. Blend at high speed until smooth and creamy.

SERVES: 2; CALORIES PER SERVING: 170; DIETARY EQUIVALENT: 2 fruit, ½ oz. protein

Nutrition Basics
I often get asked about adding protein powder to smoothies. While protein is an important component of breakfast or recovery after hard exercise, getting it from natural sources such as yogurt is healthier. There is much less processing, and, in addition to being high in protein, the yogurt also contains calcium and lactobacillus, the healthy bacteria that boosts immunity and promotes healthy gut function.

BREAKFAST GRANOLA

So easy to make, this granola has less sugar and fat than most of the commercial varieties, which often have the nutritional value of crumbled oatmeal cookies. Although that may be appealing to many of us, I truly think you will find this granola just as delicious, and your waistline will thank you. Just be sure to measure your portion—it can be addictive! It's tasty served as a topping over a bowl of fruit and nonfat Greek yogurt.

3 cups rolled oats

1 cup coarsely chopped unsalted pecans or almonds

½ cup unsweetened shredded coconut

3 tablespoons light or dark brown sugar

1 teaspoon cinnamon

½ teaspoon ground ginger

¼ teaspoon salt

⅓ cup honey

2 tablespoons canola oil

1 cup dried fruit, assorted, unsweetened

1. Preheat oven to 300°F. Line a baking sheet with parchment paper.

2. In large bowl, combine oats, nuts, coconut, sugar, cinnamon, ginger, and salt. Set aside.

3. In a small bowl, microwave the honey for 1 minute; whisk in oil until smooth.

4. Pour honey-oil mixture over oat mixture. Toss to combine.

5. Spread mixture evenly on baking sheet. Bake until golden, about 40 minutes, stirring every 10 minutes.

6. Remove from oven and cool.

7. Mix in dried fruit. Store in airtight container for up to 1 week.

SERVES: 20 (¼-cup servings—makes 5 cups); CALORIES PER SERVING: 160; DIETARY EQUIVALENT: 1 carbohydrate, 1 fat

Nutrition Basics

Nonfat Greek yogurt is twice as high in protein (as much as 2 whole eggs) as regular yogurt and lower in carbohydrates. If you're trying to lower your carbohydrate or calorie intake, buy the plain variety and stir in a small amount of natural sweetener such as stevia and a drop of vanilla extract.

QUICK BREAKFAST OATMEAL

Oatmeal is a classic breakfast staple, especially on those cool mornings. This recipe is delicious and much healthier than store-bought options. Oats, fruit, nonfat Greek yogurt, and a sprinkling of nuts all come together in a warm, cozy mix that reminds me of warm fruit pie and ice cream. Apple and cinnamon is my favorite!

1 cup water

½ cup oats

½ cup fresh or frozen berries, or sliced fresh or frozen peaches

1 teaspoon sugar or honey, or ½ teaspoon stevia

3 ounces nonfat vanilla Greek yogurt (half of a 6-ounce container)

1 tablespoon chopped unsalted almonds, walnuts, or pecans

1. Place water, oats, fruit, and sweetener in a medium microwavable bowl. (Make sure you use a 1-quart mixing bowl instead of a standard cereal bowl; the recipe foams up while cooking and it may overrun a small bowl.) Microwave for 4 minutes on high, uncovered.

2. Pour into cereal bowl, top with yogurt, and sprinkle with nuts. Serve warm.

SERVES: 1; CALORIES PER SERVING: 300; DIETARY EQUIVALENT: 1 oz. protein, 1½ carbohydrates, 1 fruit, 1 fat

VARIATION

APPLE-CINNAMON OATMEAL

1. Place 1 cup water, ½ cup oats, 1 apple (cored and diced), ½ teaspoon cinnamon, and ½ teaspoon stevia in medium microwavable bowl. Microwave on high for 6 minutes, until oatmeal is creamy and apple is soft.

2. Top with Greek yogurt and nuts. Enjoy warm.

> *Nutrition Basics*
> Use ⅓ cup oatmeal with ⅔ cup water to decrease calories to 260.

SPICED QUINOA BREAKFAST PORRIDGE

Quinoa (pronounced KEEN-wa) is actually a seed but is used like many other whole grains. It's prized for its high protein, fiber, and antioxidant content. Just five years ago, no one knew what quinoa was and now, happily, it's found in most major markets and is even showing up on casual dining menus. Whole grains make great breakfast cereals, and this one is sure to please with its nutty taste and slightly crunchy texture. The spices and vanilla add warmth to it that pairs beautifully with the dried fruit. This is a great breakfast porridge when you have a busy morning ahead of you—the protein from the quinoa, the nonfat milk, and the egg white keep you satisfied for a very long time!

½ cup quinoa, rinsed well under cold water

1 cup nonfat milk

1 cup water

½ teaspoon ground cinnamon

⅛ teaspoon ground nutmeg

⅛ teaspoon ground ginger

Pinch of sea salt

1 tablespoon honey or 1 teaspoon stevia

½ teaspoon vanilla

1 large egg white

2 tablespoons dried currants, raisins, or blueberries

SERVES: 2; CALORIES PER SERVING: 225; DIETARY EQUIVALENT: 1 carbohydrate, 1 fruit, 1 oz. protein

1. In a medium saucepan, over medium-high heat, add the quinoa. Stir until fragrant, about 2–4 minutes.

2. Stir in the milk, water, cinnamon, nutmeg, ginger, and salt. Bring to a boil, then reduce heat to simmer, stirring occasionally, until the quinoa is tender, about 20–25 minutes.

3. Remove from heat. Stir in sweetener and vanilla.

4. In a small bowl, whisk egg white with 1 tablespoon of the hot quinoa. Continue adding quinoa 1 tablespoon at a time (up to 5 additional tablespoons) until the egg white is entirely worked in. Add back to the saucepan.

5. Stir in dried fruit. Cook over medium-low heat until slightly thickened, 1–2 minutes.

6. Serve warm.

Nutrition Basics

Quinoa has 10 grams of complete protein per cup, meaning it has all nine essential amino acids that are needed to synthesize body protein. One cup of quinoa is equal to 1½ oz. of meat, fish, or chicken. Quinoa cooks quickly, but if you need to, you can cook it the night before. Just add 1 cup quinoa to 2 cups of water in a microwavable bowl, leave uncovered and pop into the microwave for 10 minutes on high. Cover and refrigerate until ready to use. You now have cooked quinoa for the porridge. To heat it up in the morning, add cooked quinoa to saucepan, add milk (omit the water) and bring to a boil. Add cinnamon, nutmeg, ginger, and salt, reduce heat to a simmer for 5 minutes and follow remainder of recipe instructions.

BLUEBERRY BANANA BRAN MUFFINS

Most muffins found in coffee shops or bakeries are large, high in sugar, and high in fat—they're really just like a piece of dense cake, with calories ranging from 500 to 800 per muffin. These Blueberry Banana Bran Muffins work into a weight loss meal plan easily, and deliciously! They're also perfect for on-the-go breakfasts. After you bake them, place in a freezer bag and freeze for later use. Just take a muffin out of the freezer bag and pop it into the microwave for 30–35 seconds and you have a hot muffin!

1½ cups all-purpose flour
1½ teaspoons baking soda
¾ teaspoon sea salt
½ teaspoon cinnamon
5 Weetabix cereal biscuits, crushed
2 tablespoons ground flaxseed
⅓ cup brown sugar
1 cup nonfat vanilla yogurt
½ cup skim milk
¼ cup egg substitute or 1 egg (beaten)
2 tablespoons canola oil
2 tablespoons natural applesauce
2 tablespoons honey
1 ripe banana, diced
1 cup frozen blueberries
Organic canola or olive oil cooking spray

1. Preheat oven to 375°F.
2. In a large mixing bowl, combine flour, baking soda, salt, cinnamon, Weetabix biscuits, flaxseed, and sugar.
3. In another mixing bowl, whisk yogurt, milk, egg, canola oil, applesauce, and honey.
4. Fold wet ingredients into dry ingredients with a spatula, being careful not to overmix.
5. Fold in banana and frozen blueberries with a spatula. (The spatula helps prevent overmixing, which creates air holes in the baked muffins.)
6. Spray muffin pan with oil or use paper muffin liners; scoop batter into liners until ⅔ full.
7. Bake for 20 minutes or until golden and a toothpick inserted into the middle of the muffin comes out clean.

SERVES: 12; CALORIES PER SERVING: 190; DIETARY EQUIVALENT: 1 carbohydrate, 1 fruit, 1 fat

Nutrition Basics

If you need to control your carbohydrate intake, remember that this muffin is equivalent to having a grain serving and a fruit serving. For a complete breakfast, add a protein (not another carbohydrate) such as low-fat cottage cheese, Greek yogurt, or eggs.

APPLE-CARROT BRAN MUFFINS

I have had one too many "healthy muffins" that were either dry with no flavor or still way too high in calories to be considered a breakfast food. I came up with this one after looking at numerous apple bran muffin recipes. The addition of carrots and oat bran made this muffin recipe taste similar to a lightly textured carrot cake.

Organic canola oil cooking spray
1 large egg + 2 egg whites, beaten
1 cup buttermilk or plain, nonfat yogurt
½ cup canola oil
¼ cup pure maple syrup
½ cup unprocessed oat bran
1½ cups unsweetened bran cereal
1 cup whole wheat pastry flour
¼ cup sugar
1 teaspoon baking soda
1 teaspoon baking powder
2 teaspoons cinnamon
½ teaspoon nutmeg
1 teaspoon sea salt
1 cup shredded carrot
1 cup shredded apple

1. Preheat oven to 350°F.
2. Lightly coat a 12-cup muffin pan with cooking spray or use paper liners.
3. In a large bowl, whisk together the eggs and egg whites, buttermilk, canola oil, and maple syrup. Stir in the oat bran and cereal; allow the mixture to sit for 5 minutes.
4. Meanwhile, in a small bowl, whisk the flour, sugar, baking soda, baking powder, cinnamon, nutmeg, and salt. Add dry mixture to the wet and stir until just combined.
5. Stir in the shredded carrot and apple.
6. Fill the muffin pan ⅔ full and bake for about 20 minutes or until the edges begin to brown and a toothpick inserted into the center of the muffin comes out clean.
7. Cool in the pan for 5 minutes then remove muffins and cool completely on a wire rack.

SERVES: 12; CALORIES PER SERVING: 185; DIETARY EQUIVALENT: 1 carbohydrate, 1 fruit, 1 fat

Nutrition Basics

Years ago, oat bran was a fad to lower cholesterol, and one that should be brought back. Eating oatmeal daily does help lower cholesterol. When not eating oatmeal, however, try adding 1–2 tablespoons of oat bran, the fiber part of the oatmeal, to your cold cereal, breakfast smoothie, or yogurt. Or, try this muffin! These muffins freeze well—just reheat in the microwave for 30–40 seconds for a warm muffin. For another variation try substituting 1 cup lite canned crushed pineapple drained with 1 cup shredded zucchini.

BREAKFAST FRITTATAS

Frittatas are similar to a crustless quiche (with much less cheese). They're so versatile—you can make them with any vegetables you have on hand, and you can eat them hot or at room temperature. While it's not a breakfast you can make "on the run," it can be prepared earlier and just reheated in the microwave for 30–40 seconds—and then you can run! Try it for a quick, easy dinner and then have the leftovers for breakfast the next morning. The spinach and sun-dried tomato combination is one of my favorites, but check out the variations here or come up with your own winning combination of vegetables. Other options might include onions, mushrooms, and red peppers, or fresh asparagus, tomato, and green onion.

SPINACH FRITTATA WITH SUN-DRIED TOMATOES AND FETA

1 tablespoon olive oil

1 cup finely chopped onion

2 (5–6-ounce) bags baby spinach

3 ounces sun-dried tomatoes, reconstituted in hot water, drained, and chopped

4 whole eggs plus 4 egg whites (or 1½ cups egg substitute)

2 tablespoons nonfat milk

½ teaspoon sea salt

½ teaspoon freshly ground black pepper

¼ cup feta cheese (can substitute goat or Parmesan cheese)

¼ cup chiffonade (thinly sliced) basil

1. Preheat oven to 350°F.

2. Heat a 10", nonstick, ovenproof sauté pan over medium heat. Add olive oil and onion. Sauté for 2–3 minutes or until soft.

3. Add spinach and sun-dried tomatoes. Cook until spinach is just wilted.

4. In a medium bowl, beat whole eggs, egg whites, milk, salt, and pepper.

5. Pour eggs over the spinach-tomato mixture and cook for 1 minute.

6. Place sauté pan in oven and bake until egg mixture is set and lightly golden, about 12–15 minutes.

7. Remove from oven, sprinkle with cheese, and garnish with basil.

8. To serve, cut into wedges.

SERVES: 6; CALORIES PER SERVING: 145; DIETARY EQUIVALENT: 2 oz. protein, ½ vegetable

Nutrition Basics

Use a combination of half whole eggs and half egg whites to lower the fat and cholesterol. You can also use egg substitute, which is really just egg whites with natural color added. Make sure you fill at least half of the sauté pan with vegetables for added volume and nutrition. Think of cheese as a condiment; use only a small amount of the ones that are low in fat but high in flavor such as feta, lite Swiss, provolone, or Parmesan.

ZUCCHINI FRITTATA WITH TOMATOES AND CHEESE

Omit spinach and add 1 medium zucchini sliced thinly; omit sun-dried tomatoes and add 2 medium tomatoes, cut into ¼" dice. (Calories: 145 per serving)

SMOKED SALMON FRITTATA WITH FRESH TOMATO

Omit sun-dried tomatoes and add 4 oz. smoked salmon, flaked, and 2 medium tomatoes, cut into ¼" dice. (Calories: 180 per serving)

MUSHROOM FRITTATA WITH TOMATOES AND GREEN ONIONS

Omit spinach and sauté 1 pound sliced mushrooms; omit onion and add 1 bunch of green onions, sliced thinly; omit sun-dried tomatoes and add 1 medium tomato, cut into ¼" dice. (Calories: 150 per serving)

Food Tip
If you do not keep fresh eggs in your fridge, store a supply of egg substitute in your freezer. (It's made with pasteurized egg whites and natural coloring.) That way you always have eggs and do not need to worry about cholesterol.

Chapter 2

Appetizers

Appetizers can be tricky; too often they are boring, unnecessary, and guilt-ridden morsels that I have often regretted eating. I often think we should just skip this ritual—but celebrations, whether casual game viewing, backyard barbecues, or more formal dinner parties, do require that little something before a meal. Generally, appetizers are high-fat, high-protein foods that leave many of us feeling too full to thoroughly enjoy the following meal, or way too regretful the next day.

Instead, I love to serve appetizers that are fresh, light, and so delicious that no one would even notice that they are healthy. I often just serve one appetizer along with a beautiful platter of crudités if a full meal is shortly following the appetizers. If appetizers are the main focus, without a meal following, I usually make three to five items to make up a small plate meal. In this case, small amounts of soup served in small glasses (also known as soup shooters) or very small plates of salads can round out the appetizers, along with a protein—such as our delicious Crab Cakes or one of the grilled shrimp recipes that can be easily eaten without plates or forks. The best part of these light appetizers is that if you're lucky enough to have any left over, you can graze the next day and not regret doing so!

GUACAMOLE

I have made many guacamole recipes over the years, but this one seems to be the favorite. I love the chopped tomatoes mixed right in; it helps the tomatoes stay on the tacos! Avocados are good fat, but like all fats, they're high in calories, so be careful with how much you consume. I add extra chopped tomatoes to give more volume without as many calories.

3 ripe avocados, diced (about 3 cups)
1 tablespoon lemon juice
2 vine-ripe tomatoes, seeded, diced
2 tablespoons diced red onion
2 tablespoons chopped fresh cilantro
¼ teaspoon sea salt

1. In medium bowl, combine avocado and lemon juice (to prevent browning).
2. Add tomatoes, onion, cilantro, and salt. Lightly mash with fork to a chunky consistency.

SERVES: 10 (¼-cup servings); CALORIES PER SERVING: 80; DIETARY EQUIVALENT: 2 fats

Food Tip

If you won't be serving the guacamole immediately, place the pit of the avocado right in the guacamole, cover it tightly with plastic wrap, and refrigerate. The pit will help hold the color and not turn brown.

SPICY GARBANZO DIP

This dip is similar to hummus, but includes more exotic Mideast flavors such as cumin, chili, and cinnamon. "Regular" sour cream–based dips have approximately 200 calories per 4 tablespoons, but this fabulous dip has less than 100 calories—plus almost no fat, compared to the 3 teaspoons of unhealthy fat in creamy dips. It's most delicious when served warm. The aromas during the making of this dip are incredible and will have everyone coming into the kitchen to see what you're cooking!

1 tablespoon olive oil
½ cup diced onion
4 garlic cloves, smashed, divided
1 dried arbol chili, crumbled
1 teaspoon fresh thyme leaves
1 bay leaf
½ teaspoon paprika
¼ teaspoon cinnamon
¼ teaspoon cayenne
½ teaspoon ground cumin
2 cups canned garbanzo beans (reserve ½ cup liquid, then rinse and drain garbanzo beans)
2 tablespoons water
1 tablespoon tahini
1–2 tablespoons lemon juice
Sea salt
Freshly ground black pepper

SERVES: 8; CALORIES PER SERVING: 85; DIETARY EQUIVALENT: ½ carbohydrate, 1 fat

1. In medium sauté pan, warm oil over medium heat. Add onion, 3 cloves garlic, chili, thyme, and bay leaf. Cook until onion softens, 3–4 minutes.

2. Stir in paprika, cinnamon, cayenne, and cumin.

3. Add garbanzo beans and water. Cook, covered, over low heat for about 10 minutes, stirring occasionally to blend flavors.

4. Remove bay leaf.

5. Add garbanzo bean mixture to a food processor with tahini, remaining garlic, and lemon juice. Purée until smooth, adding some of the reserved bean liquid until desired consistency is reached. Season to taste with salt and pepper.

6. Serve warm.

Food Tip
If you want less "heat" from the chili, do not crumble it into the sauté pan but use it whole and remove it before adding the mixture to the food processor. You still get a mild chili flavor by just sautéing, but definitely less heat!

HUMMUS WITH BAKED PITA CHIPS

We have been making this in the Wellness Kitchen for years and it's always a big hit. We have pared down the calories by using the reserved bean liquid instead of large amounts of olive oil found in the commercial varieties. It decreases the calories and gives the hummus a light, fluffy texture. Rarely do I attend a party or a social gathering where hummus isn't being served with crudités, chips, or crackers. Fortunately, it has become almost a staple in many homes, too. Vary the flavor of your hummus by adding two roasted red peppers, or add a handful of fresh parsley or cilantro for fresh flavor and more antioxidants. Hummus is one of the healthier dips; it's a vegetarian protein and has almost no saturated fat. It's great for an appetizer, and I recommend using it for a vegetarian meal if you're lucky enough to have any left! Try it for a heart-healthy vegetarian lunch on whole-wheat pita with sliced tomatoes, cucumbers, and shredded carrots.

2 (15-ounce) cans garbanzo beans (reserve ½ cup liquid, then rinse and drain beans)

¼ medium red onion, roughly chopped

2 teaspoons roughly chopped garlic

4 tablespoons lemon juice

¼–½ teaspoon cayenne pepper

1 tablespoon olive oil

¼ cup tahini (sesame seed paste)

Sea salt

4 whole-wheat pitas

Organic canola or olive oil cooking spray

1. Preheat oven to 325°F.

2. In a food processor, pulse garbanzo beans, onion, garlic, lemon juice, cayenne, olive oil, and tahini.

3. Add ¼ cup reserved liquid from garbanzo beans. Blend with a steel blade until light and fluffy. (You may need to add more reserved bean liquid.) Season to taste with salt. Place in serving bowl.

4. Cut pita into 8 wedges. Open and split each triangle to yield 16 chips from each pita.

5. Place pita chips in a single layer on baking sheets. Lightly coat chips with cooking spray and sprinkle with sea salt. Bake for 10–12 minutes or until crisp and golden brown.

6. Serve hummus with baked pita chips for an appetizer or in pita pockets for a vegan sandwich.

SERVES: 10 (¼-cup servings); CALORIES PER SERVING: 150; DIETARY EQUIVALENT: 1 protein, 1 fat

PITA CHIPS: 8 chips, 100 calories; DIETARY EQUIVALENT: 1 carbohydrate

Nutrition Basics

Beans are high in protein, fiber, calcium, and iron, and do not have the saturated fat that most animal protein has. They are a near-perfect food. Try to include them in your diet 3–4 times a week for better health and less risk of chronic disease.

KALE CHIPS

❧

I love making these for a social gathering. People are so intrigued and then so pleasantly surprised with the idea that something this healthy can be made into a chip! Lightly coated with healthy olive oil and a sprinkling of sea salt, they have that same crispness that make potato chips so addictive—only this time you do not have to feel any guilt, even if you eat the whole pan, which I have been known to do! They are best served warm right out of the oven. If you like a little heat, add a pinch of cayenne pepper before baking.

1 bunch of kale
1 tablespoon olive oil
Sea salt
Freshly ground black pepper

1. Preheat oven to 400°F.
2. Remove stems from kale and tear leaves into bite-sized pieces.
3. In a large bowl, thoroughly toss kale with olive oil, salt, and pepper.
4. Spread out on baking sheet in single layer and roast for 12–15 minutes, turning every 5 minutes until crisp.

SERVES: 6; CALORIES PER SERVING: 35; DIETARY EQUIVALENT: 1 vegetable, ½ fat

Nutrition Basics

Kale is a cruciferous vegetable like broccoli or cauliflower, with deep green curly leaves that pack a punch in the nutrition department. Kale is a great source of folic acid for heart health and antioxidants that help your body deter the effects of environmental contaminants.

ROASTED GARBANZO BEANS

Warm nuts are a fantastic party or snack food—they're so enticing but so high in calories! If you have never had roasted garbanzo beans, you are in for a treat. Similar to roasted nuts, but with very little fat, these little beans have 75 percent fewer calories than nuts, so indulging is not a problem. Try to serve them right out of the oven, hot and crispy; just make sure you have a backup pan in the oven because they are not going to last long!

2 (15-ounce) cans garbanzo beans, rinsed and drained
1 tablespoon olive oil
1 teaspoon finely chopped garlic
2 tablespoons reduced-sodium soy sauce
⅛ teaspoon cayenne pepper

1. Preheat oven to 425°F.
2. On rimmed baking sheet, toss garbanzo beans with olive oil, garlic, soy sauce, and cayenne pepper. Mix well and spread out in single layer.
3. Bake for 45 minutes, stirring a few times, until crisp. Serve hot.

SERVES: 8; CALORIES PER SERVING: 110; DIETARY EQUIVALENT: 1 carbohydrate

> *Nutrition Basics*
> It's best to rinse canned beans in cold water before using to wash off the liquid used in the canning process, which has a high sodium content. Canned beans have the same nutrition as fresh cooked beans.

VARIATIONS

Be creative and come up with new favorites! Try adding 1 tablespoon miso paste and 2 teaspoons sesame oil, or 2 teaspoons black lemon pepper or chili powder with olive oil and garlic.

WHITE BEAN AND BRUSCHETTA CROSTINI

Get ready for rave reviews when you serve this appetizer. It's so easy to prepare in just a few minutes with ingredients that you most likely have on hand. The crunch of the toasted baguette teams beautifully with the creamy bean purée, and the tomato-basil bruschetta adds freshness and fantastic flavor. This recipe can be made a day ahead and assembled just before serving so the toast does not become soggy. You can also serve the crostini, bean purée, and bruschetta separately and let guests assemble their own!

16 thin slices from a baguette
2 cans cannellini beans (reserve ½ cup liquid, then rinse and
    drain beans)
1 tablespoon plus 2 teaspoons chopped garlic, divided
2 tablespoons olive oil, divided
1 teaspoon cumin
½ teaspoon coriander
¾ teaspoon sea salt, divided
¼ teaspoon cayenne pepper
4 small vine-ripe tomatoes, seeded, cut into ¼" dice
2 tablespoons chopped basil

1. Preheat oven to 350°F.
2. Toast baguette slices on baking sheet in oven for 6–8 minutes or until golden brown. Set aside.
3. To food processor, add beans, 1 tablespoon garlic, 1 tablespoon olive oil, cumin, coriander, ¼ teaspoon salt, and cayenne. Blend until smooth.
4. Add ¼ cup reserved liquid from beans. Blend until light and fluffy. Add more liquid if needed. Place in serving bowl.
5. In a small bowl, combine the diced tomatoes, basil, and the remaining garlic, olive oil, and salt.
6. To assemble: Spread 1 tablespoon of bean purée on top of each crostino, top with bruschetta, and place on serving tray.

SERVES: 8; CALORIES PER SERVING: 175; DIETARY EQUIVALENT: 1 oz. protein, 1 carbohydrate

Nutrition Basics

This dish has many of the ingredients found in super-healthy Mediterranean cuisine, which promotes longevity and well-being! Beans, tomatoes, olive oil, and herbs are combined in a way that is sure to please everyone's taste buds.

SPINACH-STUFFED MUSHROOMS

Years ago, I was asked to bring an appetizer to a party; the hostess hesitantly noted that it didn't have to be healthy, knowing full well it would be. Not wanting to reinforce the belief that nutritious means flavorless, I wanted something impressive yet healthy, and I came up with these decadent stuffed mushrooms. It's a sophisticated appetizer full of flavor, yet easy to make. By using more spinach, the stems of mushroom, less cheese, and no bread crumbs, they are so low in calories that you can indulge! You can make these ahead and just pop them in the oven for a few minutes right before serving.

1 pound fresh medium-sized mushrooms, cremini or button

1 tablespoon olive oil

½ medium onion, finely chopped

2 teaspoons minced garlic

1 (5–6-ounce) bag baby spinach

2 tablespoons lite cream cheese

½ cup plus 2 tablespoons shredded Parmesan cheese, divided

½ teaspoon sea salt

½ teaspoon freshly ground black pepper

Pinch of cayenne

1. Wipe mushrooms clean with damp cloth. Remove stems. Chop stems into ¼" dice. Set mushroom caps on a parchment-lined baking sheet, stem side up.

2. Heat olive oil in large sauté pan over medium-high heat. Add chopped stems and sauté for 2–3 minutes. Add onion and garlic; sauté for 3–4 minutes. Remove from pan.

3. Add spinach to the sauté pan and cook until just wilted. Remove from heat and squeeze out any excess water with paper towels, so the mushroom filling is not watery.

4. Transfer onion/mushroom mixture and spinach to food processor. Add cream cheese, ¼ cup shredded Parmesan, salt, pepper, and cayenne. Mix until smooth.

5. Stuff 1 tablespoon spinach mixture into each mushroom. Sprinkle remaining 2 tablespoons Parmesan over the top of all mushrooms. Place under broiler for 2–3 minutes until cheese is lightly browned and melted.

6. Serve immediately.

SERVES: 8 (approx. 3 mushroom caps per serving); CALORIES PER SERVING: 65; DIETARY EQUIVALENT: 1 vegetable, 1 fat

Nutrition Basics

I'm often asked about mushrooms in the Wellness Kitchen; is there any nutrient value at all? My answer is always a resounding yes! Mushrooms are high in antioxidants and B vitamins, which prevent chronic disease. A mushroom is approximately 4 calories, which in my calorie-aware mind makes them very useful in cooking. They also provide a savory flavor that enhances many dishes.

FIRE-ROASTED PEPPERS STUFFED WITH FETA

These never fail to excite a crowd. I prep them ahead of time and then send a willing guest out to the grill. In about 10 minutes, a platter of the most scrumptious appetizers is ready to serve. Look for bags of red, yellow, and orange mini peppers in the produce section of your market.

12 mini sweet peppers (red, yellow, orange)
½ cup part-skim feta cheese
1 tablespoon olive oil
1 tablespoon balsamic vinegar
Sea salt
Freshly ground black pepper

1. Preheat grill to medium heat.
2. Using a paring knife, cut the top off each pepper and remove seeds and ribs.
3. Stuff each pepper with a rounded tablespoon of the feta.
4. In small bowl, whisk the olive oil into the balsamic vinegar. Season lightly with salt and pepper.
5. With a pastry brush, brush the balsamic mixture over the peppers.
6. Grill the peppers until golden and cheese is melted, about 2–3 minutes on each side.
7. Serve immediately.

SERVES: 6; CALORIES PER SERVING: 75; DIETARY EQUIVALENT: ½ oz. protein, 1 vegetable

Nutrition Basics
It's amazing that something this delicious could be so low in calories compared to most appetizers. By adding a small amount of flavorful part-skim feta cheese to a mini sweet pepper, you get the sweet/salty taste that really revs up taste buds.

SPICY MISO EDAMAME

~

Soybeans are one of the most versatile items to keep in your freezer. They're delicious added to salads, or try adding them to soups or pasta entrées in the place of green peas. Most of us are familiar with them in Japanese restaurants as an appetizer, just steamed and lightly salted. We elevated our version by adding miso, Asian chili paste, and truffle oil, making them explode with flavor in your mouth but with no worries about your waistline. That's the best kind of appetizer!

1 (14-ounce) bag frozen edamame in the pods
1 tablespoon miso paste
1 teaspoon sambal (Asian chili sauce)
2 teaspoons truffle oil or truffle-infused olive oil
½ teaspoon sea salt

1. Bring large saucepan of water to full boil. Add edamame and cook for 3–4 minutes. Drain well and pat dry with paper towel. Place in medium bowl. Set aside; keep warm.
2. In a small bowl, combine miso, sambal, and truffle oil. Mix well.
3. Pour miso mixture over edamame, add sea salt, and toss.
4. Place in serving bowl. Serve warm or at room temperature.

SERVES: 4; CALORIES PER SERVING: 140; DIETARY EQUIVALENT: 1 oz. protein, ½ protein

VARIATION

SOUTHWEST EDAMAME

Replace sambal with 1 teaspoon chipotle chili powder, ½ teaspoon cumin, and 1 teaspoon chopped garlic; replace truffle oil with 2 teaspoons olive oil. (Calories: 140 per serving)

Nutrition Basics
There have been rumors that soy intake can boost the occurrence of breast cancer in women. New studies show that it may actually lower rates of breast cancer and other types of cancer. No one should worry that one or two servings of soy foods per day increases the risk of cancer.

CRAB CAKES

Crab: it's not only so delicious, but like other seafood, it is low in saturated fat and heart healthy. Most species are low in mercury, too. Unlike what you often get when dining out, these crab cakes have more lump crab meat than breading. When I make these for a party, I make them the day before—lightly sauté and brown them, place them on a baking sheet, cover, and refrigerate. When my guests arrive, I just pop the baking sheet into the oven! Try serving these crab cakes with a sweet and spicy mango, pineapple, or orange salsa.

2 tablespoons olive oil, divided
⅓ cup finely chopped red onion
⅓ cup finely chopped celery
⅓ cup finely diced red bell pepper
¼ cup chopped parsley
1 tablespoon capers
¼ teaspoon (4 drops) Tabasco sauce
½ teaspoon Worcestershire sauce
1½ teaspoons Old Bay seasoning
½ teaspoon kosher salt
½ teaspoon freshly ground black pepper
1 pound lump crab meat
½ cup whole-grain panko crumbs (Japanese bread crumbs)
¼ cup lite mayonnaise
1 teaspoon Dijon mustard
¼ cup egg substitute (or 2 egg whites)

1. In large sauté pan, heat 1 tablespoon olive oil. Sauté red onion, celery, red pepper, parsley, capers, Tabasco, Worcestershire, Old Bay, salt, and pepper. Cook until vegetables are soft, 5–7 minutes. Set aside to cool for 10 minutes.

2. Flake the crab into a large bowl with fork; do not mash. Add panko, mayonnaise, mustard, and egg substitute and toss lightly. Add vegetables and mix well. Cover and chill for 10 minutes.

3. Shape into 2–3 oz. patties. I use a 2-oz. ice cream scoop—it's the perfect size. Just make sure to pack it in well so the crab cake is well formed before turned out of the scoop.

4. In large sauté pan, heat remaining olive oil over medium-high heat. Sauté patties until golden, about 3–4 minutes on each side. Keep warm in a 250°F oven until ready to serve.

SERVES: 4; CALORIES PER SERVING: 275; DIETARY EQUIVALENT: 4 oz. lean protein, 1 vegetable, 1 fat

Food Tip

If fresh lump crab meat is not available, use a 1-pound can of pasteurized lump crab found in the fresh fish section of your market or at large wholesale warehouse stores. Frozen crab meat is too wet and mushy to produce a really good crab cake.

Chapter 3

Salads and Vinaigrettes

Salads are an efficient way of eating wholesome foods without using a lot of fancy cooking techniques. They also don't have to be boring iceberg lettuce/Italian dressing combos. You can find a whole spectrum of flavors and textures just by layering and combining ingredients. With a wide variety of produce found in most markets year round, it's easy to put many delicious blends on your plate, whether as a side dish or a satisfying meal. Keep fresh, seasonal greens in the refrigerator and then let your imagination take over—add a can of beans, various proteins, whole grains, a small amount of cheese, nuts, blanched or grilled vegetables, or fresh fruit.

LITE VINAIGRETTE DRESSINGS

The dressing is an integral part of any salad, whether it's a simple side salad or a hearty entrée salad. Yet nothing can undermine a nutritious, healthy salad like a large dollop of high-fat, high-sodium dressing. Most commercial dressings are high in fat, and the lower-calorie ones are also low on flavor. You can make your own lite, delicious dressing with just a few staples that you probably have on hand. Traditional vinaigrettes are made with two-thirds oil and one-third vinegar, but we use one-third oil, one-third water, and one-third vinegar to keep the calories low. These dressings pack a big flavor punch, so you do not need a large amount. Remember, dressing is supposed to enhance the flavor of a salad, not be the flavor!

BALSAMIC-DIJON VINAIGRETTE

2 tablespoons balsamic vinegar

1 tablespoon water

1 teaspoon Dijon mustard

1 tablespoon olive oil

½ teaspoon sea salt

½ teaspoon freshly ground black pepper

In small bowl, whisk all ingredients. Cover and refrigerate until ready to serve. I use Mason jars with lids for mixing and storing my lite dressings, but any container with a lid will work. Homemade dressing lasts up to three days if it contains fresh ingredients such as shallots, lemon zest, or fresh herbs. If the dressing doesn't contain fresh ingredients, it will last up to 2 weeks.

SERVES: 4; CALORIES PER SERVING: 30; DIETARY EQUIVALENT: 1 fat

VARIATIONS

HONEY-LIME

Omit balsamic vinegar and Dijon. Add 1 tablespoon honey, 2 tablespoons lime juice (or the juice of 1 lime), and ½ teaspoon ground cumin. (Calories: 45 per serving)

LEMON

Omit balsamic vinegar and Dijon. Add 2 tablespoons lemon juice. (Calories: 30 per serving)

APPLE MAPLE

Omit balsamic vinegar and Dijon. Add 2 tablespoons apple cider vinegar and 1 tablespoon pure maple syrup. (Calories: 45 per serving)

HONEY-ORANGE

Omit balsamic vinegar and Dijon. Add 1 tablespoon honey and 2 tablespoons fresh orange juice. (Calories: 45 per serving)

POMEGRANATE

Omit balsamic vinegar and Dijon. Add 2 tablespoons pomegranate juice and a pinch of red pepper flakes. (Calories: 30 per serving)

ASIAN MISO

Omit balsamic vinegar, Dijon, and salt. Add 2 tablespoons miso paste, ⅓ cup orange juice, 2 tablespoons reduced-sodium soy sauce, and 2 tablespoons honey. (Calories: 75 per serving)

Nutrition Basics

Homemade dressings have fewer additives and no added preservatives, so even though we add a small amount of sea salt for flavor, the sodium is lower. Dressings can be very simple or can be made more complex by adding different oils, seeds, chopped shallots, chopped garlic, and small amounts of honey or sugar. Remember that while olive oil, canola oil, grape seed oil, and nut oils are healthy fats, they are still 120 calories per tablespoon.

COUSCOUS AND ARUGULA SALAD WITH FRESH BASIL DRESSING

When I am asked to bring something to a summer bar-becue or dinner party, this is my go-to salad. Without fail, the phone rings and rings the next day with friends asking for the recipe! The combination of spicy arugula with the charred flavor of grilled corn, the sweetness of the dried cranberries, and the saltiness of the pumpkin seeds are completely mouthwatering. When tossed with the fresh basil dressing, it's really addictive. Add grilled shrimp or grilled chicken to get a main entrée salad for a wonderful summer dinner.

8 ounces whole-grain couscous, cooked

3 cups arugula

4 vine-ripened tomatoes, diced

2 cups fresh corn (3 medium ears), grilled and cut from cob

1 avocado, diced

¼ cup salted pumpkin seeds

⅓ cup dried cranberries

½ cup fresh basil leaves, packed plus extra for garnish

½ cup buttermilk

½ cup lite mayonnaise

2 teaspoons lemon juice

½ teaspoon sea salt

½ teaspoon freshly ground black pepper

⅓ cup grated Asiago cheese

1. In large salad bowl, toss couscous, arugula, toma-toes, corn, avocado, pumpkin seeds, and cranberries. Set aside.

2. For the dressing, add basil, buttermilk, mayonnaise, lemon juice, salt, and pepper in food processor or blender until smooth. Refrigerate until ready to use.

3. When making this ahead, keep all ingredients sep-arate until just before serving so the salad retains its crispiness. To serve, toss the salad with dressing. Sprin-kle Asiago cheese over the top. Garnish with remain-ing basil leaves.

SERVES: 6; CALORIES PER SERVING: 285; DIETARY EQUIVALENT: 1 oz. protein, 2 carbohydrates, 1 fat

Nutrition Basics

Use fresh herbs whenever you can; they are much richer in antioxidants than even fruits and vegetables. Often just a couple of tablespoons of fresh herbs have the antioxidant concentration of a whole piece of fruit. This salad dressing uses a packed ½ cup of fresh basil, which means it's burst-ing with antioxidants! For the couscous in this recipe, use whole-grain couscous, which is the regular, finer texture of semolina wheat. You could also try Israeli couscous (also known as pearl couscous). Israeli couscous has a larger-sized grain, which gives it a chewier texture that goes well in this salad.

TABOULEH SALAD WITH GRILLED VEGETABLES

Every August when tomatoes reach their peak ripeness, I crave tabouleh, a Middle Eastern salad of cracked bulgur, tomato, and parsley dressed with olive oil and lemon. We came up with this version in the Wellness Kitchen when working on whole-grain recipes. I love the fact that you do not have to wait until tomatoes are in season—you can make it any time of the year with a variety of vegetables that can go on the grill: asparagus, zucchini, red and yellow peppers, onions, and mushrooms are just a few suggestions. The grilled vegetables and cracked grain are tossed with a lite lemon and olive oil vinaigrette, fresh parsley, and mint, which gives it the exotic Middle Eastern flavor that goes beautifully with a simple grilled fish or chicken.

1 cup bulgur

1 cup boiling water

2 medium zucchini, cut lengthwise into ½" thick slabs

2 onions, cut into ½" thick rounds

3 large portobello mushroom caps, wiped clean

2 cups cherry tomatoes

2 tablespoons olive oil, divided

½ teaspoon sea salt

½ teaspoon freshly ground black pepper

¼ cup walnuts, measured then chopped

3 tablespoons lemon juice

½ cup chopped parsley

½ cup chopped mint

1. Preheat grill to medium-high.

2. Place bulgur in large bowl. Add boiling water and stir. Cover and let soak, about 20 minutes. It should be al dente, not mushy, to maintain the texture and the fiber content. Fluff with fork and set aside to cool.

3. Place zucchini, onions, mushrooms, and tomatoes in single layer on baking sheet. Gently toss vegetables with 1 tablespoon oil and sprinkle with salt and pepper.

4. Grill vegetables for about 6 minutes or until just tender and golden, turning halfway through cooking time. Remove from grill and set aside.

5. Toast walnuts in small, dry sauté pan over medium heat, stirring constantly, about 2–3 minutes or until lightly toasted. Set aside.

6. Coarsely chop grilled zucchini, onions, and mushrooms (leave tomatoes whole).

7. To the cooled bulgur, mix in remaining oil, lemon juice, parsley, and mint. Add vegetables and toss gently to combine.

8. To serve, place salad on platter and sprinkle top with walnuts.

SERVES: 8; CALORIES PER SERVING: 170; DIETARY EQUIVALENT: 1 carbohydrate, 2 vegetables, 1 fat

BLACK RICE AND EDAMAME SALAD WITH MEYER LEMON VINAIGRETTE

I truly believe we eat with our eyes, not just our taste buds, and this salad is a perfect example of that. I love to serve this salad on a buffet; the black rice color is stunning, providing the perfect backdrop for green and red vegetables. The nutty flavor of the black rice complements the flavor of the vegetables with a punch from the lemon vinaigrette. Years ago, black rice—known in China as "forbidden rice"—was cultivated in very small amounts and only for the emperors' consumption, but nowadays, you can find it in most markets. Black rice's nutritional profile is much higher than any other rice, due to a high antioxidant level, making it an excellent choice for health benefits, too.

1 cup black rice, rinsed

2 cups water

¼ cup Meyer lemon juice or 3 tablespoons regular lemon juice

2 tablespoons white wine vinegar

2 tablespoons water

1 tablespoon agave nectar or honey

2 tablespoons olive oil

½ cup walnuts, measured then toasted and chopped

4 green onions, thinly sliced

1 cup frozen shelled edamame, thawed

1 cup halved grape tomatoes

1 cup thinly sliced green beans

Sea salt

Freshly ground black pepper

1. In a medium saucepan, add rice and water; bring to a boil, then cover and reduce to simmer. Cook rice until just tender, about 35–40 minutes. Drain well, spread out on a rimmed baking sheet, and let cool.

2. Whisk lemon juice, vinegar, water, and sweetener in a small bowl. Whisking constantly, gradually drizzle in the oil to emulsify.

3. In a large bowl, toss rice, walnuts, green onions, edamame, tomatoes, and green beans with the vinaigrette. Season to taste with salt and pepper.

SERVES: 8; CALORIES PER SERVING: 235; DIETARY EQUIVALENT: 1 carbohydrate, ½ oz. protein, 2 fats

Nutrition Basics
Black rice contains five times more fiber than white rice and more than double the fiber of brown rice. The black color denotes a very high antioxidant level (similar to blueberries) and has been shown to decrease cholesterol and promote heart health. Soaking black rice, like many whole grains, overnight—or even for a few hours in cold water before cooking—speeds up the cooking time.

ROASTED CARROT AND QUINOA SALAD

The colors in this salad are beautiful and impressive: the brilliant orange of the carrots, the rich red color of the quinoa, the white of the feta cheese, and the ruby color of the cranberries on a bed of dark greens. Aside from the colors, the spices in this salad (turmeric, cumin, ginger, coriander, and cinnamon) all have antioxidant properties that improve brain and heart health. The salad has a delicious, exotic Mideast flavor that complements the natural sweetness of the carrots. Quinoa is a whole, complete protein grain, so if you would like to consume this for an entrée, just add a bit more feta cheese. I love bringing this to a party—everyone is so impressed, and they think I picked it up at a gourmet takeout!

Spice Mix

2 teaspoons sweet paprika

1 teaspoon ground turmeric

1 teaspoon ground cumin

1 teaspoon ground ginger

1 teaspoon ground coriander

1 teaspoon ground cinnamon

½ teaspoon cayenne pepper

¼ teaspoon ground cardamom

1 teaspoon sea salt

1 teaspoon freshly ground black pepper

Quinoa

Organic canola or olive oil cooking spray

4 carrots, halved and then cut lengthwise into quarters, then each quarter cut into thin strips

1 red onion, thinly sliced

2 tablespoons olive oil, divided

3 tablespoons plus 1 teaspoon Spice Mix (see recipe here), divided

1 cup red quinoa

2 cups organic, reduced-sodium, fat-free chicken broth

2 tablespoons lemon juice, divided

Sea salt

Freshly ground black pepper

5 ounces mixed greens

½ teaspoon lemon zest

1 teaspoon Dijon mustard

½ cup walnuts, measured then toasted and coarsely chopped

½ cup dried cranberries

2 tablespoons chopped parsley

¼ cup crumbled feta cheese (optional)

1. Preheat oven to 400°F.

2. In small bowl, combine all spice mix ingredients. Set aside.

3. Spray a rimmed baking sheet with cooking spray. In a large bowl, combine carrots, red onion, 1 tablespoon olive oil, and 1 tablespoon spice mix. Spread vegetables in a single layer on baking sheet and roast for 20–25 minutes until golden.

4. In medium saucepan, combine quinoa, 2 tablespoons spice mix, and broth. Bring to a boil, then reduce heat to simmer for 15–17 minutes or until quinoa is tender.

5. In large bowl, whisk remaining olive oil with 1 tablespoon lemon juice. Season to taste with salt and pepper. Add mixed greens and toss to coat just before serving.

6. In a separate large bowl, combine remaining lemon juice, lemon zest, Dijon mustard, and remaining spice mix. Stir in the quinoa, roasted vegetables, walnuts, cranberries, and parsley.

7. To serve, arrange mixed greens on large platter and serve quinoa salad over top. Garnish with crumbled feta, if desired.

SERVES: 8; CALORIES PER SERVING: 205; DIETARY EQUIVALENT: ½ oz. protein, 1½ vegetables, 1 carbohydrate

Food Tip

I often cook quinoa in the microwave. Just add 1 cup of quinoa to 2 cups of water in a large microwave-safe bowl and cook on high for 10–12 minutes or just until grain is tender. I cover the bowl and place it in the refrigerator to use for the next few days. I love it for breakfast with fruit and yogurt.

FARMERS' MARKET SALAD WITH ROASTED BUTTERNUT SQUASH

I should call this the Superantioxidant Salad because of its very high antioxidant content from the pomegranate, butternut squash, and dark green arugula. Mother Nature color-coded fruits and vegetables—the more brilliant and vibrant the colors, the higher the antioxidant level. You can often find pomegranate seeds in containers in the produce aisle of your market—buying them that way does save time (I always keep a container in my freezer). I prep each ingredient beforehand and place them in ziptop bags, then all I have to do is toss the greens with the vinaigrette and assemble on a platter at the last minute. Drizzle on the pomegranate reduction right before serving for the most visual effect! Try adding roasted chicken or turkey for a complete entrée, too.

4 cups butternut squash, cut into ½" cubes

1 tablespoon olive oil

Pinch of dried red pepper flakes

1 teaspoon sea salt, divided

2 tablespoons orange juice

2 tablespoons pomegranate juice

1 tablespoon water

1 tablespoon walnut or olive oil

½ teaspoon freshly ground black pepper

1 cup pomegranate juice

1 (5-ounce) bag arugula

½ cup feta or goat cheese, crumbled

¼ cup walnuts, toasted and chopped

½ cup pomegranate seeds

1. Preheat oven to 400°F.

2. Coat squash with olive oil, red pepper flakes, and ½ teaspoon salt. Spread on baking sheet and roast for 30–40 minutes until tender and golden. Set aside to cool. (May be prepared a day in advance.)

3. In a small bowl, whisk orange juice, pomegranate juice, water, oil, remaining ½ teaspoon salt, and pepper. Set aside.

4. To make the pomegranate reduction: Place 1 cup pomegranate juice in saucepan and reduce over low heat for 20 minutes or until thick and syrupy. Watch carefully to avoid burning, because of natural sugar content. Cool completely before using. (The reduction may be kept covered in refrigerator for 3 days.)

5. To serve, toss the arugula with the dressing and place on a platter, arranging the roasted butternut squash over the top. Sprinkle with crumbled cheese, walnuts, and pomegranate seeds. Finish with a drizzle of the pomegranate reduction.

SERVES: 6; CALORIES PER SERVING: 195; DIETARY EQUIVALENT: 1 carbohydrate, 2 fats, 2 vegetables

Food Tip

For years, when I tried to peel butternut squash, I would get the knife stuck in the hard shell of the squash when I tried to cut it in half. I truly think it is one of the most dangerous tasks in the kitchen! That is, until one day I figured out how to do this safely and quickly. First, before cooking, pierce 5–6 holes in the shell with a sharp knife, just through the skin, to release the steam. This is a very important step if you do not want an explosion and a mess to clean up! Place the whole squash in the microwave and cook on high for 5–6 minutes to soften the shell and squash. Remove the skin with a vegetable peeler, and then it will cut easily in half. Scoop out the seeds and cut the squash in cubes to roast for a salad. If you are going to purée it instead, just cut in half, de-seed, and place cut side down on a baking sheet covered with parchment paper or foil. Bake at 350°F until tender (approximately 30–40 minutes, depending on the size of your squash), then scoop out the squash from the shell. Of course, there is absolutely nothing wrong with buying it already peeled and cubed at your market!

ARUGULA SALAD WITH APPLES AND MINT

Move over, kale! My new love in the salad department for the last few years has been arugula; I add handfuls to everything I can. If salads bore you (heaven forbid), this is the green for you. Known as rocket in other parts of the world, arugula's peppery flavor marries well with many flavors. It is often paired with Parmesan, tomatoes, lemon, and pears, and it is a great green to toss into pastas at the last minute. In this recipe, apples add sweetness, the walnuts a nuttiness, the feta a little saltiness, and the mint a cooling contrast to the peppery arugula. It all comes together to make this a very addictive salad indeed! Add roasted or grilled chicken to this salad and turn it into a satisfying entrée. I love to make this salad the day after "turkey day," when I definitely need lighter fare and have leftover turkey that needs to find a meal other than with mashed potatoes and gravy.

⅓ cup walnuts, measured then coarsely chopped

2 teaspoons grainy mustard

2 teaspoons honey

1 shallot, minced

2 tablespoons apple cider vinegar

1 tablespoon water

1 tablespoon olive oil

½ teaspoon sea salt

½ teaspoon black pepper

3 crisp red apples (Pink Lady or Empire), cored and cut into thin slices

5 ounces (6 cups) baby arugula, washed and dried

¼ cup coarsely chopped fresh mint leaves

2 ounces soft goat or feta cheese, crumbled

1. In a small sauté pan, over medium heat, toast walnuts. Stir frequently, until lightly toasted, about 5 minutes. Set aside to cool.

2. In a small bowl, whisk the mustard, honey, shallot, vinegar, water, oil, salt, and pepper. Set aside.

3. Place apples and arugula in a large salad bowl.

4. To serve, toss salad with dressing and top with mint, cheese, and walnuts.

SERVES: 4; CALORIES PER SERVING: 210; DIETARY EQUIVALENT: 2 vegetables, 1 fruit, 1 fat

Nutrition Basics

Arugula, in the same family as kale, was thought to be an aphrodisiac in Roman times and has been used in "love potions" for centuries. And no wonder—the health benefits are phenomenal and we all know that to be sexy one needs to be healthy. Arugula is rich in antioxidants, folic acid, iron, and vitamins A, C, and K. Vitamin K, needed for healthy bones, is low in most Americans' diets, making this salad green a top choice for improving health.

DATE, PEAR, AND GOAT CHEESE SALAD WITH POMEGRANATE VINAIGRETTE

This is a classic fall or winter salad with many variations that you probably have prepared or had when dining out. Baby greens, fall fruit, cheese, and nuts make up the basic recipe, but I love to add a bit more color to really make it pop visually and add a bit more tang to excite the taste buds. Pomegranate juice and seeds do just that, making a fantastic dressing and addition to the salad. I always say that pomegranate seeds on a bed of greens look like rubies in your salad! Besides the appealing brilliant red color, pomegranate seeds add nutritional value. One half cup of the seeds provides 50 percent of the daily vitamin C requirement, and the bright red color denotes a very high antioxidant level that helps lower risk for certain kinds of cancers.

¼ cup pomegranate juice

1 tablespoon red wine vinegar

1 teaspoon Dijon mustard

1 tablespoon honey

1 tablespoon olive oil

Sea salt

Freshly ground black pepper

8 cups mixed baby greens

2 pears, cored, thinly sliced

¼ cup Medjool dates, measured then pitted and sliced

¼ cup pomegranate seeds

2 ounces goat cheese

¼ cup walnuts, measured then toasted and coarsely chopped

1. In small bowl, whisk together the pomegranate juice, vinegar, Dijon, honey, and olive oil. Season to taste with salt and pepper. Set aside.

2. In large bowl, combine greens with half of the sliced pear.

3. Toss salad with vinaigrette.

4. Top with the remaining pear slices, dates, and pomegranate seeds. Crumble the goat cheese over the top and garnish with the nuts. Serve.

SERVES: 6; CALORIES PER SERVING: 175; DIETARY EQUIVALENT: 2 fats, 1 fruit, 1 vegetable

Food Tip

When we were children, on our way home from school my sister and I would pass a pomegranate tree that just begged us to eat its fruit. I remember my mother admonishing us for getting pomegranate juice all over our clothing, since it results in permanent stains. Over the years I tried various ways to get the seeds out of this magical fruit without totally destroying my kitchen and whatever I was wearing. I love the fact that now, when pomegranates are really in season, I can purchase them already prepared in most markets in small containers. If not, our Wellness Kitchen manager David taught me how to do it easily: just cut in half, hold over a bowl, gently tap the shell with the back of a spoon, and the seeds pop right into the bowl!

SPINACH SALAD WITH WHEAT BERRIES AND FETA

Isn't it nice to hear your family members say, "Make this again, I love it!" And it's even better when the dish is not a dessert! Expect just that when you serve this delightfully sweet, nutty salad. My favorite part is the wheat berries, which are whole kernels of wheat. When cooked, they turn into the most delightful, chewy, nutty-tasting bits that add a lot of texture to an ordinary salad. The tender baby spinach pairs beautifully with berries. I often use whatever berries are in season, mixing them or using only one type depending on what I have on hand. I pair this salad with vinaigrette made from sherry wine with origins in southern Spain. I had the opportunity to be in Spain years ago, and while the 200-year-old sherry I tasted was a bit strong for my palate, ordinary sherry vinegar has a complex, deep, slightly sweet flavor that is awesome with greens and fruit.

4 cups baby spinach

1 cup wheat berries, cooked and cooled

1 orange, sectioned

1 cup mixed fresh berries

2 tablespoons sherry vinegar

1 tablespoon water

1 teaspoon Dijon mustard

1 tablespoon walnut oil

Sea salt

Freshly ground black pepper

⅓ cup feta cheese

1. In a large salad bowl, combine spinach, wheat berries, orange, and berries.

2. In a small bowl, whisk vinegar, water, Dijon, and oil. Season to taste with salt and pepper.

3. To serve, toss salad with vinaigrette and crumble feta over the top.

SERVES: 6; CALORIES PER SERVING: 150; DIETARY EQUIVALENT: 1 vegetable, 1 carbohydrate

Nutrition Basics

Add ½ to 1 cup of cooked, cooled grains to many of your salads to increase much-needed fiber, antioxidants, and B-complex vitamins. Not only is the texture great, but these grains will keep you full for a longer time than just plain salad can. I cook whole grains in the microwave in the evening, by combining grains and water according to the proportions on the box in a large microwavable bowl and popping it into the microwave for 10–15 minutes, or until the water is evaporated and the grains are tender. Keep cooked whole grains covered for up to 3 days in the refrigerator and add to salads and soups, or you can warm them up quickly as a breakfast cereal topped with fruit and yogurt.

ROASTED BEET SALAD WITH AVOCADO, GRILLED ASPARAGUS, AND FARRO

Everything about this salad just works together: earthy beets, nutty farro, smoky grilled asparagus, and creamy avocado are all enlivened with fresh lemony vinaigrette. Pair it with grilled fish, chicken, or meats for a very satisfying, hearty meal. I fell in love with farro, an ancient grain, while taking a cooking class in Tuscany. I found bushel baskets of it in every little market I entered. It's used in soups, stews, and desserts, and served as a side dish like rice. Its nutty taste and satisfying, chewy texture, along with its stellar nutrition profile, have made it a staple in the Wellness Kitchen and at home. Farro comes in 2 forms: semi-pearled, which means that some of the outer bran has been removed, or whole-grain. If you use whole-grain, which is even higher in fiber, it's best to soak it overnight to decrease cooking time.

Salad

2 large beets, rinsed and trimmed
½ pound asparagus
1 tablespoon olive oil
Sea salt
Freshly ground black pepper
8 ounces baby arugula
1 avocado, diced
1 cup cooked farro
2 ounces feta cheese, crumbled
⅓ cup walnuts, measured then chopped

Vinaigrette

3 tablespoons lemon juice
1 tablespoon red wine vinegar
1 tablespoon water
1 tablespoon olive oil
Pinch of sea salt
Pinch of fresh black pepper

1. Preheat oven to 400°F. Preheat grill to medium-high heat.
2. Wrap beets in foil and roast for 45–60 minutes in the oven.

3. In large bowl, toss asparagus with the olive oil, salt, and pepper. Grill asparagus for 3–4 minutes. Chop into bite-sized pieces. Set aside.
4. Whisk vinaigrette ingredients in small bowl. Cover and chill until ready to use.
5. When ready to serve, toss asparagus, arugula, avocado, and farro with the vinaigrette.
6. Top salad with crumbled feta cheese and walnuts.

SERVES: 6; CALORIES PER SERVING: 225; DIETARY EQUIVALENT: 2½ vegetables, 1 fat

Nutrition Basics

Semi-pearled farro takes 20 minutes to cook and whole-grain takes 40 minutes to cook—but in either case, make sure you do not overcook whole grains. Keep them al dente, with a little chew, so the beneficial fiber stays intact. If that time frame won't work with the time you have to prepare meals, make the grain ahead of time. In addition to refrigerating already made grains, I also freeze them. I actually keep a supply of whole grains, including farro, precooked and frozen in my freezer. It's easy to cook up a batch, cool, and place a few cups in freezer bags to be taken out when needed. It can be easily thawed in the microwave or added frozen to soups, stews, etc.

ASIAN CHICKEN SALAD

I love Asian salads and I cannot imagine how many I have consumed over the years. I love this one particularly because the flavor-packed dressing with ginger and sesame oil is light, yet it stands up to the chicken and vegetables. I love using the Napa cabbage instead of the traditional iceberg lettuce—not only is Napa way healthier, but it does not wilt for hours. The snow peas, cucumbers, carrots, and edamame give this salad even more crunch and a real nutritional boost compared to the traditional iceberg lettuce and bland, fried-noodle salads of the past.

Salad

3 cups shredded cooked chicken
½ pound (about 3½ cups) shredded Napa cabbage
¼ pound snow peas, cut in 1" pieces
1 seedless cucumber, quartered and sliced
3 green onions, thinly sliced on the bias
¼ cup chopped cilantro
1 cup shredded carrots
1 cup shelled edamame
1 tablespoon black sesame seeds

Dressing

¼ cup reduced-sodium soy sauce
2 tablespoons seasoned rice vinegar
1 tablespoon sesame oil
1 tablespoon Dijon mustard
1 tablespoon chopped ginger
¼ teaspoon crushed red pepper flakes

1. Toss all salad ingredients together in large bowl except for sesame seeds.
2. Whisk all dressing ingredients together in small bowl.
3. To serve, toss salad with dressing, place in serving bowl or platter, and sprinkle with sesame seeds.

SERVES: 4; CALORIES PER SERVING: 230; DIETARY EQUIVALENT: 3 oz. protein, 1 vegetable, 1 fat

Nutrition Basics

This salad is prepared with Napa cabbage, not the usual iceberg lettuce, giving it detoxifying properties that lettuce salads do not have. Other detoxifying vegetables are broccoli, cauliflower, Brussels sprouts, bok choy, and kale. Since cabbage does not wilt quickly, leftover salad may be kept refrigerated for 24 hours.

THAI KALE SALAD

As a nutritionist, I cannot say enough about kale's health benefits; as a foodie, I sometimes wish we would move on to the next "trendy" green. I do love kale when it's cooked in braises, soups, and stews. But I think I have eaten too many tough and bitter kale salads for their health benefits without otherwise being excited about them . . . until now. The secret? Use baby kale, or micro kale (often available prewashed in bags)—it's tender, less bitter, and so much more edible. The Thai peanut dressing is well-matched to the robust flavor of the kale, so now I have seconds on a salad that is super healthy and delicious! Dress your salad lightly with this dressing; it's flavor-packed, so a small amount goes a long way. Use any leftover dressing in a vegetable stir-fry, or brush on grilled chicken for a quick Thai fix.

Dressing

¼ cup natural chunky peanut butter

1 tablespoon unseasoned rice vinegar

1 tablespoon tamari or reduced-sodium soy sauce

2 teaspoons sesame oil

1 tablespoon finely grated fresh ginger

2 teaspoons minced garlic

1 tablespoon sesame seeds

1 teaspoon Sriracha sauce

2 tablespoons water

Salad

1 pound of baby kale, or micro kale

4 scallions, sliced on the diagonal

4 large radishes, julienned or thinly-sliced half-moons

1 cup mandarin oranges packed in juice, drained

2 tablespoons salted peanuts, measured then roughly chopped

1. Combine the peanut butter, vinegar, tamari, sesame oil, ginger, garlic, sesame seeds, Sriracha, and water in a food processor or blender. Purée until smooth, adding more water if needed.

2. Place the kale in a large bowl and toss with some of the dressing. Add the scallions, radishes, and orange segments; combine well.

3. To serve, transfer the salad to a platter and garnish with peanuts. Remaining dressing may be covered and stored in the refrigerator for up to 3 days.

SERVES: 8; CALORIES PER SERVING: 80; DIETARY EQUIVALENT: 1 vegetable, fat

Nutrition Basics

If baby kale is still too much for your taste buds, try mixing it in with other greens, baby lettuces, or spinach. All dark leafy greens are rich in antioxidants and vitamins A, C, and K and folic acid, so any combination has great health benefits.

BROCCOLI SLAW

Never has broccoli tasted so good! This slaw will make the most reluctant broccoli eaters fall in love with this vegetable. The raw, shredded broccoli has a crunch, and when it's teamed with sweet peas and raisins, crunchy sunflower seeds, and a dressing that is tangy and sweet, it takes on a whole different flavor profile. If you cannot find broccoli slaw already cut in your produce section of the market, just shred raw broccoli with stems attached in a food processor using the shredding blade. Guests in the Wellness Kitchen are amazed that something so good for you can taste so good! It's a great side dish for grilled chicken or fish any time of the year.

Dressing

¼ cup sugar

⅓ cup cider vinegar

1 tablespoon olive oil

1 tablespoon water

2 tablespoons lite mayonnaise

1 tablespoon Dijon mustard

1 teaspoon Tabasco sauce

½ teaspoon salt

¼ teaspoon pepper

Slaw

1 (12-ounce) bag of broccoli slaw

1 cup frozen peas, thawed

½ cup chopped scallions

⅓ cup raisins

¼ cup dry-roasted sunflower seeds

1. To make dressing, whisk together all ingredients in small bowl.

2. Add slaw ingredients and toss to coat. Make this salad a few hours before serving so the full flavor develops. Broccoli slaw can be kept up to 3 days in the refrigerator if you're lucky enough to have any left!

SERVES: 8; CALORIES PER SERVING: 150; DIETARY EQUIVALENT: 1 carbohydrate, 1 vegetable, 1 fat

Nutrition Basics

Broccoli is a fiber-filled vegetable known to help lower cholesterol and detoxify the body of environmental contamination; it is high in vitamins A and K, which help keep vitamin D metabolism in balance. Broccoli is rich in flavonoids that lessen the impact of allergy substances in the body.

CHIPOTLE CILANTRO SLAW

We call this our "killer slaw" in the Wellness Kitchen, a description that we came up with when we developed this recipe to go on our Pulled Turkey Sandwiches with Cranberry BBQ Sauce (see recipe in Chapter 5). The "chipotle chili," which is a smoked jalapeño in adobo sauce, can be found in your market in the Mexican food section in a small can or jar. You can add more or less depending on how much heat you like. Try this spicy slaw on any turkey sandwich—it's also delicious on a fish taco.

⅓ cup lite mayonnaise
1 finely diced chipotle chili in adobo sauce
Juice of ½ lime
2 teaspoons honey or sugar
½ teaspoon salt
1 teaspoon ground cumin
3 cups finely shredded cabbage
1 cup shredded carrots
¼ cup finely chopped cilantro

1. In small bowl combine mayonnaise, chili, lime juice, sweetener, salt, and cumin; mix well.
2. Place shredded cabbage and carrots and chopped cilantro in a salad bowl, and toss with dressing, combining well.
3. Refrigerate until ready to serve.

SERVES: 8; CALORIES PER SERVING: 60; DIETARY EQUIVALENT: 1 vegetable, 1 fat

Nutrition Basics

Adding a scoop of this slaw to a sandwich is a great way to increase your fiber intake and gives your sandwich more volume for very little calories. Don't hesitate to use pre-shredded cabbage found in the produce section of the market; the convenience may be worth it if it means you eat healthier!

Chapter 4

Soups and Breads

We get rave reviews on our soups in the Wellness Kitchen, and guests are always surprised at just how easy it is to make a delicious pot of soup. I think many of us have visions of a long, drawn-out process that entails a concoction simmering on the stove for hours . . . when in fact you can make a soup in as little as 10 minutes of prep time and 20 minutes of cooking. The result? A wonderful first course or a perfect entrée paired with a salad.

Many of our recipes call for chicken or vegetable broth. Good-quality broths are now available in your local market. I really encourage you to use organic, fat-free, reduced-sodium broth—mostly because you certainly won't miss the hormones, antibiotics, added fat, or high levels of sodium. I keep a few quarts of these broths in my pantry so I can always make soup. Most of our soups are made with herbs, which gives them a real flavor boost and adds healthy antioxidants.

Few recipes are as straightforward or as healthy as puréed vegetable soups. The whole process can be as simple as a quick sauté of onion, garlic, maybe ginger or crushed red pepper flakes in a drop of olive oil, then the addition of healthy vegetables and broth, a few minutes' simmering, and then puréeing. You have a vegetable soup that is delicious and healthy, a great way to increase your vegetable intake. We often add a small amount of fat-free half-and-half and other seasonings at the end. I found that many people who do not love eating vegetables have absolutely no objection to them in these delightful soups. You won't believe how decadent Cauliflower Soup with truffle oil is or how utterly delightful the Ginger Carrot Soup is!

Many of our soups, such as the Italian Chicken Soup with Farro and Pesto, Chicken Tortilla Soup, or Spiced Pumpkin and Black Bean Soup, are actually one-pot meals that just need a side salad and maybe our Homemade Corn Bread to be a complete meal. Don't forget that you can freeze any leftover soup for another time!

PURÉED VEGETABLE SOUP

I love to see our guests' faces in the Wellness Kitchen when they first taste a rich puréed vegetable soup. The velvety texture and the wonderful subtlety of flavor make eating more vegetables so easy. I vividly remember one middle-aged male guest, who declared he does not eat vegetables . . . we had him at the first spoonful. You're sure to find one that grabs your attention in our list of variations.

1 tablespoon olive oil
1 tablespoon chopped garlic
½ onion, chopped
2 pounds vegetables, washed and trimmed, cut into bite-sized pieces
1 quart organic, reduced-sodium, fat-free chicken broth
½ cup fat-free half-and-half
Sea salt
Freshly ground black pepper

1. Heat olive oil in large soup pot. Add garlic and onion, sauté until tender, about 4–5 minutes.
2. Add vegetables and broth. Bring to a boil, cover, and simmer for 15–20 minutes until vegetables are very tender.
3. Purée soup in batches in blender, returning each to the soup pot (or use an immersion blender).
4. Reheat soup until very hot, reduce heat to a simmer, and add fat-free half-and-half. Season to taste with salt and pepper and serve.

SERVES: 6; CALORIES PER SERVING: 100–120; DIETARY EQUIVA-LENT: 2 vegetables, 1 fat

VARIATIONS

BROCCOLI CHEESE SOUP

Use 2 pounds of broccoli. Add ⅓ cup grated Parmesan cheese after adding half-and-half.

CAULIFLOWER SOUP

Use 2 pounds of cauliflower. Add 1 small fennel bulb, thinly sliced, with onion. To garnish, drizzle each serving of soup with 1 teaspoon truffle-infused olive oil.

ASPARAGUS SOUP

Use 2 pounds of asparagus. Add the zest and juice of 1 lemon before adding half-and-half.

GINGER CARROT SOUP

Use 2 pounds of carrots. Add 1½ tablespoons chopped ginger with the onions and garlic. Add ½ cup orange juice, ½ teaspoon cinnamon, and ¼ teaspoon nutmeg before adding half-and-half.

ZUCCHINI BASIL SOUP

Use 2 pounds of zucchini. Add ¾ cup loose basil leaves and ¼ teaspoon chili powder 5 minutes before puréeing the soup. Garnish each bowl with a dollop of plain nonfat yogurt and a chiffonade of basil.

> *Food Tip*
> A mirepoix consists of finely diced onion, celery, and carrot and is used to add flavor and aroma to soups, stocks, sauces, etc. When building a soup, be sure to use only one main vegetable. Too many varieties of vegetables will turn the soup an off color and the flavors become muddled when puréed. It's great to start a soup with mirepoix to add flavor, but use only 1–2 puréed vegetables in a puréed soup so the colors and flavors are not too muddled.

CHILLED AVOCADO AND CUCUMBER SOUP

This impressive soup is so easy: no cooking required! I remember the first time we made this in the Wellness Kitchen; the guest who made the soup that summer day was a total novice in the kitchen but whipped it up in no time. When this soup was served at table, he was so pleased with himself; he had rave reviews on how beautiful and delicious it was. If you make this soup ahead, refrigerate it covered and blend it again for a minute just before serving to make sure it is light and frothy; no one will know the difference. Make sure you serve this soup chilled; it's as pleasurable on a hot day as a milkshake!

1 large English cucumber, peeled, diced (about 2½ cups)
1½ cups low-fat (1%) buttermilk
1 avocado, pitted, peeled, and quartered, divided
¼ cup finely chopped red onion, divided
2 tablespoons chopped basil, divided
Sea salt
Freshly ground black pepper
1 medium vine-ripe tomato, seeded and chopped into ¼" dice
2 teaspoons lime juice
¼ cup plain nonfat Greek yogurt

1. Combine cucumber and buttermilk in blender.
2. Dice and set aside ¼ of the avocado for the salad garnish.
3. Cut remaining avocado into chunks and add to blender. Add 2 tablespoons red onion and 1 tablespoon basil. Blend until very smooth and season to taste with salt and pepper. Cover and refrigerate until chilled, about 1 hour.
4. Mix reserved ¼ avocado, remaining 2 tablespoons onions, and 1 tablespoon chopped basil, diced tomato, and lime juice in small bowl. (Can be prepared 1 day ahead; cover soup and tomato salad separately and refrigerate.)
5. To serve, ladle cucumber soup into serving bowls. Garnish with a dollop of Greek yogurt and the tomato, avocado, and basil salad.

SERVES: 4; CALORIES PER SERVING: 170; DIETARY EQUIVALENT: 1 carbohydrate, 1 fat, 1 vegetable

Nutrition Basics

While avocado is considered a fat, it's a healthy one, full of omega-3s and vitamin A. A whole medium avocado is approximately 400 calories, so use sparely on salads and sandwiches if you need to monitor calories.

BOUILLABAISSE

✈

Most guests in the Wellness Kitchen who taste this dish wonder why they have not made it before. I think it is because "bouillabaisse" sounds complicated, but it isn't! It really is a one-pot meal that can be assembled in just minutes, yet it is so impressive with its exotic flavor of saffron. When I serve this for a dinner party and guests rave over their meal, as a nutritionist I secretly relish the fact that all they had was fish, vegetables, and a small amount of healthy carbohydrates for the meal!

1 tablespoon olive oil
1 onion, diced
1 small fennel bulb, cut into small dice
2 tablespoons chopped garlic
1 (14-ounce) can peeled, diced tomatoes with juice
6 Yukon Gold potatoes, cut into small dice
1 bay leaf
¼ teaspoon saffron
6 cups clam juice or fish stock
1 pound white fish, cut into 2" pieces (halibut, tilapia, snapper, cod, bass, or grouper)
½ pound scallops
½ pound shrimp
2 tablespoons fresh chopped parsley
Rouille

1. Place large soup pot over medium heat; add olive oil, onion, and fennel. Sauté for 5 minutes or until onions and fennel are soft and golden.

2. Add garlic and sauté for 1 minute. Add tomatoes, potatoes, bay leaf, saffron, and clam juice. Bring to a boil then reduce heat to a simmer. Cook until potatoes are just tender, about 8–10 minutes.

3. Meanwhile, cut fish into bite-sized pieces.

4. When potatoes are tender, add seafood, cover, and reduce to simmer for 5 minutes until seafood is just pink (do not overcook). Add parsley. Remove bay leaf.

5. To serve, ladle into shallow bowls and top each serving with 1 tablespoon rouille.

ROUILLE

½ cup coarse fresh bread crumbs
1 tablespoon garlic, finely chopped
½ teaspoon cayenne pepper
1 tablespoon olive oil
¼ cup broth from soup
½ teaspoon salt

In food processor combine all ingredients and purée until blended.

SERVES: 8; CALORIES PER SERVING: 320; DIETARY EQUIVALENT: 5 oz. protein, 1 carbohydrate, ½ fat

Nutrition Basics

Since I also like to serve rustic bread with this entrée soup, I limit the potato to 4 oz. per person to control the calories and the amount of carbohydrate. This soup can be made ahead and just reheated, but do not add the seafood until right before serving. Just bring to a boil, turn down to a simmer, and add the fish and seafood. Cover and turn off the heat for perfect seafood that is not overcooked.

ROASTED TOMATO SOUP WITH PARMESAN CROSTINI

When my garden is overflowing with more red, juicy tomatoes than I possibly can use, I love to roast them in the oven. Oven-roasting tomatoes reduces their water content, so you are left with a very rich flavor. I let them just slightly char, giving them a nice smoky taste. Then I freeze them for later use—such as in this soup—when all the tomatoes are gone from my garden. If you or your family can't find enjoyable ways to eat more veggies, this soup is a great start. Almost everyone loves tomato soup, even those who do not like raw tomatoes! Turn it into a meal by serving it with cheesy toast (whole-grain bread with a low-fat cheese such as provolone) and a wonderful salad.

Organic olive oil cooking spray

4 pounds vine-ripe tomatoes, quartered (or 4 pounds cocktail tomatoes)

½ medium onion, sliced thin

2 teaspoons olive oil

2 tablespoons balsamic vinegar

1 teaspoon sea salt

Freshly ground black pepper

1 (3-ounce) baguette, sliced into 8 thin slices

¼ cup grated Parmesan cheese

1 quart organic, reduced-sodium, fat-free chicken broth

½ cup fat-free half-and-half

1 tablespoon chopped parsley or basil

1. Preheat oven to 375°F.

2. Spray baking sheet with nonstick spray.

3. Place tomatoes and onions on a rimmed baking sheet. Toss with olive oil, balsamic vinegar, salt, and pepper. Spread in single layer and roast for 45–60 minutes.

4. Meanwhile, slice baguette thinly and place on separate baking sheet. Place a small amount of cheese on each piece of bread. Set aside.

5. Bring broth to a boil in large soup pot.

6. When roasted, scrape tomato-onion mixture into broth and simmer 5–7 minutes.

7. Purée soup in blender or food processor in small batches; add back to soup pot.

8. Add fat-free half-and-half and adjust seasonings; add chopped parsley or basil.

9. Place Parmesan crostini under the broiler for 1–2 minutes, until cheese is melted and lightly browned.

10. To serve, divide soup between 6 bowls and place 1 crostino on top of each soup.

SERVES: 6; CALORIES PER SERVING: 150; DIETARY EQUIVALENT: 1 carbohydrate, 1 vegetable, ½ fat

Nutrition Basics

Oven-roasted tomatoes are higher in antioxidants than raw since the antioxidants really concentrate when roasted. Make sure to use the large amount of tomatoes in the recipe to get that rich tomato flavor and increased nutrition. If you're using off-season fresh tomatoes from your market, look for the vine-ripened ones. They have the most intense flavor.

CURRIED COCONUT CARROT SOUP

This soup with its beautiful color, rich texture, and exotic spices is an all-time favorite in the Wellness Kitchen. While it's Thai in origin, with the spices and lite coconut milk it pairs very well with traditional foods since it is not overwhelmingly spicy or "hot." I love to serve this at Thanksgiving—the color is amazing and the sweet carrot flavor with a touch of exotic spices is a lovely contrast to turkey or chicken. Try serving it chilled on a hot summer night too!

1 tablespoon olive oil
1 medium onion, chopped
1 large shallot, sliced
1 pound carrots, peeled and sliced
1 tablespoon chopped garlic
1 heaping tablespoon minced ginger
1 teaspoon minced serrano chili or jalapeño
1 teaspoon ground coriander
¾ teaspoon Madras-style hot curry powder
3 cups vegetable broth
½ cup lite coconut milk
1½ tablespoons fresh lime juice
Sea salt
Freshly ground black pepper
2 tablespoons chopped fresh cilantro
2 tablespoons pepitas or pine nuts, toasted

1. Heat olive oil in a large soup pot over medium heat. Add onion, shallot, and carrots. Cook, stirring occasionally, until slightly softened, about 5 minutes.
2. Add garlic, ginger, chilies, coriander, and curry powder. Cook until fragrant, about 1 minute.
3. Add vegetable broth, cover partially, and bring to a boil over high heat. Reduce to simmer for 20 minutes or until carrots are fork-tender.
4. Purée soup in a blender, working in batches, add back to soup pot. Stir in the coconut milk and lime juice; season to taste with salt and pepper.
5. Ladle into bowls. Garnish with cilantro and pepitas.

SERVES: 4; CALORIES PER SERVING: 120; DIETARY EQUIVALENT: 1 vegetable, 1 carbohydrate

CHICKEN TORTILLA SOUP

This entrée soup is a perennial favorite, and it's a healthy way to indulge in South of the Border flavors in just minutes. This is a very forgiving soup, as the flavor is not at all compromised by using canned beans, jarred tomatoes, or frozen corn. It's the kind of dish that's even better after a night in the refrigerator. Years ago when working with a school food service program, we came up with the idea of adding diced zucchini, a Southwest squash, at the last minute. We wanted to get more vegetables into the kids and figured that if we diced the zucchini very small they couldn't pick it out. And we were right! Add the zucchini at the last minute so it maintains its bright color and does not overcook. There's no need to add more chicken than the recipe calls for; the black beans and cheese add protein as well. There is a great health benefit to eating less animal protein and more beans, since beans contain no saturated fat yet are very high in nutrients.

2 boneless, skinless chicken breasts, cut in half

6 cups organic, reduced-sodium, fat-free chicken broth

1 tablespoon olive oil

1 medium red onion, diced

1 tablespoon minced garlic

2 teaspoons ground cumin

2 tablespoons ground chili powder

1½ cups frozen corn kernels

1 (15-ounce) can Mexican style chopped tomatoes

2 (15-ounce) cans black beans, rinsed and drained

4 corn tortillas

Organic canola or olive oil cooking spray

Sea salt

2 medium zucchini, cut into ¼" dice

2 tablespoons chopped fresh cilantro

½ cup shredded low-fat jack cheese

1. Preheat oven to 400°F.

2. To poach chicken; place chicken breast in saucepan, cover with 3 cups chicken broth, and place over medium heat until just boiling. Turn heat down to simmer and simmer for 10 minutes. Remove and place on cutting board to cool. Slice or shred into bite-sized pieces. Reserve poaching liquid.

3. Meanwhile, in large soup pot, heat olive oil. Add onion, garlic, cumin, and chili powder. Sauté until onions are soft (add 1–2 tablespoons water if necessary).

4. Add the poaching liquid plus the remaining 3 cups of chicken broth, corn, tomatoes, and beans. Bring to a boil, then reduce to a simmer for 5 minutes.

5. Meanwhile, stack tortillas together and slice in ¼" thin strips. Place in a single layer on baking sheet. Lightly coat with cooking spray. Season lightly with salt. Bake for 8–10 minutes or until crisp. Set aside.

6. Add cut-up chicken, zucchini, and cilantro to soup and simmer for 2 minutes. Adjust seasonings if needed.

7. To serve, ladle soup into serving bowls and top with tortilla strips and shredded cheese.

SERVES: 4 (2-cup servings); CALORIES PER SERVING: 490; DIETARY EQUIVALENT: 4 oz. protein, 2 carbohydrates, 1 vegetable, 1 fat

Food Tip

Poaching chicken in broth or even water is a quick way to have cooked chicken for soups, salads, and other entrées. Poached chicken is moist and tender compared to grilled chicken, which has a tendency to dry out. Another plus is that you have a more intensely flavored broth to add to your soup! To poach chicken breasts, cut them in quarters, place in saucepan, add water or broth to just cover, and bring to a boil. Reduce heat to a simmer and continue to cook for 10 minutes, or until chicken is no longer pink in the middle of the breast.

ITALIAN CHICKEN SOUP WITH FARRO AND PESTO

A few years ago, I had the opportunity to visit the Tuscan countryside and found farro, an ancient whole-grain wheat. It was in every little market in bushel baskets or burlap bags and on many restaurant menus. It was served in soups, added to salads, or served as a pilaf with meat, chicken, or fish. I brought a bag home with me and it was gone in no time. I was then on a mission to find a local supplier of this magnificent grain and found it in a small Italian market in my neighborhood. Now, a few years later, farro can found in most markets in the rice and bean aisle. In this soup, farro, fennel, greens, Parmesan, and pesto come together in a homey soup that brings the Tuscan countryside to your table!

1 tablespoon olive oil

1 onion, chopped

¼ teaspoon crushed red pepper flakes

4 skinless, boneless chicken breasts, cubed into bite-sized pieces

6 sprigs flat-leaf parsley, chopped

6 (3" long) strips lemon peel, cut from 1 lemon

2 quarts organic, reduced-sodium, fat-free chicken broth

1 small head fennel, thinly sliced

2 carrots, sliced

2 stalks celery, sliced

1 cup 10-minute farro or 2 cups of precooked farro

3 cups baby spinach or baby kale

Lemon juice, to taste

Sea salt

Freshly ground black pepper

¼ cup grated Parmesan cheese

Pesto, good quality, store-bought, for garnish

1. Heat the olive oil in large soup pot set over medium heat. Add the onion and crushed red pepper flakes. Cook until the onions begin to soften, about 5 minutes.

2. Add the chicken and sauté for 5 minutes. Add the parsley, lemon peel, and broth. Bring soup to a boil, then reduce heat to simmer for 5 minutes.

3. Add the fennel, carrots, and celery to the broth. Continue to simmer until the vegetables are just tender, approximately 5 minutes. Stir in the farro and cook until al dente, about 10–12 minutes. Stir in the baby spinach just until the spinach is wilted.

4. Discard the lemon peel. Stir in lemon juice and season with salt and pepper.

5. To serve, ladle the soup into serving bowls. Garnish each bowl with Parmesan and 1 teaspoon of pesto. Serve immediately.

SERVES: 4 (entrée portion); CALORIES PER SERVING: 340; DIETARY EQUIVALENT: 4 oz. lean protein, 1 carbohydrate, 1 vegetable, 1 fat

SPICED PUMPKIN AND BLACK BEAN SOUP

This soup has been a family and friend favorite for years and is now a Wellness Kitchen favorite, too. I came up with this version of black bean soup when I had a Halloween party for my then five-year-old son. I needed something that young kids and adults both would like, was easy to serve, and would be warm on a cool fall night. Pumpkin is also used in Southwest cuisine, so the addition of black beans really works well. It's best to use plain, canned pumpkin for this soup since it is precooked and smoother than what you can make out of fresh pumpkin at home. (Another option is to use puréed butternut squash, since pumpkin is part of the squash family.) Serve this homey soup with hot corn bread and a beautiful fall salad of greens, apples, grapes, and walnuts with lite cider vinaigrette.

3 (15-ounce) cans black beans, rinsed and drained

1 (15-ounce) can chopped tomatoes, drained

1 tablespoon olive oil

1 medium onion, chopped

4 green onions, thinly sliced

2 teaspoons chopped garlic

1½ tablespoons ground cumin

½ teaspoon freshly ground black pepper

2 (14-ounce) cans organic, reduced-sodium, fat-free beef broth

⅓ cup sherry

1 (16-oz.) can solid-pack pumpkin

Lite sour cream (optional)

Nutrition Basics

Beans are one of nature's most nutritious foods, supplying much of the world with a healthy protein source. The great benefit is that while they're high in protein, they do not contain the saturated fat that most other animal protein does, plus they are high in calcium and fiber. I recommend substituting beans for animal protein in meals 3 or 4 times each week to lower risk of chronic disease.

1. In blender or food processor, purée beans and tomatoes.

2. Heat oil in soup pot; add onion, green onions, garlic, cumin, and pepper. Sauté until onions are soft, 5–7 minutes.

3. Stir in bean and tomato purée, broth, sherry, and pumpkin.

4. Simmer uncovered for 20 minutes.

5. Serve with 1 tablespoon lite sour cream.

SERVES: 6 (2-cup servings); CALORIES PER SERVING: 400; DIETARY EQUIVALENT: 4 oz. protein, 1 carbohydrate, 1 vegetable

RED CARROT SOUP

We eat with our eyes as well as our taste buds. This brilliant-colored soup is wonderfully flavorful. The natural sweetness of the carrots and the earthiness of the beets make it a great accompaniment to any meal, especially roasted chicken or turkey dishes. The vibrant color also means a very high antioxidant level, which helps fight certain types of cancer.

1 tablespoon olive oil
4 large shallots, sliced
3 sprigs thyme
2 bay leaves
Pinch of dried red pepper flakes
3 pounds carrots, peeled, sliced
1 pound trimmed beets, peeled, cut into ½" pieces
2 teaspoons ground coriander
2 quarts organic, reduced-sodium, fat-free chicken broth
2 tablespoons red wine vinegar
Sea salt
Freshly ground black pepper
¼ cup plain Greek yogurt
¼ cup pumpkin seeds, toasted

1. Heat olive oil in large soup pot over medium-high heat. Add sliced shallots, thyme leaves, bay leaves, and red pepper flakes. Cook for 3 minutes.

2. Add carrots, beets, coriander, and broth. Bring to a boil, then reduce to a simmer for 20 minutes.

3. Discard the bay leaves.

4. Purée soup in batches in a blender or food processor until smooth. Return to soup pot.

5. Stir in the vinegar. Season to taste with salt and pepper.

6. Garnish with a dollop of yogurt and the toasted pumpkin seeds.

SERVES: 12; CALORIES PER SERVING: 75; DIETARY EQUIVALENT: 2 vegetables

Food Tip
Finishing a soup with a garnish always makes it more appetizing. The creaminess of the yogurt and the crunchiness of the pumpkin seeds add interest and texture in contrast to the velvety consistency of the soup.

CURRIED SQUASH AND LENTIL SOUP

Over the past few years, I've worked with our local schools to improve the nutrition and taste of their school lunch programs by going back to simple, delicious meals from scratch versus the processed foods that most schools now offer. The kids are accustomed to a menu of frozen and reheated pizza, burgers, fries, and grilled cheese sandwiches. We had to give out free samples of this Indian-inspired soup to get them to try it, but once they did, it became an all-time favorite, especially when served with warm, whole-grain, garlic naan bread! Lentils come in different varieties and color denotes texture. The brown or green ones are firm in texture when cooked. We use Indian red or yellow lentils for this soup, which are more refined in texture and produce a creamier and more beautifully colored soup.

1 tablespoon olive oil

1½ pounds butternut squash, peeled and cut into 1" pieces

1 medium onion, chopped

2 ribs of celery, chopped

1 tablespoon chopped garlic

2 tablespoons chopped ginger

1 tablespoon Madras curry powder

1 cup yellow or red lentils, rinsed

1 quart organic, reduced-sodium, fat-free chicken broth

3 cups water

1 teaspoon lemon juice

Sea salt

Freshly ground black pepper

2 tablespoons chopped cilantro

1. Heat oil in large soup pot. Add squash, onion, celery, garlic, and ginger, stirring occasionally, until vegetables are soft, approximately 15 minutes.

2. Stir in curry powder, cook for 1 minute. Add lentils, broth, and water, bring to a boil, turn down heat to a simmer, cover, and cook for 30–35 minutes until lentils are soft and tender.

3. Purée half of soup in blender and return to other half.

4. Add lemon juice, and season with salt and pepper to taste.

5. To serve, ladle into bowls and garnish with cilantro.

SERVES: 4 (entrée portion); CALORIES PER SERVING: 210; DIETARY EQUIVALENT: 3 oz. protein, 1 carbohydrate, 1 vegetable

Nutrition Basics

Millions of people worldwide exist healthily on lentils as a main source of protein. One cup of cooked lentils has the same amount of protein in 2 eggs, with no fat and loads of fiber.

TORTELLINI SOUP WITH FALL VEGETABLES

A long-time favorite in my house, I sent this soup for lunch in a wide-mouth thermos when my son started preschool at age three. We ran into his preschool teacher years later when he was in high school, and she said she remembered him asking for his tortellini soup for lunch that his mom had packed! Good organic chicken broth, whole-wheat cheese or chicken tortellini found in the cold section of your market, fresh vegetables, and a few spoonfuls of good Parmesan all come together to make this hearty, delicious entrée soup in literally 10 minutes. I even use a bag of fresh baby spinach, baby carrots, and a carton of sliced mushrooms when there is really little time to put a meal on the table. Serve it with whole-grain toast, salad, and cut fall fruit, such as pears, apples, and grapes, for a simple but complete meal.

1 (9-ounce) package cheese tortellini

1 quart plus 1 can organic, reduced-sodium, fat-free chicken broth

2 green onions, sliced thin

1 tablespoon chopped garlic

2 cups spinach leaves or kale

½ cup baby carrots, sliced thin

1 small bok choy, sliced thin

1 cup sliced mushrooms

½ teaspoon freshly ground black pepper

2 tablespoons chopped basil or 1 teaspoon dried basil

¼ cup shredded Parmesan cheese

1. Cook tortellini until al dente, drain.
2. Meanwhile, heat chicken broth until boiling in large soup pot.
3. Add onions, garlic, spinach, carrots, bok choy, mushrooms, and pepper. Simmer for 4 minutes.
4. Add tortellini and basil.
5. Serve in soup bowls and top with 1 tablespoon Parmesan cheese.

SERVES: 4; CALORIES PER SERVING: 300; DIETARY EQUIVALENT: 2 carbohydrates, 2 oz. protein, 2 vegetables

Nutrition Basics
Make sure you add enough vegetables to this soup for volume. One 9 oz. package of fresh tortellini can make 2 generous servings when teamed with vegetables, a great way for those that are calorie conscientious to have a pasta meal that is not high in calories. You can also try other leafy green vegetables such as baby kale, Swiss chard, or sliced baby bok choy.

ROASTED BUTTERNUT SQUASH SOUP WITH APPLES AND SAGE

Fall is the beginning of soup time for me, and with butternut squash and apples both in season, it's a natural fit. Butternut soup needs to be very creamy, with a light smokiness and a touch of sweet yet savory flavor. This is not hard to do when you use with cream, pancetta, and sugar, like most restaurants do. I do not like feeling guilty about eating vegetable soups, though, so I created a healthier version. I think you will be totally enamored with this one; it has all the flavor and texture of the rich recipes but is healthy enough to indulge in as often as you wish.

2 small or 1 large butternut squash
Organic canola or olive oil cooking spray
2 pieces of turkey bacon, nitrate-free
1 tablespoon olive oil
½ cup chopped onion
2 celery stalks, chopped
1½ cups apple, cut into ¼" dice
1½ quarts organic, reduced-sodium, fat-free chicken broth
3 tablespoons brown sugar
1 tablespoon fresh thyme
½ cup fat-free half-and-half or 2% milk
Sea salt
Freshly ground black pepper
2 teaspoons trans-fat-free margarine
6 fresh sage leaves, thinly sliced

1. Preheat oven to 350°F.
2. Pierce squash with sharp knife. Place in microwave to soften for 5–6 minutes. Remove from microwave; when cool enough to handle, cut lengthwise. Remove seeds and place squash halves cut side facing on foil-lined baking sheet lightly coated with cooking spray. Roast in oven for 35–40 minutes or until squash is tender. Remove. When cool, scrape out squash from shell into bowl. Set aside.
3. Cook turkey bacon in microwave until just crispy.

4. Heat olive oil in large soup pot; sauté onion, celery, and 1 cup of diced apple until soft and golden.
5. Add crumbled bacon, broth, squash pulp, and brown sugar. Bring to a boil. Turn heat to low and simmer for about 10 minutes. Add thyme and simmer for 5 more minutes.
6. Remove soup from heat and purée soup in blender in small batches or with an immersion blender.
7. Add fat-free half-and-half, and season to taste with salt and pepper. Keep warm.
8. In small sauté pan, melt margarine over medium heat. Add remaining ½ cup diced apple and sauté until tender and golden. Add sage leaves.
9. Ladle soup into bowls and garnish with 1 tablespoon of diced apples and sage.

SERVES: 8 (1-cup servings); CALORIES PER SERVING: 220; DIETARY EQUIVALENT: 1 carbohydrate, 1 fat, 1 vegetable

Nutrition Basics

Butternut squash is a starchy vegetable. I am as sorry as you are about this, but it needs to be counted as a carbohydrate. At least it's a *healthy* carbohydrate, full of fiber, vitamins, and antioxidants. Please count 1 cup of this delicious soup as 1 carbohydrate serving, which can be easily managed at any meal.

SHERRIED MUSHROOM SOUP

Nothing says richness and decadence like a puréed mushroom soup, but more likely than not, it's rich with cream. Our version from the Wellness Kitchen is every bit as satisfying, with a deep earthiness and a rich texture, but no cream. It amazes guests that a vegetable soup with a touch of nonfat dairy can be this good. Try using a variety of mushrooms instead of the usual cremini, such as porcini, shiitake, Portobello, and chanterelle for a more intense flavor. We often serve this in the fall as an entrée with whole-grain rustic bread and a great salad of greens, grapes, apples, and walnuts with a touch of goat cheese for a complete meal.

1 tablespoon no-trans-fat margarine or olive oil

1 medium onion, chopped

2½ pounds fresh mushrooms, sliced thin

⅓ cup dry sherry

2 quarts organic, reduced-sodium, fat-free beef broth

½ cup fat-free half-and-half

½ teaspoon sea salt

½ teaspoon fresh ground pepper

1. Melt margarine or olive oil in large soup pot. Add onions and sauté for 5 minutes or until onions are soft and golden. Add fresh mushrooms and sauté for 4 minutes.

2. Add sherry and continue to sauté until sherry is reduced by half. Add beef broth, bring to a boil, and lower heat to a simmer for 10 minutes.

3. Working in batches, purée soup in blender or food processor.

4. Return soup to pot and add fat-free half-and-half, season with salt and pepper, and continue heating for another 2 minutes until just hot but not boiling.

SERVES: 8; CALORIES PER SERVING: 140; DIETARY EQUIVALENT: 1 carbohydrate, 1 vegetable

Nutrition Basics
You can substitute a nondairy milk, such as plain almond or soymilk, for fat-free half-and-half.

HOMEMADE CORN BREAD

I learned to make this homey bread when I lived in Dallas—my Texas roommates grew up eating it daily. I grew up in the North, where corn bread was relatively sweet, almost cake-like, but I learned that this was not what my Texan friends called corn bread. While it's easy to reach for a mix, making this recipe is almost as easy: A bowl, whisk, and cake pan are all you need to make this homemade treat. Serve with chili or soups, or as a carbohydrate accompanying any grilled chicken meal along with a green vegetable and salad.

1 cup all-purpose flour
1 cup cornmeal
¼ cup sugar
1 tablespoon plus 1 teaspoon baking powder
1 teaspoon salt
1¼ cups buttermilk
2 eggs
⅓ cup canola oil

1. Preheat oven to 350°F. Spray 8" × 8" pan with nonstick spray.
2. In large bowl, mix flour, cornmeal, sugar, baking powder, and salt.
3. In separate bowl, combine buttermilk, eggs, and canola oil and beat 2 minutes.
4. Mix wet ingredients into dry ingredients.
5. Pour batter into pan and bake 20–25 minutes or until a toothpick inserted in the center comes out clean.
6. Cool for 10 minutes, then invert on rack. Cut into squares and serve.

SERVES: 10; CALORIES PER SERVING: 200; DIETARY EQUIVALENT: 1 carbohydrate, 1 fat

Nutrition Basics

Cornmeal contains slightly less fiber than whole-grain flour but three times more fiber than white flour. Use a monounsaturated fat, such as canola or olive oil, instead of butter to lower risk for coronary heart disease and lower overall inflammation. Speaking of butter, most of us love to smear honey butter all over hot cornbread. One trick I use with my family is to brush the top lightly with 1 tablespoon of melted healthy margarine mixed with a couple of teaspoons of honey right when the bread comes out of the oven and then cut it into squares. Amazingly, it is enough for a great taste and we are not tempted to pile on butter!

GRILLED NAAN WITH HERBS AND FETA

The employees of California Health & Longevity Institute head to the kitchen when word gets out this bread is on the menu that day, but they are lucky if there is any left after class! Don't let making homemade naan intimidate you—it's much easier than you think. Roll it out in oval or elongated shapes for a rustic look that's just perfect for this chewy, tender, perfectly charred bread with a warm cheesy-herb filling. A tablespoon of herb-cheese filling packs an incredible flavor punch that goes well with plain grilled chicken, soups, salads, or hummus.

Naan

1½ cups plus 2 tablespoons unbleached flour for dusting
1 cup whole-wheat flour
2 teaspoons baking powder
1½ teaspoons salt
1 teaspoon sugar
1 egg white
¼ cup plain nonfat yogurt
2 tablespoons olive or canola oil
¾ cup lukewarm water
Organic olive oil spray

Filling

½ cup chopped cilantro
¼ cup chopped mint
2 tablespoons blanched almonds
1½ teaspoons finely chopped garlic
1½ teaspoons finely chopped ginger
1½ teaspoons olive oil
1 tablespoon organic, reduced-sodium, fat-free broth (chicken or vegetable)
½ teaspoon sea salt
¼ cup feta or queso fresco, crumbled

1. In large bowl, combine flours, baking powder, salt, and sugar.
2. In separate bowl, whisk egg white and yogurt. Add oil; whisk well.
3. Pour egg mixture into dry ingredients; combine with fork. Slowly add lukewarm water until soft, sticky dough is formed (you may not need all ¾ cup). Lightly dust work surface with flour and knead until dough is soft and pliable.
4. Line baking sheet with parchment and sprinkle lightly with flour. Divide dough into 5 pieces, form balls, and arrange on baking sheet. Mist dough lightly with olive oil spray, cover with plastic, and let rest 1–2 hours before shaping.

Filling Directions

Combine all filling ingredients except for cheese in food processor. Pulse until finely chopped. Transfer to small bowl and add cheese, stirring with fork.

Bread Directions

1. Roll dough out on lightly floured surface to 5" diameter. Spread 1 tablespoon herb-cheese filling in middle of circle. Fold over and pinch tightly. Place on parchment-lined baking sheet.

2. Preheat lightly oiled grill to medium heat. Place dough on grill, close lid, and cook for 2–3 minutes until puffy. Turn over; cook for 3 minutes. Serve warm.

SERVES: 10; CALORIES PER SERVING: 175; DIETARY EQUIVALENT: ½ oz. protein, 1 carbohydrate, 1 fat

Food Tip
I use organic olive oil spray found in the supermarket to coat the naan bread lightly with oil before placing on the grill. It comes out in a fine mist, yet does not clog up like the home misters I have tried to use, thanks to the natural lecithin added as an emulsifier.

PUMPKIN BREAD OR MUFFINS

Tea breads and quick breads, like this pumpkin bread, are among my favorite treats—sweet but not overly so, moist and dense, and packed with flavor. This was originally my mom's recipe. It's deliciously moist and the warm spices add a depth of flavor that enhances the pumpkin perfectly. This recipe easily converts to muffins as well: Simply prepare the batter according to the directions and pour into a muffin tin that's been lightly coated with cooking spray or into paper liners; bake for about 20 minutes or until a toothpick inserted in the center of the muffin comes out clean.

Organic canola or olive oil cooking spray

1½ cups all-purpose flour

½ cup whole-wheat flour

1½ teaspoons baking soda

1 teaspoon salt

2 teaspoons pumpkin pie spice

1½ cups sugar

½ cup canola oil

2 eggs, beaten

1 cup pumpkin purée

¼ cup water

1. Preheat oven to 350°F.

2. Spray loaf pan with cooking spray.

3. In a large bowl, combine all-purpose flour, whole-wheat flour, baking soda, salt, and pumpkin pie spice. Mix well.

4. In a medium bowl, whisk sugar, oil, eggs, pumpkin purée, and water. Mix well.

5. Combine wet and dry ingredients; incorporate well, but do not overmix.

6. Pour the batter into a loaf pan and tap down to decrease air bubbles.

7. Bake for 35–40 minutes until knife comes out clean when inserted in the center of loaf.

SERVES: 12; CALORIES PER SERVING: 180; DIETARY EQUIVALENT: 1 carbohydrate, 2 fats

Nutrition Basics

One of my passions is to tweak recipes to be healthier but still taste delicious. Quick breads seem to tolerate healthy changes with little or no difference in taste or texture. Generally, you can cut the sugar by a quarter (sugar is not just added for taste but plays a significant role in texture, too), use 2 egg whites for every other egg needed, and substitute half of the white flour with whole-wheat flour. A big healthy change is to substitute a healthy fat, such as olive oil, for unhealthy butter. Olive oil is rich in monounsaturated fat, which lowers inflammation and risk of heart disease. It has a high level of polyphenols, antioxidants that are protective against chronic disease and that are lost in processed fats. Use extra-virgin olive oil, which has been the most minimally processed and is therefore the most protective. Choose a mild, fruity olive oil (not a peppery one). Olive oil can be used in place of solid butter in equal amounts. However, avoid using olive oil in place of butter when it needs to be creamed into baked goods for lightness of texture, such as in a cake. Oil will not hold the air as butter does.

Chapter 5

Quick and Easy Main Dishes

Main dishes are the centerpiece of a meal. I usually plan them first and then decide what will be the perfect complement. The entrées in this section contain a balance of carbohydrates, protein, and vegetables in them, so you only need to add a salad and fruit to make a complete meal. I've focused on entrées that do not require much prep time (generally under 30 minutes) or cooking time, since that's what most of us need; modern life does not allow for much leisurely time in the kitchen!

Making food quickly does not mean making it with less flavor, though. I have actually found the opposite to be quite true. Wholesome foods, seasonal produce, and fresh herbs and spices can all come together to make healthy, vibrant meals that are really delicious. Even if you're not an experienced chef, you can still whip up these easy dishes. You'll find that the skills you need for many of the dishes overlap, too. Master the Chicken Piccata and you will have no problem making the Chicken Marsala! In no time at all, you will develop a repertoire of weeknight standbys that are sure to keep you and your family happy and improve your health. The Salmon Wellington or the Beef in Red Wine Sauce is certainly worthy of any special occasion, but you may just find yourself serving them weeknights, too!

ASIAN FLANK STEAK WITH SWEET SLAW

While we do not prepare much red meat in the Wellness Kitchen, this recipe is an example of how it should be consumed: in smaller amounts and with the vegetables increasing the volume. This flavorful, grass-fed beef is marinated with Asian-inspired spices, grilled, and served over a spicy cabbage slaw with carrots. There's a hint of heat and a touch of sweetness. It's a flavor and texture explosion in your mouth that is so satisfying, you will not miss the smaller quantities of the meat.

¼ cup reduced-sodium soy sauce

1 tablespoon olive oil

2 tablespoons minced ginger, divided

1 tablespoon chopped garlic

1¼ pounds grass-fed flank steak

2 tablespoons sugar

3 tablespoons seasoned rice vinegar

1 tablespoon finely chopped jalapeño

5 cups Napa cabbage, thinly sliced

2 medium carrots, shredded

6 green onions, thinly sliced on the bias

Sea salt

Freshly ground black pepper

1 tablespoon sesame seeds, toasted

1. Preheat grill to medium-high heat (10 minutes before ready to cook).

2. Add soy sauce, olive oil, 1 tablespoon ginger, and garlic to large ziptop bag. Add flank steak and marinate 30 minutes or overnight.

3. Add sugar and rice vinegar to small saucepan and heat until sugar dissolves. Remove from heat. Stir in jalapeño and remaining ginger. Let cool.

4. Place cabbage, carrots, and green onions in a large bowl. Toss with vinegar mixture. Season to taste with salt and pepper. Let slaw stand at room temperature while grilling steak.

5. Remove steak from marinade. Grill 5–7 minutes on each side, until medium-rare (130°F–135°F) or to

desired doneness. Let rest 10 minutes and then slice steak thinly against the grain.

6. To serve, mound slaw on platter, arrange steak slices on slaw, and sprinkle with sesame seeds.

SERVES: 5; CALORIES PER SERVING: 370; DIETARY EQUIVALENT: 4 oz. protein, 2 vegetables, 1 fat

Nutrition Basics

Although grass-fed beef is three times higher in heart-protecting omega-3s, one could argue that there are better sources of this important nutrient. I think the real reasons to eat grass-fed beef are that it's leaner overall, it's raised in a cleaner way (generally without the hormones and antibiotics used in commercial feed lots), it's better for the environment, and, of course, it's better for the cows. Make sure to marinate grass-fed beef; it can dry out during cooking or grilling due to its lower fat content. Grill to a medium-rare 130°F–135°F for optimal flavor. Yes, you will pay more for it, but you can probably buy less overall. Americans consume much larger portions of meat than needed for good health because we have been able to produce it so cheaply. Unfortunately, our bodies and our land pay the cost! I hope that needing to pay a bit more for better quality discourages overconsumption and helps reduce the risk of chronic disease that is associated with consuming large amounts of red meat.

PEPPER STEAK WITH SUMMER CHOPPED SALAD

While I do advocate limiting red meat to twice a week to lower the risk of coronary heart disease and cancer, pairing a small amount of red meat with a wonderful salad is another great way to indulge without feeling so guilty. If you can't find arugula, try Romaine lettuce, thinly sliced.

1 tablespoon finely chopped garlic

1½ teaspoons sea salt, divided

2 teaspoons freshly ground black pepper, divided

2 pounds grass-fed sirloin steak (1½" thick)

2 cups arugula

3 vine-ripe tomatoes, chopped

½ cup chopped red onion

3 tablespoons pitted, chopped Kalamata olives

1 tablespoon red wine vinegar

1 tablespoon water

1 tablespoon olive oil

½ jalapeño, seeded and finely chopped

⅓ cup crumbled feta cheese

1. Preheat grill to medium-high heat (10 minutes before ready to cook).

2. In small bowl, combine garlic, 1 teaspoon salt, and 1½ teaspoons pepper. Rub mixture over steak and let stand at room temperature for 1 hour.

3. Grill steak 5–7 minutes on each side, until medium-rare (130°F–135°F), or to desired doneness. Let rest 10 minutes and then slice steak thinly against the grain. Set aside; keep warm.

4. Meanwhile, in a medium-sized bowl, combine arugula, tomatoes, red onion, and olives.

5. In a small bowl, whisk the vinegar, water, olive oil, jalapeño, and remaining salt and pepper.

6. Toss salad with dressing right before serving.

7. To serve, place tossed salad on a platter and arrange steak slices over the salad. Crumble the feta over the top.

SERVES: 6; CALORIES PER SERVING: 345; DIETARY EQUIVALENT: 4–5 oz. protein, 1 vegetable, 1 fat

Nutrition Basics
Add a can of rinsed cannellini beans or the kernels from two grilled ears of corn for your healthy carbohydrate and enjoy a quick, complete meal.

MARGARITA STEAK WITH TOMATILLO SALSA

Our meat-loving executives are very happy when they see steak on our summertime Wellness Kitchen menu! They expected to have to give up their favorite dishes in order to be healthy, so are relieved when they discover they can indulge occasionally. Our Margarita steak is sliced in thin strips for portion control and served over a roasted tomatillo salsa that will have you craving the salsa more than the steak. Marinades definitely improve the flavor of meats, and this one is packed with flavor—cilantro, garlic, citrus, tequila—which means you can cook with less salt. Serve it with warm corn tortillas, black beans, and a generous fresh garden salad for a completely satisfying meal. Grill fresh pineapple for dessert and you'll conquer a sweet tooth as well.

Zest and juice from 1 lime, divided
1 tablespoon orange juice
3 tablespoons tequila
1 tablespoon canola oil
1 tablespoon minced garlic
3 tablespoons chopped cilantro, divided
Pinch of dried red pepper flakes
½ teaspoon sea salt
1 pound grass-fed skirt steak or flank steak (marinated 1–24 hours)
½ ripe avocado, diced
2 tablespoons minced red onion
1 jalapeño, seeded and minced
½ pound (6–7) tomatillos, husked and rinsed
1 yellow bell pepper
1 tablespoon olive oil
Freshly ground black pepper, to taste

1. Preheat grill to medium-high heat (10 minutes before ready to cook).
2. In a 9" × 13" glass baking dish, add half the zest and half the lime juice. Whisk in the orange juice, tequila, canola oil, garlic, 2 tablespoons cilantro, red pepper flakes, and salt.
3. Add the steak to the marinade and coat well. Cover and refrigerate for 1–24 hours.

4. In a medium bowl, combine the remaining lime zest and juice, avocado, onion, jalapeño, and remaining cilantro. Set aside.
5. Brush tomatillos and yellow bell pepper with olive oil. Grill tomatillos for 5–6 minutes until lightly charred. Remove from grill. Cool slightly, dice into ¼" pieces, and add to avocado mixture.
6. Grill the yellow pepper until charred all over, about 8–10 minutes. Remove from grill, place in small bowl, and cover tightly with plastic wrap. Set aside for 5 minutes.
7. Remove charred skin and seeds from the pepper, cut into ¼" dice, add to avocado mixture. Adjust seasonings with salt and pepper.
8. Remove steak from marinade. Grill 5–7 minutes on each side, until medium-rare (130°F–135°F) or to desired doneness. Let rest 10 minutes and then slice thinly against the grain.
9. To serve, place steak slices on platter and serve with tomatillo salsa on the side.

SERVES: 4; CALORIES PER SERVING: 465; DIETARY EQUIVALENT: 4 oz. protein, 1 vegetable, 1 fat

Food Tip
If you cannot find fresh tomatillos in your local market, use canned ones or a green (verde) sauce. Add the remaining fresh ingredients, but leave out the salt. You may want to double the salsa ingredients in order to have leftovers for grilled shrimp or chicken—it's that good!

SPICY BEEF WITH HOISIN AND CUCUMBER RELISH

Even though I am not much of a red meat eater, I will admit nothing smells better than steak on a grill. This one has not only a great flavor but also a wonderful texture. The grilled meat is topped with a flavor-packed Asian sauce and then served with a platter of char-grilled onions and a cool crunchy cucumber relish. We always try to pair a protein entrée with vegetables, whether it is a chopped salad topped with grilled meat, thinly sliced beef with a slaw, or a vegetable relish such as this recipe. If you use grass-fed meat (which has not been fed a high-grain diet), it's leaner to begin with, so do not overcook on the grill. Lean beef is better when cooked to medium-rare so it does not dry out.

2 tablespoons olive oil, divided

4 medium shallots, thinly sliced

1 tablespoon minced garlic

1 tablespoon plus 1 teaspoon finely grated ginger, divided

¼ teaspoon dried red pepper flakes

⅓ cup chopped cilantro

¼ cup hoisin sauce

3 tablespoons reduced-sodium soy sauce

½ cup organic, reduced-sodium, fat-free chicken broth

2 tablespoons honey

2 pounds strip steak

2 large sweet onions, sliced into ½" rings

Sea salt

Freshly ground black pepper

2 English or hothouse cucumbers, sliced ¼" thick

¼ cup seasoned rice wine vinegar

1 tablespoon sesame seeds, toasted

1. Preheat grill to medium-high heat (10 minutes before ready to cook).

2. In small saucepan, heat 1 tablespoon olive oil over medium heat. Add shallots, garlic, 1 tablespoon ginger, dried red pepper flakes, and cilantro. Cook until softened, about 5 minutes.

3. Add hoisin sauce, soy sauce, and broth. Turn heat to high and boil for 5 minutes until thickened. Add honey and remove from heat.

4. Brush steak and onions with remaining 1 tablespoon olive oil. Season with salt and pepper. Grill steak on one side for 5–7 minutes, turn over, and brush with hoisin mixture.

5. Grill until medium-rare (130°F–135°F), about 5–7 minutes. Let rest 10 minutes and then slice thinly against the grain.

6. Grill onions for 4 minutes on each side. Remove from heat.

7. Meanwhile, in a medium bowl, toss the cucumbers, vinegar, remaining ginger, and sesame seeds together. Refrigerate until ready to serve.

8. To serve, arrange steak and grilled onions on one side of the platter and cucumber relish on the other side. Serve with remaining hoisin sauce on the side.

SERVES: 6; CALORIES PER SERVING: 340; DIETARY EQUIVALENT: 4–5 oz. protein, 1 vegetable, 1 fat

Nutrition Basics

After working with thousands of people, I realize many of us are not willing to give up red meat entirely, nor do I think you have to for health. I do advocate learning how to eat red meat more healthily, which means less quantity, better quality (avoid hormones and antibiotics), and limit frequency to twice a week.

BEEF IN RED WINE SAUCE

Guests often ask, "How can beef in wine sauce be healthy?" I actually love the challenge of making a "not so healthy" dish much healthier while still maintaining the original recipe's flavors and integrity. It must have been all those hours in my college years spent in food chemistry, under the watchful eye of Dr. Chen, who tried to instill in us that food is really just chemistry. The secret to this dish: more vegetables than meat! Plus, the sauce is rich just from the reduction of the wine, with no butter added. The wine adds flavor without calories since the alcohol cooks off.

1 tablespoon olive oil

2 pounds grass-fed flatiron steak, trimmed and cut into 1" cubes

Sea salt

Freshly ground black pepper

1 cup finely chopped onion

1 tablespoon finely chopped garlic

1 tablespoon flour

1 (750-milliliter) bottle dry red wine

2 bay leaves

1 thyme sprig

4 slices nitrate-free turkey bacon

1 tablespoon trans-fat-free margarine

15 pearl or small cipollini onions, peeled

15 cremini mushrooms

15 baby carrots, peeled

¼ cup water

2 tablespoons chopped fresh parsley

1. Preheat the oven to 350°F.

2. In a large Dutch oven, over medium-high heat, add the olive oil. Season the beef with salt and pepper. Add to pan and brown on all sides, about 8 minutes.

3. Add the onion and garlic. Cook until the onion is softened, 5 minutes, stirring occasionally.

4. Add the flour, coat the meat, and incorporate well.

5. Add the wine, bay leaves, and thyme sprig. Bring to a boil; stir to dissolve any brown bits stuck to the bottom of the pot.

6. Cover the pot and transfer it to the oven. Cook for 1–1½ hours or until the meat is very tender and the sauce is rich and flavorful.

7. Microwave the turkey bacon until crisp. Crumble and set aside.

8. In sauté pan melt margarine. Add pearl onions, mushrooms, carrots, and water.

9. Bring to a boil; cover and simmer until almost all of the water has evaporated, about 7–8 minutes. Uncover and cook over high heat, tossing, until the vegetables are tender and nicely browned, about 2 minutes. Season to taste with salt and pepper.

10. To serve, stir crumbled bacon and vegetables into the stew. Top with parsley.

SERVES: 6; CALORIES PER SERVING: 395; DIETARY EQUIVALENT: 5 oz. protein, 1 vegetable serving, 1 fat

FISH IN PARCHMENT

We discovered that many of our guests visiting the Wellness Kitchen were unfamiliar with this classic way to cook fish. Now we always include this recipe in our Simplicity of Fish class. It is, indeed, simply fish, aromatics, and vegetables wrapped in parchment and placed in the oven to steam. The sauce used in this recipe infuses amazing flavor into the fish. We have come up with a variety of tastes from around the world that will entice your palate. I love serving this with a whole grain, such as a scoop of brown rice, barley, or quinoa, to make this dish a complete meal. Try serving this dish to company—it's so easy and impressive. Assemble as directed and place a baking sheet with parchment packets of fish in the refrigerator until 30 minutes before serving. Bring to room temperature for 15 minutes and bake as directed.

4 (5-ounce) fish fillets (sea bass, halibut, salmon, branzino, black cod, or raw, large, peeled shrimp)

½ teaspoon sea salt

½ teaspoon freshly ground black pepper

Sauce (see recipe variations)

Vegetables (see recipe variations)

4 (14") sheets parchment paper

2 tablespoons finely chopped parsley

1. Preheat oven to 375°F.

2. Rinse fish in cold water and pat dry with paper towels. Season with salt and pepper.

3. Combine sauce ingredients in small bowl. Set aside.

4. Prep the vegetables.

5. Place ½ cup vegetables in center of parchment. Place fish fillet over vegetables. Add ¼ of the sauce over each fish fillet. Bring the two long sides of parchment together, fold over 2–3 times, and fold under to seal parchment packet.

6. Arrange packets on baking sheet and place in oven for 10–15 minutes until fish is cooked through. The fish is done when flakey and opaque. (The thicker the fillet, the more cooking time needed.)

7. To serve, open packet and transfer to platter or individual plates with all juices and vegetables. Garnish with chopped parsley.

SERVES: 4; CALORIES PER SERVING: 180–200; DIETARY EQUIVALENT: 4 oz. protein, 1 vegetable

VARIATIONS

MEDITERRANEAN

1. Whisk 1 tablespoon olive oil, zest of 1 lemon, 1 teaspoon minced garlic, and ¼ cup dry white wine in a small bowl.

2. Prepare the vegetables: 1 julienned medium carrot and 1 julienned red or yellow pepper or 1 vine-ripe tomato, thinly sliced. Add a few thinly sliced pieces of fennel bulb, and 2 thinly sliced green onions.

ASIAN

1. Whisk together 2 teaspoons sesame oil, 2 tablespoons reduced-sodium soy sauce, ¼ cup finely chopped cilantro, 1 tablespoon minced fresh ginger, 1 teaspoon minced garlic, and 2 finely chopped green onions.

2. Prepare the vegetables: 4 baby bok choy, ends trimmed and cut in half, and 2 green onions, thinly sliced.

THAI

1. Whisk 1 tablespoon minced fresh ginger, 2 teaspoons minced garlic, ½ of a seeded, minced red jalapeño pepper or Thai red pepper, ½ teaspoon chili powder, 1 tablespoon ground coriander, ¼ teaspoon turmeric, ½ cup lite coconut milk, and 2 tablespoons fresh chopped cilantro.

2. Prepare the vegetables: 1 julienned carrot, 1 julienned red pepper, 1 thinly sliced small zucchini or yellow summer squash, and 2 thinly sliced green onions.

Nutrition Basics

The steaming method used in this dish requires very little fat and the sauces are just bursting with flavor. This technique creates a moist, healthy, and delicious fish every time. Don't use the same fish every time, though—experiment with different tastes and textures. Eating a variety of fish will also decrease your chance of mercury exposure, which is more likely to occur if you continually eat just one or two types of fish.

FRESH AHI AND SOBA NOODLE SALAD WITH CUCUMBER AND COCONUT DRESSING

❧

Take cool, fresh fish and noodles, season them just right, add crisp vegetables and toss with flavorful coconut dressing—and you have the perfect dinner for a hot night! While this dish seems exotic, everyone is always surprised at how little time and preparation it actually takes to produce such a show-stopper. Make sure you use sushi-grade ahi tuna for this dish. "Sushi-grade" means that it has been frozen at a particular temperature for a specific amount of time to kill any possible microbes found in raw fish, making it safer to consume. If you don't eat raw fish, this salad is delicious with any cold, cooked seafood; shrimp, crab, or scallops; or even crispy tofu for a vegetarian version.

4 ounces soba noodles, cooked according to package directions, drained

2 teaspoons sesame-chili oil, divided

1 teaspoon reduced-sodium soy sauce

1 pound fresh, sushi-grade tuna, cut into ½" dice

¼ cup unsweetened dried coconut flakes

1 cup unsweetened lite coconut milk

3 tablespoons fresh lime juice

2 tablespoons Asian fish sauce

1 tablespoon brown sugar

Crisp lettuce leaves (leave whole for serving)

1 seedless cucumber, julienned

1 lime cut into wedges for garnish

1. Preheat the oven to 350°F.

2. In a medium bowl, add the cooked, drained soba noodles with 1 teaspoon sesame-chili oil. Set aside.

3. In a large bowl, combine the remaining sesame-chili oil and soy sauce. Toss in the tuna. Cover and refrigerate for 20 minutes.

4. Meanwhile, place the coconut flakes on a sheet pan and bake for about 5 minutes, or until golden brown.

5. In a medium bowl, whisk the coconut milk, lime juice, fish sauce, and brown sugar until combined.

6. To serve, place a large lettuce leaf on the center of each plate. Top with the soba noodles, ¼ of cucumber julienne, and ¼ of the tuna. Drizzle with the dressing. Sprinkle the toasted coconut over the top, and garnish with lime wedges. Serve immediately.

SERVES: 4; CALORIES PER SERVING: 255; DIETARY EQUIVALENT: 4 oz. protein, 1 carbohydrate, 1 vegetable, 2 fats

Nutrition Basics

You can easily control the calories and carbohydrates in this dish by cooking exactly the amount of soba noodles you should have. One ounce dry is 1 carb serving and makes ½ cup cooked; 2 ounces dry is 2 carb servings, 1 cup cooked. Soba noodles are typically sold in 8-ounce packages, so it's easy to determine the amount you should prepare.

GRILLED FISH TACOS WITH GUACAMOLE AND CABBAGE SLAW

I have prepared fish tacos many ways and this is one of my favorites! The combination of spicy fish, creamy guacamole, and crunchy slaw makes eating healthy really easy. (You can also try this recipe with shrimp and chicken.) The recipe is also healthy because corn tortillas, for the most part, are unprocessed. They contain ground corn with no fat versus flour tortillas with lard or hydrogenated fat. (Two corn tortillas are the caloric equivalent to one piece of bread.) I often serve this to friends and family with a side of black beans, a squeeze of lime, and a few tablespoons of fresh cilantro. The dry rub is so easy, yet gives plain grilled fish a Mexican flavor that makes a big impact on this taco's taste. Olé!

Guacamole

1 ripe Hass avocado, halved, pitted, and peeled
1 tablespoon nonfat plain Greek yogurt
½ small jalapeño, seeded and minced
¼ cup finely chopped red onion
2 tablespoons chopped cilantro
Juice from 1 lime, divided
1 medium vine-ripe tomato, diced
Sea salt
Freshly ground black pepper

Slaw

2 cups (1 small head) finely shredded Napa cabbage
1 tablespoon plus 2 teaspoons canola oil, divided
Sea salt
Freshly ground black pepper

Spice Rub

1 tablespoon paprika
1 teaspoon garlic powder
1 teaspoon dried oregano
1 teaspoon sea salt
¼ teaspoon cayenne pepper

Fish Tacos

1 pounds snapper fillets, cut into 10 strips (can use mahi-mahi or halibut)
8 (6") corn tortillas
Hot sauce (optional)
Lime wedges (optional)

1. Preheat grill to medium-high heat.
2. For the guacamole: In a small bowl, mash avocado with fork. Add yogurt, jalapeño, red onion, cilantro, ½ lime juice, and tomatoes. Season with salt and pepper. Cover with plastic wrap directly on surface of guacamole. Set aside.
3. For the slaw: Combine cabbage, 1 tablespoon canola oil, and remaining lime juice in small bowl. Season to taste with salt and pepper. Set aside.
4. For the spice rub: In a small bowl, mix together paprika, garlic powder, oregano, salt, and cayenne pepper.
5. Brush both sides of fish lightly with remaining canola oil. Sprinkle spice rub on both sides of fillets.
6. Grill 4–5 minutes on each side. Slice fish into bite-sized pieces.
7. To assemble tacos, place fish in tortilla and top with slaw, guacamole, and hot sauce and lime, if using.

SERVES: 4 (2 tacos each); CALORIES PER SERVING: 385; DIETARY EQUIVALENT: 4 oz. protein, 1 carbohydrate, 1 vegetable, 1 fat

PAN-SEARED HALIBUT WITH UMAMI SAUCE, SUGAR SNAP PEAS, AND MUSHROOMS

Umami is the fifth taste sensation that we recognize (the other four being sweet, salty, sour, and bitter). It's that very savory taste that you find in anchovies, mushrooms, Parmesan cheese, and soy sauce. Umami sauce is terrific on sandwiches, burgers, grilled chicken, or tossed with steamed vegetables or salads. It takes only a tablespoon or two for a major flavor boost! (Leftover sauce can be stored in the refrigerator, covered, for up to 3 weeks.) In this recipe, we pair halibut with a sauce made from nutritional yeast that is very high in umami flavors. The combination of sweet snap peas, earthy roasted mushrooms, and a drizzle of this addictive sauce makes eating more fish delightful! We use a variety of vegetables when we make this in the Wellness Kitchen—but we always include the roasted mushrooms, which add even more umami flavor.

¼ cup apple cider vinegar

3 tablespoons tamari or reduced-sodium soy sauce

1 cup nutritional yeast flakes

2 tablespoons finely chopped garlic

¼ cup water plus 2 tablespoons, divided

¼ cup olive oil

1 pound sugar snap peas, trimmed and cut on the bias

4 (5–6-ounce) halibut steaks

Sea salt

Freshly ground black pepper

2 tablespoons canola oil, divided

8 ounces mushrooms (cremini, shiitake, oyster, or maitake), quartered

1 tablespoon lemon zest

1 tablespoon lemon juice

1 tablespoon peeled and finely grated fresh ginger

2 scallions, white part only, finely minced

½ teaspoon sambal oelek (chili paste found in the International/Asian section of most markets)

1. Preheat oven to 400°F.

2. To prepare the Umami Sauce: In a food processor or blender, add the vinegar, tamari, nutritional yeast flakes, garlic, and ¼ cup water; mix well. With the machine running, slowly drizzle in the olive oil until the mixture emulsifies. Set aside.

3. Place the snap peas in a microwave-safe bowl with 1 tablespoon of water and cover with plastic wrap. Microwave for 3 minutes. Transfer to a colander and rinse under cold water until cool; allow to drain. Set aside.

4. Pat the halibut steaks dry with a paper towel and season with salt and pepper. Heat an ovenproof skillet over medium-high heat. Add 1 tablespoon of canola oil and wait until it shimmers. Then sear the fish for 3 minutes on each side, being careful to not move it around in the pan. Transfer fish to a rimmed baking sheet and roast for 5 minutes or until opaque and flakey.

5. Heat another skillet over medium-high heat. Add the remaining canola oil and sauté the mushrooms until just starting to soften. Stir in the snap peas, lemon zest, lemon juice, ginger, scallions, and sambal oelek. Add the remaining water and cook until evaporated. Add 2 tablespoons of the Umami Sauce and toss to coat.

6. To serve, divide the snap peas and mushrooms among 4 plates. Top each with a halibut steak and drizzle 1 tablespoon Umami Sauce over the fish.

SERVES: 4; CALORIES PER SERVING (including 1 tablespoon sauce): 390; DIETARY EQUIVALENT: 5 oz. protein, 2 fats, 2 vegetables

UMAMI SAUCE YIELDS: 1½ cups (serving size is 1 tablespoon); CALORIES PER SERVING: 48; DIETARY EQUIVALENT: 1 fat

Nutrition Basics

Nutritional yeast is a dry, flakey food supplement found in health food markets that is high in protein, B vitamins, and iron but low in sodium. It is considered a probiotic and is often used in vegan meals. Try it sprinkled on popcorn for a delicious healthy alternative to butter or cheese.

CRISPY FISH STICKS WITH HOMEMADE BREAD CRUMBS

❧

I made these years ago for my son when he was a toddler. As many young moms know, it's hard to get toddlers to eat protein, but anything breaded is always a winner with that age group. I have found that many adults who think they do not like fish really enjoy these fish sticks, too. The fish is mild in flavor and the crispy Parmesan coating adds just the right amount of crunch. In fact, this recipe tastes just like traditional restaurant fish and chips, but they are baked, not fried. I prefer to use fresh bread crumbs for this recipe; they are lighter and less finely ground than the packaged ones. Using whole-grain bread to make them adds fiber and a unique nutty flavor.

Organic canola or olive oil cooking spray
¾ cup fresh bread crumbs (2 slices of whole-grain bread pulsed in food processor)
¼ cup grated Parmesan cheese
⅛ teaspoon cayenne pepper
1 pound cod, cut into strips
1 egg, beaten
1 lemon, cut into wedges

1. Preheat oven to 375°F.
2. Spray a rimmed baking sheet with cooking spray.
3. In a shallow dish, mix bread crumbs, Parmesan, and cayenne.
4. Dip the fish into beaten egg. Coat with bread crumb mixture and place on prepared baking sheet. Do not crowd.
5. Spray fish with cooking spray.
6. Bake for 20 minutes until browned and crispy. Serve with lemon wedges.

SERVES: 4; CALORIES PER SERVING: 210; DIETARY EQUIVALENT: 4 oz. protein, ½ carbohydrate

---

Food Tip

Omit or adjust the cayenne pepper if making these for very young children or pepper-sensitive adults. They may not appreciate the heat that the cayenne gives to the fish sticks.

PAN-ROASTED HALIBUT WITH BUTTERNUT SQUASH AND TOMATO

Guests in the Wellness Kitchen always lament that they wish they could cook fish like a restaurant does. Well, this elegant fish entrée is the one to try! The roasted vegetables are caramelized and slightly sweet, the vibrant orange and red color of butternut squash and the roasted tomatoes are beautiful to the eye, and the wine sauce is fabulous. You really can cook a delicious fish entrée very easily and healthily!

1 small butternut squash
Organic canola or olive oil cooking spray
1 pint cherry or grape tomatoes
2 tablespoons olive oil, divided
¼ cup sherry vinegar, divided
Sea salt
Freshly ground black pepper
4 (5-ounce) halibut fillets (1¼ pounds)
1 lemon, juiced
½ cup dry white wine
½ cup organic, reduced-sodium, fat-free chicken broth
2 tablespoons fresh marjoram leaves

1. Preheat oven to 400°F.
2. With sharp knife, pierce squash 5–6 times and place in microwave for 5–6 minutes or until somewhat soft. Peel squash, cut lengthwise and scoop out seeds. Cut into bite-sized cubes. Place on rimmed baking sheet and lightly coat with cooking spray. Roast until the squash is tender, 20–30 minutes. Set aside.
3. Meanwhile, place the tomatoes in a small baking dish and drizzle with 1 tablespoon of olive oil and 2 tablespoons of sherry vinegar. Season with salt and pepper. Toss to coat. Roast for 20 minutes or until soft, slightly browned, and wrinkled.
4. Pat the fillets dry with paper towel and season with salt and pepper.
5. Heat an ovenproof sauté pan over medium-high heat until very hot. Add remaining 1 tablespoon olive oil; swirl oil around pan. Place fillets in hot pan and sear until browned, about 2–3 minutes. Turn fillets over carefully and continue to brown for about 2–3 minutes. Place fillets in oven to finish cooking, about 5 minutes or until just opaque and flakey. Transfer fish to a platter; cover loosely with foil to keep warm, and set aside.
6. Add the lemon juice, wine, broth, and remaining sherry vinegar to the pan the fish was cooked in. Place over medium heat; bring to a boil for 2–3 minutes until the sauce thickens slightly. Remove from heat.
7. To the pan sauce, add the butternut squash, tomatoes, and marjoram; combine well. Adjust seasonings if needed.
8. To serve, plate the fish and spoon the squash tomato mixture over and around the fish.

SERVES: 4; CALORIES PER SERVING: 410; DIETARY EQUIVALENT: 4 oz. lean protein, 2 carbohydrates, 1 fat

Nutrition Basics

Butternut squash is very nutritious, but it is a starchy vegetable. A half cup is considered 1 carbohydrate serving. I like to serve butternut squash with a green vegetable such as broccoli or green beans—not only does this help keep calories in line, but it makes the whole plate a work of art!

CEDAR-GRILLED SALMON WITH FRESH HERBS

In the Wellness Kitchen, we serve salmon in myriad ways because of its amazing omega-3 health benefits. This recipe is one of our favorite ways to serve this fish. Many guests who are not particularly fond of salmon are surprised to discover that they love this dish. The freshness of the herbs combined with the warmth of the cedar gives the salmon a remarkable taste and a hint of smokiness that is delectable! Cedar planks are now available in most large grocery markets or barbecue stores. Make sure you really soak them for at least 2 but as long as 24 hours so they do not burn while on the grill. You can reuse them a few times; just wash with soapy water, rinse well, and pat dry.

4 (5-ounce) salmon fillets

3 tablespoons finely chopped fresh parsley

3 tablespoons finely chopped fresh basil

1 tablespoon minced garlic

Zest of ½ lemon

Juice of ½ lemon

1½ tablespoons olive oil

½ teaspoon sea salt

½ teaspoon freshly ground black pepper

Cedar planks, soaked in water for at least 2 hours

1. Preheat grill to medium–high heat.
2. Rinse fish under cold water and pat dry with paper towels.
3. In a small bowl, mix together parsley, basil, garlic, lemon zest, lemon juice, olive oil, salt, and pepper.
4. Place salmon on a plate and spread herb mixture evenly on top of fish; refrigerate for 20 minutes or longer, up to 2 hours.
5. Transfer fillets to cedar planks. Place on grill for 3–5 minutes, until planks begin to smoke. Close the lid, turn grill off, and cook for 6–8 minutes or until fish is cooked to desired doneness or turns opaque in the center.

SERVES: 4; CALORIES PER SERVING: 200; DIETARY EQUIVALENT: 4 oz. protein

Nutrition Basics

It's best to eat wild fish when available. Salmon season runs May through September. The rest of the year, look for farm-raised salmon from Alaska, Canada, and Northern European countries such as Norway or Scotland. They have tighter farm regulations, similar to the United States'. Our regulations are not perfect, but are better than most.

HONEY-MUSTARD SALMON WITH SPINACH AND LENTILS

This dish is simple and satisfying, and reminds me of a little French bistro in Paris. It's sophisticated, yet homey—a French version of comfort food! The implication with comfort food is that it is usually somewhat less than healthy . . . but not this dish. The fish is high in omega-3s, the lentils are packed with fiber and protein, and the spinach is full of antioxidants and heart-healthy vitamins. Be sure you use Indian red or yellow lentils, which take on a creamy texture when cooked, unlike the green and brown ones, which stay firmer when cooked. The honey-mustard glaze on the salmon adds just the right spicy sweetness to stand up to the earthiness of the lentils.

1 tablespoon olive oil

½ onion, finely chopped

1 cup Indian red or yellow lentils, rinsed well

1 quart organic, reduced-sodium, fat-free chicken broth

8 ounces baby spinach, roughly chopped

½ teaspoon sea salt, divided

½ teaspoon freshly ground black pepper, divided

2 tablespoons honey

2 tablespoons Dijon mustard

4 (5-ounce) salmon fillets, skinless

1. Preheat oven to 400°F.

2. Heat oil in medium sauté pan over medium heat; add onion and sauté 5 minutes, until onion is soft and slightly golden.

3. Add lentils and chicken broth to sauté pan, bring to a boil, and then simmer, covered, for 20 minutes.

4. Remove cover, add spinach, and continue to simmer, uncovered, for 10 more minutes or until lentils are creamy and tender. Season with ¼ teaspoon salt and ¼ teaspoon pepper. Set aside; keep warm.

5. In small bowl, combine honey and mustard.

6. Place salmon on parchment-lined baking sheet; season with remaining salt and pepper. Roast in oven for 8 minutes. Remove from oven, brush salmon fillets thoroughly with honey-mustard glaze, and return to oven. Cook for another 2–3 minutes or until opaque.

7. To serve, divide lentils on 4 dinner plates and top with roasted salmon fillet.

SERVES: 4; CALORIES PER SERVING: 340; DIETARY EQUIVALENT: 4 oz. protein, 2 carbohydrates, 2 vegetables

Nutrition Basics

I often prepare double the amount of lentils so I can set some aside for a great vegetarian lentil meal for the next day or two. Top ½ cup to 1 cup of cooked whole grain such as barley or brown rice with a cup of lentil mixture and you have another super healthy "comfort food" meal! You can also try making the lentil part of this dish the night before or earlier in the day. It reheats wonderfully, and then all you have left to do is roast the salmon and toss a salad.

HOISIN SALMON BURGER WITH GINGER AIOLI

Before you reach for another pound of ground beef or turkey, switch it up with fresh salmon to create a seriously delicious burger with an Asian twist! Combining fresh salmon with ginger, garlic, a touch of hoisin sauce, and cilantro creates a flavorful burger that will make even the most discriminating burger lover very happy. My family loves the ginger aioli with extra heat, but you can adjust the Asian chili paste to suit your taste. This burger pairs well with baked sweet potato fries tossed with a sprinkle of lime juice and sea salt.

1 pound skinless, boneless salmon fillet, cut into 2" pieces

1 tablespoon chopped cilantro

1 tablespoon hoisin sauce

½ teaspoon garlic

1 teaspoon ginger paste or peeled and grated fresh ginger, divided

½ teaspoon sea salt

½ teaspoon freshly ground black pepper

⅓ cup panko (Japanese bread crumbs)

Organic canola or olive oil cooking spray

¼ cup lite mayonnaise

1 teaspoon Asian garlic chili paste (optional)

1 teaspoon lemon juice

2 teaspoons reduced-sodium soy sauce or hoisin sauce

4 whole-wheat hamburger buns

1 cup baby greens

1 ripe tomato, sliced

1. Preheat broiler to medium-high and set the rack 4" from heat source.

2. In a food processor, pulse the salmon 3–4 times, just enough to rough chop, not purée. Make sure not to overprocess the salmon.

3. Place chopped salmon in a medium bowl and add cilantro, hoisin sauce, garlic, ½ teaspoon ginger, salt, pepper, and panko bread crumbs. Mix well.

4. Form chopped salmon into 4 patties. Place on a sheet pan lightly coated with cooking spray. Cover and refrigerate if using later.

5. Make the ginger aioli by whisking together the mayonnaise, Asian garlic chili paste, lemon juice, soy sauce, and remaining ginger.

6. Place salmon patties under broiler for 3–5 minutes on each side, or until just opaque.

7. To serve, place each patty on a whole-wheat bun and top with 1 teaspoon of ginger aioli. Top with baby greens and tomato slice.

SERVES: 4; CALORIES PER SERVING: 410; DIETARY EQUIVALENT: 3 oz. lean protein, 2 carbohydrates

Nutrition Basics

For those who need to limit carbohydrates, eliminate the bun and serve with a side of baked sweet potato fries, which are high in fiber and lower on the glycemic scale.

GRILLED SALMON WITH BALSAMIC GLAZE

Can something so easy be so good? Yes it can, and this recipe for grilled salmon will not disappoint! While I am a big fan of salmon cooked any way, especially from a nutritionist's point of view, I too get tired of plain fish. This glaze is sweet yet tangy and holds up well to the stronger flavor of salmon. We love serving this in the Wellness Kitchen on top of an arugula salad with cherry tomatoes drizzled with a little olive oil, squeeze of fresh lemon, and pinch of salt and pepper.

½ cup balsamic vinegar
2 tablespoons pure maple syrup
2 tablespoons Dijon mustard
1 teaspoon minced garlic
4 (5-ounce) salmon fillets (1½ lbs.)
1 tablespoon olive oil
Sea salt
Freshly ground black pepper

1. Heat grill to medium heat.
2. In a small saucepan, heat balsamic vinegar, maple syrup, Dijon, and garlic. Bring to a boil, then reduce to a simmer over low heat for approximately 15–17 minutes, until syrupy. Set aside.
3. Brush salmon fillets with olive oil and season with salt and pepper.
4. Grill salmon 5 minutes on one side, turn over, and continue to grill for another 4 minutes or until salmon is flakey and opaque.
5. Brush salmon with balsamic glaze; continue grilling for 1 more minute. Remove from grill.
6. To serve, plate the salmon and lightly brush with additional glaze if desired. Refrigerate any leftover glaze and use on grilled chicken or grilled vegetables. Leftover glaze can be refrigerated up to 2 weeks.

SERVES: 4; CALORIES PER SERVING: 250; DIETARY EQUIVALENT: 4 oz. protein, ½ fat

Nutrition Basics
All sugars are approximately 54 calories per tablespoon, and really none of them is good for us in large amounts—even the pure maple syrup used here. We limit sugar in all of our recipes as much as possible, adding just enough to improve flavor but little enough not to be a health issue.

MISO GRILLED SALMON WITH BOK CHOY

The sweet and savory salmon pairs well with the charred smokiness of the bok choy, creating a perfectly balanced dish. I get hungry just thinking about beautiful glazed pink salmon sitting on a platter of light green and white bok choy! Bok choy is known as Chinese cabbage, but it does not have the strong flavor we associate with cabbages. This nutrient-packed cruciferous vegetable helps your body detoxify. Four servings of cruciferous vegetables (broccoli, kale, cauliflower, bok choy, Brussels sprouts, cabbage) per week can reduce the risk of colon cancer by 30 percent. You can make this dish with sea bass or black cod as well.

¼ cup golden miso

½ cup sweet mirin (sweet Japanese wine)

2 tablespoons rice vinegar

1 tablespoon sugar

3 tablespoons reduced-sodium soy sauce

1 teaspoon minced ginger

1 teaspoon minced garlic

1 teaspoon sesame oil

4 salmon fillets (5–6 oz. each) rinsed, patted dry

1 pound baby bok choy, halved

1 tablespoon sesame seeds, toasted

1. Preheat a clean, lightly oiled grill to medium-high heat.

2. In a medium baking dish, whisk together miso, mirin, vinegar, sugar, soy sauce, ginger, garlic, and sesame oil.

3. Place the salmon in the marinade; coat fish well, and refrigerate for 20 minutes or up to 2 hours.

4. Remove fish from marinade (reserve marinade). Grill salmon for 4–5 minutes on each side or until salmon is opaque and flakey. Set aside; keep warm.

5. Brush bok choy with remaining marinade. Grill until golden brown and tender.

6. To serve, place bok choy on platter, arrange salmon over top, and sprinkle with toasted sesame seeds.

SERVES: 4; CALORIES PER SERVING: 175; DIETARY EQUIVALENT: 4 oz. protein, 1 vegetable

Food Tip

Miso (fermented soy bean paste) can be easily found in the refrigerated Asian section of your market. It has a sweet savory flavor and comes in light yellow, light brown, and darker brown colors, taking on a stronger flavor with the darker colors. I prefer to use the light- or medium-colored one and make sure I use just enough to not overpower the dish with a too-strong salty taste. Try adding a tablespoon of miso to your soups or salad dressings for added health and flavor benefits.

SALMON WELLINGTON

❧

We serve this for a winter holiday meal in the Wellness Kitchen, but it's perfect for any special occasion, any time of the year. It's stunning in flavor and in presentation. This elegant fish entrée is typically very high in calories because of high fat content and puff pastry. We came up with a delicious filling of sautéed mushrooms and spinach held together with just a bit of lite cream cheese, giving it a creamy, rich taste. We only wrap the puff pastry on the top of the fish, which saves calories and eliminates the problem of soggy crust underneath. Orange-glazed baby carrots and puréed cauliflower are the perfect accompaniments to this special entrée.

1 tablespoon olive oil

2 leeks, thinly sliced, white part only

1 tablespoon chopped garlic

1 cup sliced mushrooms

3 (5–6-ounce) bags baby spinach

1 teaspoon sea salt

1 teaspoon freshly ground black pepper

1 teaspoon fresh thyme leaves (or ½ teaspoon dried thyme)

4 ounces lite cream cheese

¼ cup grated Parmesan cheese

1 tablespoon Dijon mustard

1 (2½–3-pound) boneless, skinless salmon fillet

1 sheet prepared puff pastry, thawed but chilled in fridge

1 egg, beaten

1. Preheat oven to 375°F.

2. In a large sauté pan, heat oil over medium heat. Add leeks; reduce heat to medium-low and sauté for 8–9 minutes until golden. Add garlic and mushrooms, and sauté for 1 minute. Remove to bowl, set aside.

3. Add spinach to sauté pan and sauté until wilted, 3–4 minutes. Place in colander and squeeze out excess moisture with paper towels. Add spinach to leek and mushroom mixture, season with salt, pepper, and thyme, mixing well. Add lite cream cheese, Parmesan, and Dijon, blending well into the spinach mixture.

4. Rinse and pat dry salmon. Place salmon in middle of parchment-lined upside down baking sheet. Spread spinach mixture evenly over salmon. (Salmon may be prepared ahead to this point; just cover with plastic wrap and bring to room temperature for 30 minutes before placing pastry sheet on salmon and baking.)

5. Remove puff pastry sheet from refrigerator and roll out wide and long enough to cover salmon fillet.

6. Cover salmon fillet with puff pastry and tuck edges under salmon to seal. Cut 5–6 small slits in pastry to allow steam to escape. Brush lightly with beaten egg.

7. Bake salmon for 20–25 minutes or until the pastry is golden brown.

8. To serve, let rest 10 minutes. Slide salmon onto platter, slice into 8 servings.

SERVES: 8; CALORIES PER SERVING: 485; DIETARY EQUIVALENT: 5 oz. protein, 2 fats, ½ vegetable

Food Tip

Make sure you do not take the puff pastry out of the refrigerator until ready to use or it will not "puff" when baking. Placing the salmon on an upside down baking sheet makes it easy to slide off onto the platter for serving.

Chapter 5: Quick and Easy Main Dishes   133

SPICE-RUBBED SALMON WITH POMEGRANATE RAITA

✦

The first time we made this in the Wellness Kitchen was for a class that featured spices. It was a beautiful fall day, a little crisp but bright and sunny, and we had a group of ladies who were celebrating a friend's birthday by taking a cooking class together. This Indian-inspired fish dish was the perfect entrée! The spice rub gave the fish a beautiful red color when pan-seared. When placed on a platter, topped with the raita (an Indian yogurt sauce) then garnished with pomegranate seeds and mint, it looked like a magazine cover, exotic and scrumptious! The unique flavor of this raita made with cilantro and mint is the perfect complement to the warm spiciness of the fish. Plain nonfat Greek yogurt gives the raita a creamy texture similar to real sour cream, but it is fat-free and contains twice as much protein as regular yogurt. Plain Greek yogurt can be used in place of sour cream in many dishes at a fraction of the calories.

Spice Rub

2¼ teaspoons caraway seeds

2¼ teaspoons cumin seeds

1½ tablespoons ancho chili powder

¾ teaspoon garlic powder

1½ teaspoons sea salt

Salmon

1 tablespoon olive oil

4 (5-ounce) or 1½ pounds salmon fillets

Raita

1 cup plain nonfat Greek yogurt

¼ cup finely chopped cilantro

¼ cup finely chopped mint

⅛ cup (about 2) minced scallions

1½ teaspoons freshly squeezed lemon juice

½ cup pomegranate seeds

½ teaspoon sea salt

½ teaspoon freshly ground black pepper

1. Preheat oven to 425°F.

2. In a small skillet, toast the caraway and cumin seeds over moderate heat until fragrant, about 2 minutes. Let cool.

3. Transfer caraway and cumin seeds to a blender or food processor, or grind with a mortar and pestle. Add the chili powder, garlic powder, and salt.

4. Brush the fish with olive oil. Rub the fish with the spice mixture, creating a paste. Set aside until ready to cook.

5. Place fish on a parchment-lined rimmed baking sheet. Roast fish for about 7–10 minutes, depending on the thickness of the fillet, until just opaque and tender.

6. Meanwhile, in a medium bowl, combine the yogurt, cilantro, mint, scallions, and lemon juice. Gently fold in pomegranate seeds. Season to taste with salt and pepper.

7. Transfer the fish to a platter. Top each piece with 1 tablespoon of raita. Serve remaining raita on the side.

SERVES: 4; CALORIES PER SERVING: 315; DIETARY EQUIVALENT: 4½ oz. protein, ½ fat, ½ carbohydrate

Food Tip

This is a great "company" dish—you can prepare it ahead except for roasting the fish. Place spice-rubbed fish on a baking sheet, cover, and refrigerate. Make raita ahead of time, place in covered bowl, and refrigerate. About 25 minutes before serving, remove fish from refrigerator, bring to room temperature for 15 minutes, then place in the oven to roast. I love to serve this fish on platter of baby greens; the colors are magnificent and so impressive!

ASIAN SHRIMP MEATBALLS AND CABBAGE

Years ago, when my son was a Cub Scout, my fellow troop leader and I took our group of seven Cub Scouts to the Los Angeles Music Center to a children's music program and then to Chinatown for dim sum. By the time we arrived at the restaurant, they were in high gear after sitting for two hours in the auditorium. Containing the energy of seven eight-year-old boys was proving to be challenging, to say the least. Yet when the waiter brought the first order of dumplings, they were so infatuated that we hardly heard a word out of them. One of their favorite dumplings was a shrimp one, which I went home and tried to duplicate the next day. I could not believe how easy it was—a few ingredients, nothing overly exotic, and requiring merely the basic Asian bamboo steamer I already had, which can be found in many import stores or kitchen stores for very little money. Try these with a stir-fry vegetable dish and cut fruit for a complete meal, or as impressive appetizer.

1 pound raw shrimp, peeled, deveined, tails removed
4 green onions, thinly sliced
1 tablespoon reduced-sodium soy sauce
½ teaspoon finely chopped ginger
½ teaspoon finely chopped garlic
1 cup cooked brown rice, cooled
Cabbage leaves
¼ cup ponzu sauce or hoisin sauce, for dipping

1. Place half of the raw shrimp in food processor and pulse until finely chopped.

2. Add the remaining shrimp to food processor and pulse just a few times to combine.

3. Transfer shrimp to a large bowl. Add green onions, soy sauce, ginger, garlic, and rice. Mix well. Form shrimp mixture into 1½" balls.

4. Line steamer with cabbage leaves. Place shrimp balls in steamer for 6–7 minutes until shrimp turns pink.

5. To serve, place cooked cabbage leaves on platter, arrange shrimp balls on cabbage, and place dipping sauce on platter.

SERVES: 4; CALORIES PER SERVING: 185; DIETARY EQUIVALENT: 4 oz. protein, ½ carbohydrate, 1 vegetable

Nutrition Basics

Shrimp is only 30 calories per ounce and has one of the lowest mercury levels for seafood. It is also no longer restricted on a low-cholesterol diet. Recent research has showed that, thanks to its very low saturated-fat content and the protective factor of omega-3 fatty acids, shrimp does not raise human cholesterol. Very few markets get fresh shrimp, unless you are lucky enough to live near an area where they fish for it. Instead, most markets get it frozen and thaw it before they put it in the fish case. For convenience and for fresher product, buy frozen seafood and thaw when you need it.

BBQ SHRIMP

If you want seafood packed with flavor, this is the dish for you! This shrimp dish will seem like something you'd eat at a picnic table in New Orleans on a hot balmy night with a very cold glass of iced tea or beer. It couldn't be much easier to prepare—just add spices to a bowl, squeeze lemon over the shrimp, give it a good toss, and head for the grill. For less heat, cut the amount of ancho chili in half.

1 tablespoon Spanish smoked paprika
2 teaspoons ancho chili powder
1 tablespoon brown sugar
½ teaspoon ground cumin
1 teaspoon sea salt
½ teaspoon freshly ground black pepper
1 tablespoon chopped garlic
1 tablespoon olive oil
2 pounds large shrimp, deveined and peeled
1 lemon
6 green onions, sliced thinly

1. Preheat grill to medium-high heat.
2. In a large bowl, combine the paprika, chili powder, sugar, cumin, salt, pepper, garlic, and olive oil. Mix well.
3. Add shrimp to bowl of spices and toss well.
4. Cut lemon in half and squeeze one half over the shrimp. Cut the remaining half into wedges. Grill shrimp until just pink, about 2–3 minutes per side.
5. To serve, place on platter, sprinkle with sliced green onions, and garnish with lemon wedges.

SERVES: 6; CALORIES PER SERVING: 150; DIETARY EQUIVALENT: 5 oz. protein

Nutrition Basics

For a very easy, light-on-the-calories meal, just serve this shrimp alongside sliced rustic bread that has been lightly brushed with olive oil and grilled, and a large green salad tossed with Lite Honey-Lime Vinaigrette (see recipe in Chapter 3). Be sure to grill only the right amount of bread per person to keep carbohydrate portions in check!

THAI GRILLED SHRIMP

This is one of the easiest, most flavorful shrimp recipes ever! The shrimp are sweet, salty, and tart all at the same time, which is so very typical of Thai food. The recipe is so easy that you can go from freezer to platter in under 30 minutes. You can take these shrimp in many directions—serve as a lite appetizer or as an entrée with sesame peanut noodles and cut tropical fruit.

8 skewers (wood, soaked for 2 hours in water)
1½ pounds large raw shrimp, peeled, deveined
1 tablespoon olive oil
½ teaspoon sea salt
1 tablespoon fish sauce
3 tablespoons lime juice
2 teaspoons sugar
¼ cup coarsely chopped lightly salted peanuts
2 tablespoons finely chopped cilantro

1. Preheat grill to medium heat.
2. Place shrimp in medium bowl and toss with olive oil and salt. Place shrimp on skewers.
3. In small bowl, mix fish sauce, lime juice, and sugar. Set aside.
4. Place shrimp on grill and cook until just pink and opaque, approximately 3–4 minutes on each side.
5. Remove from grill and place on serving platter.
6. To serve, brush shrimp liberally with lime juice mixture and sprinkle with chopped peanuts and cilantro.

SERVES: 4; CALORIES PER SERVING: 220; DIETARY EQUIVALENT: 5 oz. protein

Nutrition Basics
Since grilled shrimp are so low in calories, a 6-ounce portion is not excessive for those watching their weight. If shrimp are frozen, just place in bowl of cold water for 15 minutes to unthaw. Dry the shrimp well with paper towels before tossing with olive oil and grilling.

HONEY-CHILI GRILLED SHRIMP WITH NECTARINE SALSA

As soon as nectarines hit the markets, I make this fabulous shrimp dish. It's light and flavorful, just what I love to eat on a hot summer night. (I actually sometimes make this in the winter when I need a tropical fix. Just substitute a fresh pineapple half, diced in ½" pieces, for the nectarines, and use a cup of frozen grilled corn, which is available in most markets in the freezer section.) The combination of lime juice, honey, garlic, and chili gives these grilled shrimp a slightly spicy, sweet, and tart taste that everyone loves!

Salsa

2 ears fresh corn
2 ripe nectarines, diced with skins on
2 tablespoons slivered almonds
1 tablespoon olive oil
½ teaspoon sea salt
1 tablespoon fresh chopped cilantro

Shrimp

8 bamboo skewers, soaked in water 2 hours prior to grilling
1 pound large shrimp, peeled and deveined

Glaze

1 tablespoon olive oil
1 tablespoon honey
1 tablespoon lime juice
2 teaspoons chopped garlic
1½ teaspoons ground chili powder
1 tablespoon water
1 teaspoon salt

1. Heat grill to medium.
2. Add corn to grill; cook approximately 6–8 minutes. Turn every few minutes until slightly charred and golden. Remove from grill.
3. In medium bowl, gently toss the nectarines, almonds, oil, salt, and cilantro.
4. Remove corn kernels from cob and combine with other salsa ingredients. Set aside.

5. Place shrimp on bamboo skewers.
6. In a small bowl, whisk all ingredients for the glaze.
7. Brush the shrimp with the glaze.
8. Place shrimp on grill for 3–4 minutes, then turn over and continue to grill for another 2–3 minutes until opaque and just cooked through. Remove from grill.
9. To serve, place nectarine salsa on platter and arrange shrimp skewers on top of salsa.

SERVES: 4; CALORIES PER SERVING: 335; DIETARY EQUIVALENT: 4 lean protein, 1 carbohydrate, ½ fruit, 1 fat

Nutrition Basics
A ½ cup portion of the salsa should be counted as 1 carbohydrate serving since it contains corn and fruit.

CRAB ENCHILADAS

These seemly decadent enchiladas never fail to impress my guests, especially when the guests hear that the enchiladas are not as unhealthy as they taste! Crab is a very low-fat, low-calorie seafood that only needs a bit of lite cream cheese to make a decadent filling. I avoid frying the corn tortillas and instead dip them in the green sauce, then top with a smaller amount of a lite Mexican cheese blend. I always put out a bowl of finely shredded romaine to add on top—I love the crunch and it adds volume with virtually no calories. I do not serve rice and beans with these enchiladas because they can easily add 500–700 more calories to a meal. Instead, I serve a green salad with bite-sized pieces of citrus fruit and Lite Honey-Lime Vinaigrette (see recipe in Chapter 3).

Organic canola or olive oil cooking spray
16 oz. lump crab meat
4 green onions, thinly sliced
4 ounces lite cream cheese
2 tablespoons diced Ortega chilies (optional)
1 cup grated low-fat jack cheese or lite Mexican blend
12 corn tortillas
1 (15-ounce) can green enchilada sauce, divided
1 (6-ounce) can pitted black olives
Shredded lettuce
Reduced-fat sour cream (optional)

1. Preheat oven to 350°F.
2. Spray 9" × 13" baking dish with nonstick spray.
3. Break crab into smaller pieces.
4. In small bowl, combine green onion and cream cheese, and chilies, if using. Gently add the crab, being careful to not overmix.
5. Pour half of the green enchilada sauce in a shallow dish and dip each tortilla in sauce. Spread 2 tablespoons crab and 1 tablespoon grated cheese on each tortilla. Roll up and place in baking dish.

6. Pour remaining sauce over enchiladas. Top with remaining cheese and olives. Cover with foil and bake for 30 minutes.
7. Serve with shredded lettuce and reduced-fat sour cream, if using.

SERVES: 6 (2 enchiladas each); CALORIES PER SERVING: 425; DIETARY EQUIVALENT: 4 oz. protein, 2 carbohydrates, 1 fat

Food Tip

If fresh crab meat is unavailable or too expensive, look for vacuum-packed crab (found at the fish counter at your market in the refrigerator section) for these enchiladas. It comes in a 1-pound can, and is pasteurized, contains nice whole lumps of crab, and keeps in the refrigerator for weeks. Avoid the frozen crab if you can; it generally is too mushy in texture when thawed.

ULTIMATE GRILLED CHICKEN

Grilled chicken has become a somewhat mundane entrée for many of us. As a nutritionist I certainly recommend it for its health benefits; it's a great source of lean protein. As a foodie, I am tired of dried-out grilled chicken with no flavor. I think the dried-out part often results from leaving the chicken breast too long on the grill; it's hard to cook it to doneness inside without overcooking the outside because of the thickness of the chicken. By pounding the chicken flat, it takes just minutes on the grill to cook. Brining adds moisture to the chicken; just be sure to rinse well so it does not have an overly salty flavor.

¼ cup sugar

2 tablespoons kosher salt

½ cup boiling water

1 quart (4 cups) cold water

2 pounds skinless, boneless chicken breast or thighs

¼ cup lemon juice

2 teaspoons chopped garlic

2 teaspoons finely chopped fresh rosemary

½ teaspoon dried red pepper flakes

1 tablespoon water

2 tablespoons olive oil, divided

Lemon wedges, for garnish

Fresh rosemary sprigs, for garnish

1. Preheat grill to medium-high (10 minutes before ready to cook).

2. To brine chicken, in a small bowl, dissolve sugar and salt in boiling water. Transfer to a large container with lid. Add cold water. Place raw chicken pieces in brine and refrigerate for 2 hours or longer, up to overnight.

3. Remove chicken from brine and rinse well with cold water. Pat dry.

4. In small bowl, whisk together lemon juice, garlic, rosemary, red pepper flakes, water, and 1 tablespoon olive oil.

5. Pound chicken to ¼" thickness between two sheets of plastic wrap on cutting board. Brush both sides of chicken with remaining olive oil.

6. Grill for 4–5 minutes on one side, turn over, and brush with lemon vinaigrette. Cook an additional 4–5 minutes.

7. Brush with remaining vinaigrette.

8. Transfer chicken to platter. Garnish with lemon wedges and fresh rosemary sprigs.

SERVES: 6; CALORIES PER SERVING: 230; DIETARY EQUIVALENT: 4 oz. protein

Nutrition Basics

Pounding skinless deboned chicken breast is a great way to fool your mind. A four-ounce chicken breast pounded thin tricks your brain into thinking you're eating a much larger portion. It's funny how the visual appearance of how much food you have on your plate affects how satisfied you feel after you eat it! If you happen to have extra chicken breasts left over, use them to make tasty panini (Italian-style sandwiches) the next day. Spread a tablespoon of pesto over whole-grain rustic bread; add chicken, a slice of provolone cheese, and tomato. Mist the bread with olive oil and grill until warm and toasty.

CHICKEN PARMESAN WITH BASIC TOMATO SAUCE

The chicken in this Italian classic is usually fried, which makes it the not-so-healthy way to eat chicken. Our Wellness Kitchen revision is sure to please everyone—and it takes less than 40 minutes from start to finish, so it's doable on a weeknight. I prefer to make my own bread crumbs from whole-grain bread. Not only is it healthier, but the crumbs have a crisper, lighter texture than the finely ground prepared ones, which tend to have a gritty texture. Oven-frying allows for a crisp, cheesy crust, and you can make the Basic Tomato Sauce while the chicken bakes in the oven. If you're really pressed for time, use a good-quality jarred marinara sauce in place of the homemade sauce. Better yet, make homemade tomato sauce when time allows and keep frozen in 2-cup portions to be defrosted in the microwave when needed quickly.

Organic olive oil or canola cooking spray
4 boneless, skinless chicken breasts
3 pieces whole-grain bread (or ¾ cup prepared bread crumbs)
¼ cup grated Parmesan cheese
1 tablespoon finely chopped fresh basil
¼ teaspoon sea salt
¼ teaspoon freshly ground black pepper
1 whole egg or 2 egg whites
2 cups Basic Tomato Sauce or marinara sauce
4 slices low-fat provolone cheese or mozzarella cheese
2 tablespoons shredded Parmesan cheese

1. Preheat oven to 350°F. Spray 9" × 13" baking dish with olive oil spray.
2. Place chicken breasts on plastic wrap, cover with another sheet, and pound chicken with flat side of meat mallet until ¼" thick.
3. Tear bread slices into quarters. Place in food processor and pulse until bread becomes medium crumbs.
4. Combine bread crumbs, grated Parmesan cheese, basil, salt, and pepper in a large shallow bowl; mix well.
5. In medium bowl, whisk egg with fork. Dip each chicken breast in the egg and transfer to the bread crumb mixture; coat lightly. Transfer breaded chicken to prepared baking dish. Repeat process with remaining chicken breasts, arranging in a single layer.
6. Spray breaded chicken with organic cooking spray to increase browning and crispiness of the chicken.
7. Place chicken in oven and bake for 18–20 minutes, until lightly browned.
8. Remove from oven and top each piece with ½ cup Basic Tomato Sauce or marinara sauce and 1 slice of low-fat cheese.
9. Sprinkle with shredded Parmesan cheese.
10. Return chicken to oven and bake for 5 minutes, or until sauce is bubbly and cheese is melted. Serve immediately.

SERVES: 4; CALORIES PER SERVING: 310; DIETARY EQUIVALENT: 5 oz. protein, 1 vegetable

Nutrition Basics
Try serving the Chicken Parmesan with our Roasted Spaghetti Squash with Parmesan (see recipe in Chapter 6) or shredded zucchini as an alternative to pasta for a tasty, lighter meal.

BASIC TOMATO SAUCE

1 tablespoon olive oil
½ large onion, diced
½ cup shredded carrots
1 tablespoon minced garlic
¼ teaspoon dried red pepper flakes
2 (28-ounce) cans diced plum tomatoes (reserve juice)
¼ cup finely chopped basil leaves, divided
1 tablespoon fresh thyme leaves or 1½ teaspoons dried thyme
Sea salt
Freshly ground black pepper

1. Heat olive oil in medium saucepan over medium heat.
2. Add onion, carrots, garlic, and red pepper flakes. Sauté for 2–3 minutes.
3. Add tomatoes with juice.
4. Bring to a boil, and then reduce heat to simmer for 15 minutes until sauce has thickened slightly.
5. Add half of the basil and all of the thyme. Carefully blend sauce in blender or food processor in batches.
6. Return to saucepan; season with salt and pepper and garnish with remaining basil.

YIELDS: approx. 6 cups; CALORIES PER ½ CUP: 40; DIETARY EQUIVALENT: 1 vegetable

CHICKEN SAUTÉ

How many times have you heard "Chicken again??" at your house? Americans do eat more chicken than any other meat—about 90 pounds per person, per year—and it can get boring! A great technique to master is sautéing chicken breast. It turns everyday chicken into a memorable meal. Start with a small amount of oil to brown the chicken, adding great color and flavor; then finish cooking the chicken by adding 1 tablespoon of water for a quick steam, which guarantees that your chicken will be moist and tender every time—without using lots of oil. Finish with one of our pan sauces for a delicious, healthy, gourmet dish. One of my family's favorites for a birthday dinner is Chicken Piccata; I was surprised how many young children love the bright, lemony taste with the saltiness of the capers.

4 boneless, skinless chicken breasts
2 tablespoons all-purpose flour
1 teaspoon sea salt
½ teaspoon freshly ground black pepper
1 tablespoon olive oil
1 tablespoon water

1. Place chicken breasts on plastic wrap, cover with another sheet, and pound chicken with flat side of meat mallet until ¼" thick.
2. Place flour, salt, and pepper in 9" × 13" baking dish. Add one chicken breast and lightly coat both sides with the flour mixture, shake off extra flour, and place on a clean plate. Repeat with remaining chicken breasts.
3. In large nonstick sauté pan, heat olive oil over medium heat. Add chicken and brown for 3 minutes, turn over, and brown other side for 1 minute.
4. To finish cooking the chicken through, add 1 tablespoon water to sauté pan lid and quickly place on pan to steam chicken breast for 1 minute. (Putting the water in the lid and quickly covering the pan allows the steam to stay *in* the pan, cooking the chicken quickly and making it very moist.) Remove lid and transfer chicken to clean platter.

VARIATIONS

CHICKEN PICCATA

Juice of 2 lemons
⅓ cup white wine
2 tablespoons capers
2 tablespoons finely chopped parsley

1. Return sauté pan from cooking chicken back on burner over medium-low heat.
2. Add lemon juice, wine, and capers to sauté pan, scraping the flavorful brown bits from the bottom of the pan. Simmer for 1 minute.
3. Return chicken to sauté pan. Turn chicken breast over to coat with sauce on both sides and simmer for another 2 minutes or until sauce has thickened.
4. Sprinkle with chopped parsley.

CHICKEN MARSALA

1 tablespoon trans-fat-free margarine
2 cups sliced mushrooms
2 teaspoons minced garlic
⅓ cup Marsala wine
½ cup organic, reduced-sodium, fat-free chicken broth
2 tablespoons chopped parsley

1. Return sauté pan from cooking chicken back on burner over medium-low heat.
2. Add margarine and melt over medium heat.
3. Add mushrooms and garlic; sauté for 2–3 minutes or until softened.
4. Add Marsala wine and broth; cook for an additional 2 minutes.
5. Return chicken to sauté pan. Turn chicken breast over to coat with sauce on both sides and simmer for another 2 minutes or until sauce has thickened.
6. Sprinkle with chopped parsley.

CHICKEN DIJON

2 tablespoons Dijon mustard

¼ cup white wine

¼ cup organic, reduced-sodium, fat-free chicken broth

2 tablespoons chopped parsley

1. Return sauté pan from cooking chicken back on burner over medium-low heat.

2. Add Dijon, wine, and broth to sauté pan, scraping the flavorful brown bits from the bottom of the pan. Cook for 1 minute.

3. Return chicken to sauté pan. Turn chicken breast over to coat with sauce on both sides and simmer for another 2 minutes or until sauce has thickened.

4. Sprinkle with chopped parsley.

SERVES: 4; CALORIES PER SERVING: 220 calories for Marsala, 220 for Piccata, 190 for Dijon; DIETARY EQUIVALENT: 4 oz. protein, 1 fat

Nutrition Basics

I frequently get asked if it's necessary to buy organic chicken. My response to this much-disputed subject is yes, if you can afford to. Look for chicken that has no synthetic products, no antibiotics, and no hormones for cleaner, less contaminated protein that can have only positive benefits to your health. I have found that many of the large warehouse stores have organic chicken at much lower prices than the regular markets. One way to balance out the cost of organic chicken is to make sure you have some vegetarian protein meals each week that consist of less expensive protein. For example, one night it's organic chicken, but the next night a bean soup, which benefits not only your wallet but your health as well.

PERFECT ROASTED CHICKEN WITH BROCCOLI RABE AND POTATOES

It's a surprise to all of us in the Wellness Kitchen that many of our guests have never cooked a whole chicken. People think it's an intimidating process, but once you do it a few times, it'll be no big deal. We created the perfect roasted chicken recipe, moist and flavorful. By cooking the whole chicken in a super-hot oven for half the time, the chicken sears and does not dry out. Organic chickens tend to be leaner and smaller than factory-produced chickens, so a 2½-pound chicken should feed 4. Most men and teen boys need no more than 5–6 ounces of protein at dinner and women and children no more than 3–4 ounces of protein at dinner. Too much animal protein can raise cholesterol and can be the source of unneeded calories. I love this recipe because so little time is spent in prep. I can pop it in the oven and go do other things. Your family will think you slaved away, but good cooks know that simplicity is always the best for good food.

1 (2½–3) pound whole chicken

1½ tablespoons olive oil, divided

1½ teaspoons sea salt, divided

1½ teaspoons freshly ground black pepper, divided

1 tablespoon chopped garlic

8 parsley sprigs

1 lemon, cut in half

1 pound broccoli rabe (rapini) stems, cut into ½" pieces, leaves coarsely chopped

4–6 Yukon Gold potatoes, cut into ½" pieces

2 tablespoons water

½ cup organic, reduced-sodium, fat-free chicken broth

¼ cup dry white wine

¼ cup chopped parsley

1. Preheat oven to 450°F.

2. Place ovenproof roasting pan or skillet in oven to heat.

3. Remove giblets and neck from inside chicken. Rinse chicken and pat dry. Place chicken, breast side up, on cutting board.

4. Mix ½ tablespoon olive oil, 1 teaspoon salt, 1 teaspoon pepper, and garlic into a paste. Rub paste evenly under the skin of chicken by gently lifting the skin.

5. Place parsley sprigs and half of the lemon into the cavity of the chicken.

6. Remove hot pan from oven and place chicken in pan. Cross legs to keep them together. Roast for 30 minutes at 450°F.

7. Meanwhile, place broccoli rabe and potatoes in microwavable bowl with 2 tablespoons water, cover with plastic wrap, and microwave on high for 5 minutes to par-cook.

8. Drain microwaved vegetables. Toss with remaining olive oil, salt, and pepper. Spread on rimmed baking sheet.

9. When chicken has roasted for 30 minutes, place potatoes and broccoli rabe on bottom rack in oven, and turn off oven completely. Continue to roast chicken, potatoes, and broccoli rabe for another 30 minutes.

10. Remove chicken and vegetables from oven. Make sure chicken has reached an internal temperature of 165°F or that juices run clear, not pink, when chicken is pierced with a fork. Move chicken to cutting board and tent with foil to keep warm. Tent vegetables with foil; keep warm.

11. Pour pan juices from roasting pan into a measuring cup. Let fat rise to top; spoon off fat. Add pan juices, broth, and white wine to saucepan and bring to boil for 2 minutes. Add the juice from the remaining lemon half into the sauce. Add chopped parsley.

12. To serve, carve chicken, place on one side of a large platter, and drizzle with pan sauce. (To carve: Slice off breast meat first, then detach legs and cut leg thighs in half.) Spoon roasted potatoes and broccoli rabe onto other half of platter. Serve immediately.

SERVES: 4; CALORIES PER SERVING: 425; DIETARY EQUIVALENT: 4 oz. protein, 1–2 carbohydrates, 1 vegetable, 1 fat

Food Tip

I often prepare two whole chickens on Sunday, reserving the meat from one to use in meals for the upcoming week. This roasted chicken can be used in homemade chicken and vegetable soups, pasta, sandwiches, or salads. It makes cooking for the next few days so much easier! Cooked proteins should be consumed within 3 days. If you know you cannot use before then, debone and cut into bite-sized pieces and freeze for later use.

CHICKEN TINGA MINI TOSTADAS

Everyone loves this spicy chicken filling, especially when you team it with a crispy corn tortilla and top it with shredded lettuce and a dollop of great guacamole! I love it because it's simple, healthy food but tastes adventurous. Though this recipe calls for chicken breast, you could also use skinless, well-trimmed chicken thigh meat. While it contains slightly more calories and fat than the white meat, it does have higher iron, zinc, and B-vitamin levels than the white meat. You may want to double the recipe and put half in the freezer for another time. Everything in this recipe can be made ahead. Store the crispy tortillas in an airtight container and just warm them in the oven for a few minutes while reheating the filling. The filling can be stored in the refrigerator up to 3 days (the flavor actually improves), or can be frozen up to 3 months.

3 boneless, skinless chicken breasts, cut in half

1 white onion, finely chopped, divided

2 teaspoons chopped garlic

3 tomatoes

2 teaspoons olive oil

½ (7-ounce) can chipotle peppers in adobo sauce

16 mini 3" corn tortillas or 8 6" corn tortillas

Organic canola or olive oil cooking spray

2 cups finely shredded lettuce

4 ounces Cotija cheese, crumbled (a low-fat cheese similar to a feta)

Guacamole (see recipe in Chapter 2)

1. Preheat oven to 350°F.

2. In a large pot over medium heat, add chicken, half of the chopped onion, garlic, and enough water to cover the chicken. Bring to a boil, then reduce to simmer.

3. Poach chicken for about 10–12 minutes, until the chicken is no longer pink. Remove chicken, cool slightly, and shred the meat. Set aside.

4. To the poaching liquid, add whole tomatoes and bring to a boil. Cook until the skins split open, approximately 6–8 minutes. Remove and set aside.

5. In a large sauté pan over medium heat, add olive oil and the remaining onion; sauté until translucent. Set aside.

6. In a blender, combine poached tomatoes with chipotle peppers. Purée until smooth. Add puréed mixture to the pan with the sautéed onions. Add the shredded chicken; heat through.

7. Place tortillas on baking sheet and spray with cooking spray. Bake for 8–10 minutes or until tortillas are crisp. Remove from oven and set aside.

8. To serve, spoon chicken on each tortilla, top with shredded lettuce, sprinkle with Cotija cheese, and top with 1 tablespoon Guacamole.

SERVES: 4 (4 3" or 2 6" tortillas per serving); CALORIES PER SERVING: 300; DIETARY EQUIVALENT: 4 oz. protein, 1 carbohydrate, 1 fat

ULTIMATE CHICKEN WITH CHIMICHURRI SAUCE

Before you plate another grilled chicken breast, check out this easy sauce that will make an ordinary staple extraordinary. I have come to the conclusion that it's all about the sauce—a good one can make bland, everyday fare special. This one takes just a few minutes to prepare with fresh herbs, garlic, and lemon. Pounding chicken very thin before placing on the grill allows the chicken to cook quickly . . . and less time on the grill means no more dried-out chicken breast!

2 pounds skinless, boneless chicken breast or thighs
1 cup (packed) fresh Italian parsley leaves
¼ cup (packed) fresh cilantro
2 tablespoons olive oil
2 tablespoons organic, reduced-sodium, fat-free chicken broth
2 tablespoons sherry vinegar
1 tablespoon garlic, chopped
¼ teaspoon dried red pepper flakes
1 teaspoon lemon zest
¼ teaspoon ground cumin
1 teaspoon sea salt
1 teaspoon freshly ground black pepper
2 lemons cut in wedges for garnish

1. Preheat grill to medium heat (10 minutes before ready to cook).
2. Cover cutting board with sheet of plastic wrap. Place chicken breast on plastic wrap, cover with another sheet, and pound chicken with flat side of meat mallet until ¼" thick. Repeat with remaining chicken breasts. You can also cut the breasts horizontally if you prefer. If you place the chicken breasts in the freezer for 20 minutes, it firms up the chicken and makes it much easier to slice thinly.
3. Add parsley, cilantro, olive oil, broth, vinegar, garlic, red pepper flakes, lemon zest, cumin, salt, and fresh ground pepper to food processor and pulse until finely chopped, but not puréed. Place in small bowl and set aside.
4. Place chicken breast on grill and grill for 4–5 minutes on each side until golden.
5. To serve, transfer chicken to platter, top with spoonfuls of chimichurri sauce, and garnish with lemon wedges.

SERVES: 6; CALORIES PER SERVING: 210; DIETARY EQUIVALENT: 4 oz. lean protein

Nutrition Basics

Fresh herbs have a high level of antioxidants, even higher than most vegetables, so we use handfuls of them not only to flavor food but to increase the health benefits of recipes. We have reduced the amount of olive oil typically used in this type of sauce and substituted a small amount of chicken broth to lower the calories, but no one will know the difference!

HONEY-PECAN CRUSTED CHICKEN

These chicken strips never fail to please kids of all ages, as well as adults. Their preparation technique is similar to Shake 'n Bake, but there's no comparison in terms of taste. The corn flake crumbs and pecans give it a great nutty taste and add a crunchy texture. Coating the chicken with just a bit of honey and Dijon imparts a sweet-spicy flavor that makes these chicken strips irresistible. Spraying the chicken strips lightly with olive oil before popping them into the oven ensures a great crispy texture without frying. If I am lucky enough to have leftovers, which is rarely the case, I throw them on a salad with baby greens, apples, grapes, and a lite honey-mustard dressing.

Organic canola or olive oil cooking spray
4 boneless, skinless, chicken breasts (1 pound)
2 tablespoons honey
1 tablespoon Dijon mustard
1 cup crushed cornflakes
1 teaspoon sea salt
½ teaspoon cayenne pepper
¼ cup finely chopped pecans

1. Preheat oven to 350°F.
2. Spray a rimmed baking sheet with cooking spray. Set aside.
3. Cut each chicken breast into 4 strips.
4. In a small bowl, add honey and Dijon. Microwave 10 seconds to loosen honey. Whisk together.
5. In a shallow bowl, mix cornflake crumbs, salt, cayenne pepper, and pecans.
6. Dip each chicken strip in honey-mustard mixture. Shake off excess.
7. Lightly coat each chicken strip in cornflake mixture and place in single layer on prepared baking sheet. Repeat with remaining chicken strips.
8. Spray chicken strips lightly with cooking spray. Bake for 25 minutes until crisp.

SERVES: 4; CALORIES PER SERVING: 250; DIETARY EQUIVALENT: 4 oz. protein, 1 carbohydrate, ½ fat

Nutrition Basics

You do not need to "pack on" the cornflake/pecan mixture—a lighter coating means fewer calories, but there will still be plenty of crunch! You can easily make these ahead. Just put them on a baking sheet, cover with plastic wrap, and refrigerate, but do not bake until about 20 minutes before serving. Spray with olive oil right before placing in the oven for the crunchiest strips.

TEXAS BBQ CHICKEN

Here's an incredible rub that makes everyday grilled chicken taste like your favorite barbecue place. I dream about opening a chicken stand every time I make this barbecue chicken . . . I think I could make a fortune, it's that good! I did an internship in Texas and was introduced to great barbecue that was different than the sweet, sticky sauce I was accustomed to. Guests in the Wellness Kitchen are always surprised to find out how easy it is to make a dry rub that can add so much flavor to grilled chicken. I like to use a whole chicken cut in half, but if I have a larger group or want leftovers, I just add a few extra chicken breasts, considering that most people prefer white meat anyway. Serve it with our Chipotle Cilantro Slaw (see recipe in Chapter 3) and baked sweet potato fries for a real treat.

1½ teaspoons salt
1 tablespoon pepper
1 tablespoon chili powder
1½ teaspoons cumin
1 teaspoon thyme
1½ teaspoons finely chopped rosemary
8 pieces chicken, or 2½–3-pound whole chicken split in half
1 tablespoon olive oil

1. Preheat grill to high heat. Preheat oven to 400°F.
2. Combine salt, pepper, chili powder, cumin, thyme, and rosemary in small bowl and mix well.
3. Brush chicken with olive oil.
4. Sprinkle half of the dry rub over chicken and under skin.
5. Grill chicken pieces for 5–6 minutes on each side (10 minutes on each side if cooking a whole split chicken).
6. Transfer to baking sheet and finish cooking in oven for 10–15 minutes or until chicken reaches an internal temperature of 165°F.

SERVES: 4; CALORIES PER SERVING: 230; DIETARY EQUIVALENT: 4 oz. protein

Nutrition Basics

I recommend removing the skin after grilling, so it doesn't dry out and to lower the saturated fat content of the chicken. Make sure to get most of the dry rub under the skin so the flavor is in the meat, not just on the skin. You may want to double this rub recipe, especially if using more chicken. Store any leftover rub in a covered container for 6 months.

SPINACH-STUFFED TURKEY MEATLOAF

Years ago, I came up with this variation of the old standby meatloaf I remembered eating as a child. I distinctly recall the top of the meatloaf with the ketchup on it being the best part. Over the years I have tweaked this recipe, and from the feedback I have received in the Wellness Kitchen and at home, I think I finally achieved "meatloaf nirvana." Combining very lean ground beef with ground turkey not only lowers the fat but improves the texture as well. The sautéed garlic, spinach, and onion in the stuffing are just the right flavors to complement the homey traditional dish. And yes, I still left the ketchup on the top, because that little sweetness makes the ordinary fabulous!

1 tablespoon olive oil

1 cup finely chopped onion

1 teaspoon chopped garlic

2 (5–6-ounce) bags fresh baby spinach

⅛ teaspoon nutmeg

1 pound ground turkey breast

1 pound ground sirloin or lean ground beef

2 teaspoons sea salt

1 teaspoon freshly ground black pepper

1 teaspoon chopped fresh thyme

2 tablespoons Worcestershire sauce

¼ cup organic, reduced-sodium, fat-free chicken broth

1 tablespoon plus ½ cup ketchup, divided

½ cup bread crumbs made with whole-grain bread

1 whole egg plus 1 egg white, beaten

1. Preheat oven to 350°F.

2. Heat olive oil in large sauté pan over medium-high heat. Add onions and sauté for 6–8 minutes or until soft and golden. Add garlic and sauté for 1 minute. Transfer to large bowl.

3. Add spinach leaves to sauté pan and cook until wilted, 3–4 minutes. Using paper towels, squeeze excess water out of spinach. Season with nutmeg. Add onions and garlic. Set aside.

4. Combine ground meats, salt, pepper, thyme, Worcestershire sauce, broth, 1 tablespoon ketchup, bread crumbs, and egg in a large bowl.

5. On sheet of plastic wrap or wax paper, shape meat mixture into a rectangle, about 12" × 9", 1" thick. Spread spinach mixture over meat in a thin layer. Roll up meatloaf, jellyroll-style.

6. Place sheet of foil or parchment paper on a rimmed baking sheet. Place meatloaf seam side down, turning ends under. Spread remaining ketchup evenly over top.

7. Bake for 45 minutes. Remove from oven, tent with foil, and let rest for 10 minutes before slicing.

SERVES: 8; CALORIES PER SERVING: 270; DIETARY EQUIVALENT: 4 oz. protein, 1 vegetable

Nutrition Basics

Filling the meatloaf with vegetables keeps it moist and increases your vegetable intake. Make sure you squeeze all the water out of the spinach after sautéing so your meatloaf is not soggy. You can use two packages of frozen spinach, which is just as nutritious as fresh; again take care to squeeze the water out. I have also used steamed cut carrots instead of spinach. Be sure to cook the carrots to just crisp-tender, since they will cook longer in the meatloaf. This makes a large meatloaf, enough for 2 meals or sandwiches for the next few days. Freeze any leftovers for a later time as well.

FRENCH CHICKEN IN A POT

Anytime a recipe mentions "French," many people think it's going to be overly complicated and difficult. This couldn't be further from the truth! A quick rough chop of onion, lemon, and garlic, then a quick browning in the pot . . . add the wine, cover, and pop into the oven. An hour or so later, you have perfect moist, flavorful chicken that is so tender it falls off the bone! I love this dish served alongside roasted root vegetables and garlic-roasted potatoes. To make them, place bite-sized vegetables and potatoes on separate baking sheets, toss with 1 tablespoon olive oil, a pinch of sea salt, and freshly ground pepper, and place in the oven at the same time as the chicken. All you have to do is add a salad for a complete, delicious dinner.

1 (2½–3 pound) whole chicken

2 teaspoons sea salt

½ teaspoon freshly ground black pepper

½ onion, chopped

1 celery rib, chopped

6 cloves of garlic, peeled

1 bay leaf

2 sprigs fresh rosemary

1 lemon, sliced

1 tablespoon olive oil

1 cup dry white wine

1. Preheat oven to 325°F.

2. Rinse and pat chicken dry with paper towels. Season with salt and pepper.

3. Place onion, celery, garlic, bay leaf, rosemary, and lemon inside chicken cavity.

4. Heat large Dutch oven over medium-high heat. Add olive oil and swirl to cover bottom of pot. When oil is hot, place chicken breast side down and lightly brown, about 5 minutes. Using a wooden spoon inserted into the cavity, flip chicken over and brown for another 5 minutes.

5. Pour white wine into the bottom of pan and cover tightly with lid.

6. Place in oven for 60–70 minutes or until internal temperature reaches 165°F in thickest part of the thigh.

7. Transfer chicken to cutting board and let rest 15 minutes.

8. Remove skin from chicken and carve meat. Serve on platter with roasted vegetables.

SERVES: 4–6 (4-oz. servings); CALORIES PER SERVING: 175; DIETARY EQUIVALENT: 4 oz. lean protein

Nutrition Basics

Feel free to enjoy the white or dark meat of poultry; there is actually very little difference in calories. The white meat is about 8 calories an ounce less than the dark, with the skin removed. A 6-ounce piece of chicken with the skin on is 100 calories more because the skin is primarily fat.

SLOW COOKER TURKEY BREAST WITH BARLEY

When the temperature starts to drop and you can smell fall in the air, it's time for warm, substantial fare. It's also the time of year when many guests ask me about cooking in their slow cookers, and now I have a new favorite way to use this helpful kitchen appliance. I love Thanksgiving flavors and would be happy eating them more than just one day out of the year . . . but clearly, I'm not so interested in trying to pull that off on a busy weeknight. So I came up with this delicious recipe using a slow cooker that is very reminiscent of Thanksgiving. Hearty, healthy barley, white meat of turkey, onions, apples, and cranberries along with spices and seasoning all come together beautifully. After only a few minutes of prep time in the morning, you will have a meal as flavorful as a Thanksgiving feast, with almost no work!

1½ cups pearled barley, soaked in cold water for 2–24 hours, then drained

1 onion, peeled, chopped

½ cup dried cranberries

¼ cup chopped pecans

2 unpeeled apples, cored, chopped

3 cups organic, reduced-sodium, fat-free chicken broth

1 teaspoon dried thyme

1 teaspoon sea salt

½ teaspoon freshly ground black pepper

½ teaspoon poultry seasoning

2½–3 pounds boneless turkey breast, unthawed

2 tablespoons chopped fresh parsley

Nutrition Basics
Barley was the first grain cultivated by man. The nutty, chewy texture of this supergrain is high in fiber that lowers cholesterol and it metabolizes slowly, which aids in controlling blood sugars. It is considered the "grain of choice" to prevent or treat diabetes.

1. Place soaked barley, onion, cranberries, pecans, apples, broth, thyme, salt, pepper, and poultry seasoning in slow cooker. Mix well.

2. Place turkey breast on top of barley mixture. Cover slow cooker and cook on low for 8–9 hours until turkey is thoroughly cooked and barley is tender.

3. Remove turkey from slow cooker. Remove skin and slice. Spoon barley on platter, top with sliced turkey, and sprinkle with parsley.

SERVES: 8 (5 oz. lean turkey, ¾ cup barley per serving); CALORIES PER SERVING: 430; DIETARY EQUIVALENT: 5 oz. lean protein, 1½ carbohydrate, ½ fruit, ½ fat

PERFECT ROASTED TURKEY

Roasted turkey is a great meal and the leftovers can be used in so many tasty, nutritious ways. One of my favorites is a turkey sandwich with lite cranberry mayonnaise on hearty whole-grain bread. Turkey meat is low in fat and about 45 calories an ounce, making it a good choice if you want to consume lean protein. It's considered a white meat, meaning that it's low in N-nitroso, a compound in red meat that is associated with an increased cancer risk. It's best to choose organic turkey or at least one produced with no hormones or antibodies for a healthier meal. To debunk the myth that turkey makes you sleepy: turkey is not any higher in the amino acid tryptophan than beef, lamb, or fish. A high-fat and refined-carbohydrate intake is what makes us want to sleep after the holiday meal, but the lean turkey is not the culprit!

1 (12-pound) whole organic fresh turkey, at room temperature
2 tablespoons olive oil
1 tablespoon chopped garlic
2 teaspoons finely chopped fresh rosemary
2 tablespoons fresh thyme leaves removed from stems
2 tablespoons finely chopped fresh sage leaves
1½ teaspoons sea salt
1 teaspoon freshly ground black pepper
2 stalks celery, cut to fit inside cavity
1 medium onion, quartered
1 carrot cut in half

1. Preheat oven to 500°F.

2. Remove and discard giblets and neck. Thoroughly rinse the turkey inside and out. Pat dry with paper towels.

3. In a small bowl combine the olive oil, garlic, rosemary, thyme, sage, salt, and pepper. Gently lift the skin and rub olive oil–herb mixture under the skin and on the outside of the turkey.

4. Add the celery, onion, and carrot to the cavity. Put the turkey in a V-shape rack (which will lift the turkey off the bottom and brown the underside) and place within a large, heavy roasting pan about 2" deep (no deeper or the turkey will steam). If you don't have a rack, twist three feet of heavy-duty aluminum foil and snake around the bottom of the roaster to create one.

5. Roast for 30 minutes at 500°F, then reduce oven temperature to 325°F. The turkey is done in approximately 2–2½ hours for a 12-pound turkey, or when the thermometer reaches 165°F when placed in the turkey thigh. Juices should run clear, not pink, when thigh is pierced with fork.

6. Remove turkey from roaster to serving platter, tent with foil, and let rest 15–20 minutes before carving.

SERVES: 6–8 servings (4-oz. serving); CALORIES PER SERVING: 200; DIETARY EQUIVALENT: 5–6 oz. protein

Food Tip

Cooking the turkey on high heat for the first 30 minutes sears the turkey and keeps the juices in, giving you a juicier bird. Traditional basting every 20–30 minutes actually will result in a drier turkey: Since the skin of the turkey is impermeable it absorbs no basting liquid, and every time you open the oven to baste, the temperature drops, lengthening the cooking time and resulting in a drier turkey. If the turkey starts browning too much, tent with aluminum foil. Consider roasting a turkey breast along with a whole turkey and you'll have more white meat available for your guests.

APRICOT HONEY–GLAZED TURKEY BREAST

For a casual family meal or smaller holiday gathering, try roasting a deboned, tied turkey breast. I get them at my local market, but if you can't find one, just ask the meat department to prepare one for you. They are usually 3–5 pounds with very little waste. I typically plan on three servings to the pound, and I often buy a larger turkey breast so I have leftovers for meals throughout the week. Starting the turkey breast in a very hot oven sears in the juices and results in nicely moist turkey. The white meat, when thinly sliced, makes excellent turkey sandwiches without the higher sodium and preservative levels found in deli sliced turkey.

Organic canola or olive oil cooking spray
1 onion, quartered
2 carrots
2 celery stalks
Fresh herbs such as parsley, sage, rosemary, or thyme
1 (3–4 lb.) rolled turkey breast
1 tablespoon olive oil
1 teaspoon sea salt
1 teaspoon freshly ground black pepper
½ cup white wine

1. Preheat oven to 500°F. Spray roasting pan with nonstick spray. Add vegetables and herbs to the bottom of the pan to infuse the turkey with flavor and to act as a rack for the turkey breast.
2. Rinse and pat turkey dry with paper towels, then brush with oil and season with salt and pepper. Insert meat thermometer into the thickest part of turkey. Place on top of vegetable rack. Add white wine to pan. Tent loosely with foil.
3. Place in oven for 25 minutes at 500°F, then reduce temperature to 325°F. Continue cooking for 55 minutes for a 3-pound turkey breast or 1 hour and 25 minutes for a 4-pound turkey breast. Remove from oven when thermometer reads 165°F.
4. Remove turkey from pan and let rest for 15 minutes before slicing to keep juices in.
5. To serve, arrange sliced turkey on platter and drizzle with Apricot Glaze (see following recipe).

SERVES: 8–10 (4-oz. serving with 2 tablespoons apricot honey glaze); CALORIES PER SERVING: 160; DIETARY EQUIVALENT: 4 oz. protein

Nutrition Basics
Roasted turkey breast is only 30 calories an ounce, making it a great choice for those watching their weight and saturated fat. If you have more leftover turkey than you can eat in the next 3 days, place it in a freezer bag and freeze up to 3 months. Remove from freezer and thaw in refrigerator overnight.

APRICOT GLAZE

I came across this recipe a few decades ago when I was looking for something different for Thanksgiving dinner. With a healthier revision, it has turned out to be a real favorite at my home and in the Wellness Kitchen. This glaze offers a hint of Southwest flavor with the jalapeño and a touch of sweetness from the apricot preserves, with the aromatic rosemary adding pizzazz and flavor to your turkey.

½ cup apricot preserves (fruit only, no sugar added)
½ jalapeño, finely diced
2 tablespoons red wine vinegar
2 tablespoons Dijon mustard
1 tablespoon honey
1 teaspoon chopped garlic
1 teaspoon chopped fresh rosemary, chopped or ½ teaspoon of dried rosemary
½ teaspoon sea salt
½ teaspoon black pepper

1. Whisk all ingredients in medium mixing bowl.
2. Microwave glaze for 3 minutes until boiling.
3. Brush glaze on turkey the last 10–15 minutes of roasting. Serve remaining glaze as a sauce on the side.

SERVES: 12 (2-tablespoon servings); CALORIES PER SERVING: 20

> *Food Tip*
> This glaze is equally good on roasted or barbecued chicken or pork tenderloin. Or use a tablespoon on the ordinary turkey sandwich—delicious!

TURKEY BURGERS WITH TZATZIKI

Burger fans often turn their noses up at turkey burgers, complaining that they are dry and tasteless. I wish I could take credit for this recipe, but the secret to the Wellness Kitchen's delicious, moist turkey burgers was the brilliant idea of Chef Mario Alcocer, a Four Seasons chef whom I had the pleasure to work with. The white spots of low-fat cottage cheese may look a little strange when uncooked but they disappear when cooked, resulting in a moist and light burger that melts in your mouth. Since Chef Mario is a personal convert to healthy eating, he won't mind one bit that I share this recipe with you! The tzatziki sauce adds a whole other layer of flavor—but it's so light and healthy, you can indulge as much as you wish.

1 pound ground white meat turkey
½ cup low-fat cottage cheese
2 scallions, finely chopped
2 teaspoons chopped garlic
1 tablespoon Dijon mustard
1 tablespoon Worcestershire sauce
Sea salt
½ teaspoon fresh ground black pepper
Organic canola or olive oil cooking spray
4 whole-grain buns
Romaine lettuce leaves
1 large tomato, sliced thin
Tzatziki Sauce (see recipe here)

1. Preheat grill to medium–high.
2. Mix all ingredients (except buns, tzatziki sauce, lettuce, and tomato) in large bowl lightly with fingers.
3. Form 4 patties and lightly spray each side of patties with canola or olive oil spray.
4. Grill burgers for 4–5 minutes on each side. Remove from grill.
5. To serve, place burgers on whole-grain buns, add lettuce and tomato slices, and top with a heaping tablespoon of tzatziki sauce.

SERVES: 4; CALORIES PER SERVING: 310 (including 2 oz. bun); DIETARY EQUIVALENT: 4 oz. lean protein, 2 carbohydrates, 1 vegetable

Food Tip
Make sure the grill is at medium-high heat to start with, to sear the meat and prevent sticking to the grill.

TZATZIKI SAUCE

Use tzatziki sauce on sandwiches, as a dip for raw veggies, or on grilled chicken.

1 medium cucumber, peeled, seeded, and finely chopped
8 ounces plain nonfat Greek yogurt
1 teaspoon sea salt
2 teaspoons chopped garlic
1 tablespoon olive oil
2 teaspoons red wine vinegar
5 mint leaves, finely minced

1. Place chopped cucumber in 2–3 paper towels and squeeze to remove liquid.
2. In medium bowl, combine cucumber, yogurt, salt, garlic, olive oil, vinegar, and mint. Mix well.

SERVES: 8 (¼-cup servings); CALORIES PER SERVING: 55; DIETARY EQUIVALENT: 1 vegetable

PULLED TURKEY SANDWICHES WITH CRANBERRY BBQ SAUCE

My son ordered these sliders made with pork in a trendy restaurant for dinner and loved them. He asked if I could make these for him at home—which I did, but I wanted them to be healthier, so I used a turkey breast instead of the pork. He loved them just as much! This is the kind of dish I love to make the night before, especially when I am having a houseful of guests over for a game. I put the turkey and seasoning in a baking dish, pop into the oven for a few hours, cool, and then refrigerate. The next day, I just have to shred the turkey and combine with the sauce, toss the slaw, and wait for rave reviews!

2½–3 pounds fresh turkey breast
½ cup chicken stock
1 tablespoon chipotle chili powder
½ cup Masterpiece Original Barbecue Sauce
½ cup jellied cranberry sauce
10 whole-grain buns
Chipotle Cilantro Slaw (see recipe in Chapter 3)

1. Preheat oven to 300°F.
2. Place turkey breast, chicken stock, and chipotle powder in baking pan, cover tightly with foil, and bake for 1½–2 hours, until turkey is very tender.
3. Meanwhile, in a small saucepan, combine barbecue and cranberry sauces. Stir over medium-low heat until cranberry sauce is completely melted. Remove from heat and set aside.
4. Remove all fat and skin from turkey. Place turkey in a medium bowl and shred with 2 forks. Add sauce and mix well.
5. Serve pulled turkey on a toasted bun with Chipotle Cilantro Slaw or other spicy slaw.

SERVES: 10–12 (3–4 oz. servings); CALORIES PER SERVING: 450 (including bun and slaw); DIETARY EQUIVALENT: 2 carbohydrates, 3 oz. protein, 1 fat, 1 vegetable

Nutrition Basics
The crunch and flavor of the slaw is a must on these sandwiches, but not just for taste alone. The cabbage contains antioxidants that help the liver detox, ridding your body of environmental contaminants.

SOUTHWEST TURKEY CHILI

I tasted a version of this recipe years ago at Stein Erikson Lodge in Deer Valley, Utah. Unlike traditional chili, this is a white chili, meaning it doesn't have tomatoes. That doesn't mean it's lacking in flavor, though! Red and yellow peppers, onions, a good amount of chili powder, and jalapeños come together in a delicious Southwest version of chili. Corn is used both whole and puréed to give this chili a creamy consistency that pairs so well with the flavor of the jalapeños. My food processor makes quick work of chopping the peppers, celery, and onions. Just make sure that you pulse to get even chopping and that you do not overprocess. Serve up a bowl of this chili on a cold rainy night and you will be lucky to have leftovers for lunch the next day.

1 tablespoon no-trans-fat margarine

½ small can jalapeño chilies, chopped

⅔ cup chopped red onion

⅔ cup chopped red pepper

⅔ cup chopped celery

1½ tablespoons chopped garlic

1½ tablespoons oregano

1 pound ground turkey breast (white meat only, "extra lean")

⅓ cup all-purpose flour

1 quart organic, reduced-sodium, fat-free chicken broth

1 package frozen corn, divided

2 tablespoons chili powder

¼ cup finely chopped cilantro

2 tablespoons ground cumin

½ teaspoon salt

¼ teaspoon sugar

2 (15-ounce) cans of black beans, rinsed and drained

Low-fat cheese, grated

Lite sour cream

1. Melt margarine in large Dutch oven over medium-high heat.

2. Sauté jalapeños, onion, pepper, celery, garlic, and oregano for 10 minutes until softened.

3. Add turkey to Dutch oven and brown.

4. Add flour, mix well.

5. Stir in broth, bring to a boil, and reduce to a simmer.

6. Purée half of the corn in food processor or blender.

7. Add puréed corn, remaining whole corn, chili powder, cilantro, cumin, salt, sugar, and beans to Dutch oven. Simmer for 15 minutes.

8. To serve, top with low-fat cheese and lite sour cream.

SERVES: 6; CALORIES PER SERVING: 335; DIETARY EQUIVALENT: 4 oz. lean protein, 2 carbohydrates, and 1 vegetable

Nutrition Basics

I love a recipe that can be made vegetarian without losing flavor, and this is one! Just omit the turkey and double up on the black beans. For those whose digestive tract cannot tolerate beans, just make with turkey, omit the beans, and add one additional cup of corn.

TURKEY MEATBALLS AL FORNO

A good meatball needs the proper texture. Soaking the bread in milk is an old Italian tradition that makes meatballs moist and lighter in texture. The sauce is not the usual red sauce that is cooked for two hours, but a much lighter version that is done in 15 minutes. Placing the sauce in the blender gives it a wonderful, smooth texture that is so right for the light, tender meatballs.

½ cup finely diced day-old bread, crust removed

¼ cup nonfat milk

¾ cup grated Parmesan cheese, divided

½ cup finely chopped onion

½ cup finely chopped parsley

1 whole egg plus 2 egg whites, beaten

2 tablespoons chopped garlic

¼ teaspoon dried red pepper flakes

2 pounds ground turkey breast

Organic canola or olive oil cooking spray

1 quart Basic Tomato Sauce (see Chicken Parmesan recipe earlier in this chapter)

2 tablespoons chopped fresh basil

1. Preheat oven to 350°F.
2. Combine bread in small bowl with milk; let soak for 5 minutes.
3. In large bowl, combine ½ cup Parmesan, onion, parsley, eggs, garlic, and red pepper flakes. Mix to combine.
4. Using hands, squeeze bread to press out the milk. Add soaked bread and ground turkey to onion mixture. With fingertips, combine all ingredients without overmixing.
5. Using a 2-ounce scoop (or by hand), form mixture into 2" meatballs. Place meatballs on parchment-lined baking sheet.
6. Spray meatballs lightly with cooking spray. Bake in oven for 20–25 minutes or until lightly browned.
7. Place meatballs on platter, spoon over Basic Tomato Sauce, and sprinkle with remaining Parmesan cheese and basil.

SERVES: 8; CALORIES PER SERVING: 315; DIETARY EQUIVALENT: 4 oz. protein, 1 vegetable, 1 fat

Nutrition Basics

I often serve these meatballs with our Roasted Spaghetti Squash with Parmesan (see recipe in Chapter 6) instead of the usual pasta. The spaghetti squash is 35 calories a cup, the pasta 220 calories a cup. Not only does the squash have fewer calories but I found the crunchy texture of the squash the perfect background for the meatballs. If you have leftover meatballs from this meal, just place in a freezer bag and freeze up to 6 months. Try them in an Italian bean and vegetable soup, topped with a sprinkle of Parmesan and fresh basil for a hearty meal that can be made in minutes.

SPINACH-STUFFED TURKEY BREAST WITH TART CHERRY SAUCE

This elegant, easy entrée is healthy and delicious, and tastes nothing like Thanksgiving turkey. It can be prepped the day before and popped into the oven 1–2 hours before eating, depending on the size of turkey breast. If you're intimidated by the butterflying, ask your butcher at the meat counter to do it for you. I find most of them very willing to do the added service, which makes this entrée so easy to prep. The spinach filling with the dark red cherry sauce is perfect for other winter holidays!

1 (2½–3 pound) boneless, skinless turkey breast
2 tablespoons olive oil, divided
1 onion, finely chopped
1 teaspoon minced garlic
2 (5–6-ounce) bags fresh baby spinach
1 teaspoon salt, divided
½ teaspoon freshly ground black pepper, divided
¼ cup pine nuts, toasted
1 cup organic, reduced-sodium, fat-free chicken broth
Tart Cherry Sauce (see recipe here)

1. To butterfly turkey breast: Cover cutting board with a sheet of plastic wrap. Place turkey breast lengthwise on cutting board. Holding knife parallel to the turkey breast, cut along the length of the breast but not all the way through. Unfold turkey breast as if opening a book. Cover with plastic wrap and pound with a meat mallet until turkey breast is of uniform thickness (about ½"). Set aside.

2. Heat 1 tablespoon olive oil in large sauté pan over medium-high heat. Add onion and garlic; sauté for 3–4 minutes until soft. Transfer to large bowl.

3. Add spinach leaves to sauté pan and cook until wilted, 3–4 minutes. Press with paper towels to remove any excessive moisture. Season with ½ teaspoon salt and ¼ teaspoon pepper. Combine the spinach with the onion and garlic mixture. Add the pine nuts.

4. Spread spinach mixture evenly over turkey breast. Roll breast tightly around spinach stuffing and tie with kitchen twine.

5. Heat the remaining 1 tablespoon olive oil in large sauté pan until hot. Add turkey breast and brown on each side for 3–4 minutes.

6. Transfer turkey breast to roasting pan with rack coated with cooking spray. Season with ½ teaspoon salt, and ¼ teaspoon pepper. Add chicken broth to pan, cover with foil, and roast until internal temperature of the turkey breast reaches 165°F (30 minutes per pound).

7. Prepare Tart Cherry Sauce (recipe here).

8. Transfer to cutting board and cover with foil to rest for 10 minutes. Snip off kitchen twine before slicing.

9. Arrange on platter and spoon Tart Cherry Sauce over turkey.

SERVES: 6–8; CALORIES PER SERVING: 245; DIETARY EQUIVALENT: 4 oz. lean protein, ½ vegetable, ½ fruit

TART CHERRY SAUCE

½ cup tart or Bing cherry preserves (fruit only)
1 teaspoon to 1 tablespoon finely chopped jalapeño
    (depending on how much heat is desired)
1 teaspoon finely chopped rosemary
½ cup dried cherries
¼ cup port wine

1. Place all ingredients in medium saucepan and simmer on medium heat until slightly reduced, about 3 minutes.

2. Spoon over turkey or serve on the side.

SERVES: 8 (1½-tablespoon servings); CALORIES PER SERVING: 35; DIETARY EQUIVALENT: ½ fruit

Nutrition Basics
The filling of this entrée is heart healthy: The spinach is high in folic acid and the pine nuts are an excellent source of omega-3 fats and vitamin E. All that plus very lean protein makes this entrée a winner!

TOFU STIR-FRY WITH SPICY GINGER-SESAME SAUCE

Tofu is always a hard sell for non-vegetarians, but if you do not find this dish as flavorful as one that uses chicken, I would be surprised. Plain tofu is bland and somewhat flavorless, but that's the beauty of this healthy plant-based protein. The bland palette allows you to be creative with spices and sauces and make a flavor-packed entrée with great versatility. Make sure you use extra-firm tofu in this dish so it does not crumble. Drain and wrap in paper towels for a few minutes, to remove most of the moisture so the tofu stays firm during cooking. The sauce on this crispy tofu dish is perhaps the best stir-fry Asian sauce I have ever tasted! Many people wrinkle up their noses when tofu is mentioned in the Wellness Kitchen . . . so I love to see their faces when they taste this dish.

3 tablespoons reduced-sodium soy sauce

1 tablespoon sugar

½ teaspoon dried red pepper flakes

2 teaspoons chopped garlic

4 teaspoons sesame oil, divided

2 teaspoons finely chopped fresh ginger

14 oz. extra-firm tofu

1 tablespoon canola oil

4 cups broccoli florets, or 4 baby bok choy, sliced

½ red bell pepper, finely diced

2 tablespoons water

2 scallions, thinly sliced

1 tablespoon sesame seeds, toasted

1. In small bowl, combine soy sauce, sugar, red pepper flakes, garlic, 2 teaspoons sesame oil, and ginger. Set aside.

2. Slice tofu crosswise into 8 thin slabs. Dry tofu with paper towels, pressing until no moisture remains.

3. In a large nonstick skillet, heat canola oil over medium heat. When pan is hot, add tofu and cook, turning once, until browned and crisp, about 4–5 minutes per side. Drain on paper towels.

4. Using same pan, add remaining sesame oil and sauté broccoli and red pepper for 3 minutes. Add 2 tablespoons water and cover for 1 minute to steam.

5. Arrange broccoli and red pepper on serving platter; top with crispy tofu. Spoon sauce over tofu and broccoli and sprinkle with scallions and sesame seeds.

SERVES: 4; CALORIES PER SERVING: 190; DIETARY EQUIVALENT: 3 oz. protein, 1 vegetable, 1 fat

Nutrition Basics

Change your vegetables and use whatever is on hand or in season. The more colors this dish contains, the higher the antioxidant levels. Mother Nature color-coded fruits and veggies—the more brilliant and vibrant the colors, the more nutrients. Try sliced baby bok choy with green beans and red peppers, or sugar snap peas with yellow peppers.

TOFU FRIED RICE WITH EDAMAME

Almost all of us love Asian fried rice, but most of us know it's not the best choice for health—it's got too much white starch, and frying isn't exactly a way to improve your health. Well, fried rice lovers rejoice: You have a new version that is healthy and delicious! Start with cold brown rice (yes, you can use the frozen precooked version), a hint of garlic and green onions, crisp vegetables, whole eggs and egg whites, tofu, and a touch of reduced-sodium soy and you have a delicious fried rice any Asian restaurant would be proud to serve. You're probably assuming this is a side dish, but with the edamame and tofu added for protein and the ratio of vegetables to rice higher than usual, this is a great entrée that will not sacrifice your waistline!

10 ounces extra-firm tofu, well drained

Organic canola or olive oil cooking spray

2 whole eggs plus 2 egg whites, beaten

2 tablespoons canola oil

8 green onions, sliced

1 cup finely diced carrots

4 baby bok choy, sliced

1 tablespoon chopped garlic

3 cups cooked brown rice, chilled

1 cup shelled edamame

¼ cup reduced-sodium soy sauce

SERVES: 6; CALORIES PER SERVING: 320; DIETARY EQUIVALENT: 4 oz. protein, 1 carbohydrate, 2 vegetables

1. Dry tofu with paper towels, pressing until no moisture remains. Dice into bite-sized pieces. Set aside.

2. Coat nonstick sauté pan with cooking spray. Over medium heat, pour in eggs—spread thinly to cover pan, like a crepe. Cook until lightly browned, then turn over and finish cooking. Remove from pan and cool on cutting board. When cool, roll up and thinly slice.

3. In a large sauté pan, over medium-high heat, heat oil. Add onion and carrot and sauté for 2 minutes. Add bok choy and garlic and stir-fry for 2 more minutes.

4. Add brown rice. Sauté for 3 minutes, stirring occasionally. Add tofu, edamame, soy sauce, and sliced egg; toss and heat through.

Nutrition Basics

If you really want to make this dish super heart-healthy without saturated fat, use egg substitute that is made of egg whites exclusively (with natural color added). You really will not know the difference! You can also substitute finely shredded cabbage, found in the produce section of your market, for the baby bok choy, and there is nothing wrong with purchasing those small bags of shredded carrots either. It makes the cooking go ever-so-quickly, and you are more likely to use more vegetables if they're already prepped.

TOFU CURRY WITH SUMMER VEGETABLES

I have always loved Thai food; the flavors in the dishes are like no other cuisine. I had the opportunity to visit the Four Seasons in Chiang Mai, Thailand, a few years ago and cooked with Chef Pitak in his cooking school, and I learned just how easy it is to make some of those exotic dishes that I have had in restaurants. This particular recipe is so versatile; once you make the curry sauce, you can use just about any combination of vegetables and proteins you have on hand. Think of this recipe seasonally—curried tofu with summer vegetables, with fall vegetables, and so on. You can use different proteins such as seafood, cooked chicken, or pork as well as the tofu. I have tweaked it a bit, substituting the readily available lite coconut milk for the coconut milk and reduced-sodium chicken broth to cut the calories, fat, and sodium, but you will not notice a difference in taste!

1 (14-ounce) can lite coconut milk
1 cup organic, reduced-sodium, fat-free chicken broth
1 lemongrass stalk, mashed
1 tablespoon plus 1½ teaspoons chopped fresh ginger
1 tablespoon Thai red curry paste
2 tablespoons brown sugar
1 Kaffir lime leaf, torn or 1 teaspoon lime zest
1 tablespoon freshly squeezed lime juice
4 sprigs cilantro
3 fresh basil leaves
⅓ teaspoon curry powder
⅛ teaspoon sea salt
3 ounces shiitake mushrooms, stemmed and sliced
1 small onion, thinly sliced
2 cups baby carrots
1½ cups sugar snap peas, trimmed
8 thin asparagus spears, cut in 1" pieces on the bias
12 ounces extra-firm tofu, drained and pressed, then cut into 1" dice
4 cups steamed brown rice or whole grain
½ cup chopped roasted unsalted cashews (optional)
¼ cup chopped fresh cilantro

1. In a large Dutch oven, over medium heat, combine the coconut milk, broth, lemongrass stalk, ginger, curry paste, brown sugar, Kaffir lime leaf, lime juice, cilantro sprigs, basil leaves, curry powder, and salt. Bring to a boil, then reduce to simmer. Continue simmering for 30 minutes, do not let boil. Strain the broth using a mesh strainer into a large saucepan.
2. To the saucepan with the curry broth, add the mushrooms, onion, and carrots. Cook over medium heat (do not boil) until just tender.
3. Add the sugar snap peas and asparagus; cook for another 2 minutes. Adjust the seasonings if needed.
4. Gently add the tofu.

5. To serve, divide the rice among 4 bowls, top with curry, and garnish with the chopped cashews (if using) and chopped cilantro.

SERVES: 4; CALORIES PER SERVING: 450; DIETARY EQUIVALENT: 4 oz. protein, 1 carbohydrate, 2 vegetables, 2 fat

VARIATIONS

TOFU CURRY WITH CAULIFLOWER AND YUKON GOLD POTATO

Omit sugar snap peas and asparagus. Substitute 2 cups cauliflower florets and 2 medium Yukon Gold potatoes cut into bite-sized pieces. (Calories: 490 per serving)

TOFU CURRY WITH SWEET CORN, GREEN BEANS, AND RED PEPPER

Omit carrots, sugar snap peas, and asparagus. Substitute 2 ears of fresh corn removed from cob, 18 oz. fresh green beans cut into bite-sized pieces, and 1 red bell pepper cut into thin strips. (Calories: 490 per serving)

Nutrition Basics
The lite coconut milk is about 65 percent lower in calories and in fat, so be sure to use the lite version. (Freeze any leftover lite coconut milk for later use, or use in fruit smoothies for a tropical treat.) Try serving this curry over whole grains such as barley or quinoa in place of the rice for ⅓ less calories and added nutrition.

TOFU, CASHEW, AND BUTTERNUT SQUASH CURRY

Every time fall rolls around and I am at a farmers' market, I start to crave this dish. And no wonder—it's spicy, sweet, hot, and creamy, all the taste and textures to wake your taste buds in a healthy vegetarian meal! Originally this was a high-calorie dish, because butternut squash is a carbohydrate (albeit a healthy one), and coconut milk and cashews are high in fat and calories. After tasting the original recipe, I was determined to make it work healthwise. By roasting instead of pan-browning the butternut squash to caramelize, you cut the fat to less than half; using lite coconut milk did not alter the flavor one bit; and ½ cup of cashews is more than enough for flavor and texture.

3 pounds butternut squash, pumpkin, or winter squash, peeled and cut in 1½" cubes

2 tablespoons olive oil, divided

1 teaspoon sea salt, divided

1 onion, halved and cut into half-moons

1–2 red or green serrano chilies, seeds removed, finely chopped

1 cinnamon stick

20 fresh curry leaves or 6 dried bay leaves

1 teaspoon turmeric

2 teaspoons cumin seeds

1 (14-ounce) can lite coconut milk

½ cup organic, reduced-sodium, fat-free vegetable or chicken broth

12 ounces extra-firm tofu, cut into 1" cubes

½ cup salted roasted cashews

1 tablespoon lemon juice

4 cups steamed brown rice or whole grain

1. Preheat oven to 400°F.
2. Toss squash cubes with 1 tablespoon olive oil and season with ½ teaspoon salt. Spread on baking sheet and roast for 30–40 minutes or until just tender and golden.
3. In a large sauté pan, heat the remaining oil over medium heat. Sauté onion, stirring occasionally, until golden, 12–15 minutes.
4. To the onion, add the serrano chilies, cinnamon stick, and curry leaves. Cook, stirring often, until curry leaves are fragrant, about 2 minutes. Add turmeric, cumin seeds, and remaining salt. Cook until spices are fragrant, about 1 minute.
5. Add butternut squash, coconut milk, and broth. Gently add the tofu. Bring to a boil, then cover and reduce heat to simmer, for about 6–8 minutes.
6. Stir in cashews and lemon juice. Adjust seasonings if needed.
7. Serve over 1 cup hot rice or whole grain.

SERVES: 6; CALORIES PER SERVING: 370 (without rice); DIETARY EQUIVALENT: 2 carbohydrates, 2 fats, 2 vegetables

Nutrition Basics

1 cup cooked butternut squash is equal to 2 carbohydrate servings, the right amount for most of us at a mealtime, so you may want to serve over green veggies such as broccoli florets or green beans instead of brown rice. It's delicious and satisfying either way.

SPICY TOFU WITH GREEN HARISSA

In Latin cuisine, "Sofrita" is a fragrant blend of herbs and spices used in a braised or sautéed dish. We came up with this version of the blend for a "Meals That Heal" Wellness Kitchen class and it proved to be a hit for those who thought they did not like tofu. Firm tofu is the right texture, and with the right combination of spices, it makes a delicious filling for burritos and tacos, or a topping for bean and rice bowls. Green harissa is a nutrient-, antioxidant-, and flavor-packed sauce that, once you taste it, you'll want on everything!

1 pound firm tofu (drain well and wrap in paper towel to remove excess water)
1 tablespoon canola oil
1 teaspoon red pepper powder
1 teaspoon ground coriander
1 teaspoon ground cumin
1 teaspoon minced ginger
1 teaspoon minced garlic
1 teaspoon sea salt
1 teaspoon Sriracha sauce
1 tablespoon rice vinegar
2 tablespoons chopped fresh cilantro
Green Harissa (see recipe here)

1. Dice tofu into ¼" pieces.
2. Heat a nonstick pan until hot, add canola oil and diced tofu, and let brown for about 2–3 minutes until tofu starts to get golden around edges. Turn tofu over and continue to brown, stirring occasionally.
3. When tofu is golden brown, add all the seasonings except Sriracha and vinegar. Continue to sauté for another 2 minutes.
4. Add Sriracha and vinegar and continue sautéing for 1 minute.
5. Add fresh cilantro and serve over a bean and rice bowl or as taco/burrito filling. Serve with Green Harissa.

SERVES: 4; CALORIES PER SERVING: 120; DIETARY EQUIVALENTS: 3 oz. protein

Food Tip
Drain tofu well, wrap in 2 or 3 paper towels, and let sit for 2–4 hours to drain further. This gives the tofu an even firmer texture so it holds together better when browning.

GREEN HARISSA

1 cup cilantro, large stems removed
1 cup baby spinach leaves
1 tablespoon fresh lemon juice
1 tablespoon olive oil
1 tablespoon chopped garlic
2 scallions, roughly chopped
2–3 jalapeños, seeded, roughly chopped
¼ teaspoon ground coriander
¼ teaspoon ground cumin
1 teaspoon sea salt
¼ cup olive oil mayonnaise

1. Add cilantro, spinach, lemon juice, olive oil, garlic, scallions, jalapeño, coriander, cumin, and salt to food processor and pulse until combined, stopping once to scrape the side of the bowl.
2. Add mayonnaise and process until smooth. Store in refrigerator, covered, up to 3 days.

SERVES: 16 (2-tablespoon serving size); CALORIES PER SERVING: 20; DIETARY EQUIVALENT: ½ vegetable

TOFU EGG SALAD

I love egg salad, but given its high cholesterol level, I am always hesitant to make it. When I tasted this at a local health food store, I was so impressed that I bought tofu right then to make my own. This is a cholesterol-free, unsaturated-fat-free version, and it took just minutes to make! Tofu, like egg, does not have a lot of flavor, so whatever you add to it will give the tofu its taste. Make it your own by adding your choice of Dijon mustard, capers, pickle relish, diced dill pickle, onion, celery, celery seed, or chopped black olives. Use a small amount of olive oil mayonnaise, which is healthy fat.

1 (14-ounce) package firm tofu, rinsed and well drained
⅓ cup olive oil mayonnaise
1 teaspoon lemon juice
½ teaspoon turmeric
1 teaspoon Dijon mustard
¼ teaspoon cayenne pepper
½ teaspoon salt
2 celery ribs, finely chopped
¼ cup chopped green onion

1. In a small bowl, coarsely mash tofu with a fork.
2. In a medium bowl, whisk mayonnaise, lemon juice, turmeric, Dijon, cayenne pepper, and salt. Fold in tofu, celery, and green onion. Combine well. Serve with rustic whole-grain bread, lettuce, and vine-ripened tomato. (Will keep in the refrigerator for up to 3 days.)

SERVES: 4; CALORIES PER SERVING: 165; DIETARY EQUIVALENT: 3 oz. protein, 1 fat

Food Tip
Not *all* fat is bad fat. Olive oil–based mayo is a good fat that you can use, but watch your portion size because it's high in calories (as are all fats).

Chapter 6

Vegetables

I do think more people would eat healthy vegetables if they were made flavorful and delicious more often. I always tell my Wellness Kitchen guests, who are somewhat dubious that vegetables can really be made the star of each meal, that the concept of plain, steamed broccoli being the only thing healthy is just wrong, dead wrong. The charm of this food group is that vegetables are incredibly versatile, with way more texture and flavor than a chicken breast or grilled piece of fish. Once you learn a few simple cooking methods and ways to play off those wonderful flavors and textures, you'll look at vegetables in a whole new light.

While I do steam some vegetables in the Wellness Kitchen and at home, I have found that other cooking methods, such as roasting or grilling, give vegetables new dimensions of flavor and texture. I have witnessed the amazement of adults and children alike when tasting Roasted Green Beans with Pine Nuts or Honey-Roasted Root Vegetables. The Cauliflower Purée is such a hit, we can never seem to make enough! For health and weight loss benefits, vegetables should take up half of your dinner plate. With a little creativity, these low-cal wonders can become the most delectable part of a meal. The addition of a dusting of Parmesan, a drizzle of olive oil, zest of orange or lemon, or a sprinkling of nuts is not going to change them into something that you need to monitor your intake of. No one can attribute his or her weight issue to carrots, even when glazed with a tablespoon of brown sugar!

Try to buy local, in-season vegetables as often as possible, for added health benefits and the best flavor. Shipping vegetables halfway around the world means that they are drained of some flavor and/or nutrition by the time you get them to your plate. Look for produce grown in the United States, which has lower contamination levels than imported. Feel free to use some frozen produce as well when fresh is in short supply; it's just as nutritious as the fresh, since it's flash frozen within hours after picking.

ROASTED VEGETABLES

Roasting vegetables in a drop of olive oil with a sprinkling of salt and pepper is a great basic recipe. You can get more creative by adding exotic spices, warm chili powders, savory garlic, or a squeeze of citrus. Roasting caramelizes the natural sugars and imparts a candy-sweet taste to just about any vegetable. The kids in our Wellness Kitchen summer programs eat all of these by the handful.

ROASTED GREEN BEANS WITH PINE NUTS

1 pound green beans, washed and trimmed
1 tablespoon olive oil
½ teaspoon sea salt
½ teaspoon freshly ground black pepper
2 tablespoons pine nuts

1. Preheat oven to 375°F.
2. Place green beans on rimmed baking sheet, drizzle with olive oil, salt, and pepper. Mix well and spread in single layer, then sprinkle with pine nuts. (Do not crowd on top of each other or roasted vegetables become soggy.) Roast in oven 20–25 minutes or until green beans and pine nuts are golden.

SERVES: 4; CALORIES PER SERVING: 80 calories; DIETARY EQUIVALENT: 1 vegetable

VARIATIONS

ROASTED BROCCOLI WITH LEMON AND PARMESAN

Substitute 1 pound of broccoli florets for the green beans. Toss with olive oil, salt, and pepper. Spread on rimmed baking sheet in single layer. Roast in oven for 25–30 minutes until slightly golden. Remove from oven, squeeze the juice of ½ lemon over them, and sprinkle with 2 tablespoons Parmesan cheese; toss well. (Calories: 60 per serving)

ROASTED CAULIFLOWER WITH PARMESAN

Substitute 1 pound cauliflower florets for green beans. Toss with olive oil, salt, and pepper. Spread on rimmed baking sheet in single layer. Roast for 30–35 minutes until golden. Remove from oven and sprinkle with 2 tablespoons Parmesan cheese. (Calories: 60 per serving)

ROASTED BRUSSELS SPROUTS WITH LEMON AND HAZELNUTS

Substitute 1 pound of Brussels sprouts, washed and cut in half. Toss with olive oil, salt, and pepper. Spread on rimmed baking sheet in single layer. In a small bowl combine the juice of ½ lemon, 1 tablespoon honey, and ½ teaspoon dried thyme. Pour over

Brussels sprouts, mix well, and spread in single layer. Roast in oven for 30–35 minutes until golden. (Calories: 80 per serving)

ROASTED CARROTS AND CUMIN

Substitute 1 pound of baby carrots or carrots cut thinly diagonally. Spread carrots on rimmed baking sheet in single layer. Toss with olive oil, salt, pepper, 1 tablespoon honey, and 1½ teaspoons cumin; mix well. Cover baking sheet with foil and roast for 15 minutes. Remove foil and continue to roast for another 20–25 minutes until carrots are tender and slightly golden. (Calories: 90 per serving)

ROASTED WINTER SQUASH

Substitute 1 pound of peeled, bite-sized, cubed winter squash. Spread on rimmed baking sheet in single layer. Toss with olive oil, salt, pepper, 1 tablespoon honey, and 1 teaspoon chili powder. Cover with foil and roast for 15 minutes. Remove foil and continue to roast for another 20–25 minutes or until squash is tender and golden. (Calories: 95 per serving)

Nutrition Basics

All cooking methods change the nutrient content of the vegetable, which means you do lose some nutrients in the cooking process. But it does not mean you should only eat raw vegetables. Cooking, including roasting, can concentrate certain antioxidants and often makes certain nutrients easier for your body to absorb because of the slight decrease in fiber. It's best to have a large amount of antioxidants and fiber in your diet every day! The following vegetables roast very well. Times may vary slightly depending how large the pieces of vegetables are.

- Cauliflower
- Brussels sprouts
- Broccoli
- Baby bok choy
- Beets
- Asparagus

- Carrots
- Parsnips
- Turnips
- Green Beans
- Yams

LIME-GLAZED ROASTED YAMS

This is the potato to eat! Thank goodness science has proved that yams (and sweet potatoes) are very healthy carbohydrates. The bright orange color denotes a high antioxidant level, which helps protect your body from chronic diseases. The fiber content of this potato makes it the ideal choice: The fiber slows down the absorption of starches and sugar, meaning that the glucose load is low, which makes you feel full for a longer period of time. This simple way to roast yams results in wonderful sweet caramelized flavor; the lime adds a touch of tartness, and with just a sprinkling of salt you have the most delicious (even somewhat addictive) potato. I serve these yams for holiday meals and they are wonderful with roasted chicken.

Organic canola oil cooking spray
2 yams (12 ounces each), peeled and cut into 1" pieces
2 tablespoons no-trans-fat margarine
2 tablespoons brown sugar
1 tablespoon lime juice
½ teaspoon sea salt

1. Preheat oven to 350°F.
2. Spray 9" × 13" baking dish or rimmed baking sheet with canola oil spray.
3. Add yams and dot with margarine.
4. Bake for 25 minutes, turning once after 10 minutes to coat in margarine.
5. Remove from oven, sprinkle with brown sugar, lime juice, and salt.
6. Return to oven and bake 15–20 minutes longer, until lightly browned and caramelized.

SERVES: 6; CALORIES PER SERVING: 145; DIETARY EQUIVALENT: 1 carbohydrate, 1 fat

---

Nutrition Basics

Four oz. of potato is equivalent to a 1 carbohydrate serving, so a large yam could be equivalent to a 4 carbohydrate serving. Most of us need 4–8 ounces of potato for a portion of carbohydrates for meals. If you're running short on time, place cut yams with 2 tablespoons water in covered microwave bowl and microwave on high for 5 minutes. Then drain and add to baking sheet. Add margarine, brown sugar, lime juice, and salt and place in oven for 20 minutes until golden.

HONEY-ROASTED ROOT VEGETABLES

We are addicted to roasting fall and winter vegetables in the Wellness Kitchen. The natural sugars in these root vegetables, along with the touch of honey, caramelizes the vegetables, giving them a sweet, nutty flavor that is divine. The sherry vinegar added at the end of roasting gives them a warm tang, keeping them from being overly sweet. While root vegetables are slightly higher in calories than other vegetables because of their starch content, they still are a great value when weight watching, averaging 60 calories a cup versus grains at 200 calories a cup. The flavor of these vegetables is delightful with a simple roasted chicken or with turkey for a holiday meal.

1¼ pounds parsnips, peeled, sliced, and cut into ½" dice

1¼ pounds carrots, peeled, sliced, and cut into ½" dice

1¼ pounds celery root, peeled, quartered, and cut into ½" dice

1¼ pounds golden beets, peeled and cut into ½" dice

1 tablespoon olive oil

2 tablespoons honey

6 thyme sprigs

½ teaspoon sea salt

½ freshly ground pepper

Organic canola or olive oil cooking spray

2 tablespoons sherry vinegar

1. Preheat oven to 425°F.

2. In large bowl, toss vegetables with oil, honey, and thyme; season with salt and pepper. Spray nonstick spray on two baking sheets; spread vegetables in single layer on sheets.

3. Cover with foil and roast for 40 minutes, shifting pans once, until vegetables are tender. Remove foil and roast for 10 minutes longer, until glazed.

4. Return vegetables to bowl, add vinegar, and toss.

SERVES: 6; CALORIES PER SERVING: 60; DIETARY EQUIVALENT: 1 vegetable, 1 fat

Food Tip

Try to cut all the vegetables in similar sizes so they are tender at the same time. Make sure the vegetables are spread in a single layer; if too crowded they'll steam instead of roast, resulting in soggy vegetables.

ROASTED SPAGHETTI SQUASH WITH PARMESAN

I find this amazing vegetable in the produce section of my market from early summer into winter. It gets its unique name from the texture—once cooked, it separates into long fibrous strands, hence the name. You could cut it in half and microwave it, but I find roasting it in the oven gives the squash much more flavor and a slightly drier texture. Spaghetti squash is definitely not pasta, but can be a great substitute for pasta at some meals. Since plain spaghetti squash is only 35 calories a cup versus the 200 in a cup of pasta, I often team it with my turkey meatballs or chicken parmesan and forgo the pasta for a healthier, lighter meal. It has a high antioxidant level, and is high in fiber, making it a great choice nutritionally, too.

1 medium spaghetti squash
Organic olive oil cooking spray
1 tablespoon no-trans-fat margarine
½ teaspoon sea salt
½ teaspoon freshly ground black pepper
¼ teaspoon nutmeg
⅓ cup Parmesan cheese

1. Preheat oven to 350°F.
2. With a sharp knife, pierce squash 4–6 times. Place in microwave for 5–6 minutes to soften slightly. When cool enough to handle, cut lengthwise and remove seeds. Place face down on a rimmed baking sheet coated with olive oil cooking spray. Roast in oven for 30 minutes until soft and lightly browned.
3. Remove from oven and cool slightly. Over a bowl, run a fork lengthwise down the squash, creating spaghetti-like strands, until all of the flesh is removed.
4. Add margarine, salt, pepper, nutmeg, and Parmesan cheese, tossing well.

SERVES: 6; CALORIES PER SERVING: 85; DIETARY EQUIVALENT: 1 vegetable, 1 fat

Nutrition Basics
Spaghetti squash is high in potassium, which helps your body regulate kidney function and lowers your blood pressure.

ORANGE-GLAZED CARROTS

I always think of ways to make vegetables the star of the meal, so that everyone will love them and want more. These orange-glazed carrots get just that reaction. The sweetness of the carrots is enlivened with the orange and the touch of ginger adds a soft warmth. The best part? It all comes together in the sauté pan in just 3 minutes!

2 pounds baby carrots, peeled (or sliced regular carrots, peeled and cut into ¼" slices)
2 tablespoons water
1 tablespoon no-trans-fat margarine
1 teaspoon fresh chopped ginger (optional)
Zest of 1 orange
Juice of ½ orange
1 tablespoon brown sugar
½ teaspoon sea salt
½ teaspoon freshly ground black pepper
¼ teaspoon ground nutmeg

1. Place carrots in large microwavable bowl. Add 2 tablespoons water to bowl, cover and microwave for 4–5 minutes or until almost tender (al dente).
2. In a large sauté pan, heat margarine until melted. Add ginger and sauté for 1 minute. Drain carrots and add to sauté pan; mix well. Add orange zest, juice, and brown sugar; stir until carrots are well heated and evenly glazed. Season to taste with salt, pepper, and nutmeg.

SERVES: 4; CALORIES PER SERVING: 105; DIETARY EQUIVALENT: 2 vegetables, 1 fat

Nutrition Basics

Over the years I have had many guests tell me that they try to avoid carrots, because of their natural sugar content and calories. Carrots are 70 calories a cup cooked, which is a little more than other vegetables—but the few additional calories are worth the nutrient benefits. A cup of carrots contains 4.5 grams of fiber and is extremely high in vitamin A and the antioxidants that prevent chronic disease. In 32 years, I have never met anyone with a weight issue that comes from carrots!

If you're pressed for time, partially cooking hard vegetables in the microwave for 4–6 minutes will speed up preparation time. You'll cut the cooking time in half or less for a quick pan sauté or if roasting in the oven.

SAUTÉED BALSAMIC BRUSSELS SPROUTS

Brussels sprouts used to have a bad reputation, due to the old method of just boiling or steaming them. Of late they have become a trendy vegetable, and that's a good thing! They are so versatile; there are so many delicious recipes for roasting them. We found another favorite method in the Wellness Kitchen: We par-steam the Brussels sprouts in the microwave, then finish with a quick sauté in a rich balsamic glaze. Do not overcook the Brussels sprouts in the sauté pan—the little bit of brown sugar in the glaze can burn easily. Take them off the heat as soon as the glaze thickens and coats the Brussels sprouts.

2 pounds Brussels sprouts
2 tablespoons water
1 tablespoon no-trans-fat margarine
1 tablespoon minced garlic
2 tablespoons balsamic vinegar
1 tablespoon brown sugar
Sea salt
Freshly ground black pepper

1. Place Brussels sprouts in large microwavable bowl. Add 2 tablespoons water to bowl, cover with plastic wrap, and microwave for 4 minutes or until crisp but tender (al dente).

2. In a large sauté pan, heat margarine and garlic. Add drained Brussels sprouts to sauté pan along with balsamic vinegar and brown sugar; mix until sprouts are well heated and glazed. Season to taste with salt and pepper.

SERVES: 6; CALORIES PER SERVING: 45; DIETARY EQUIVALENT: 1 vegetable, ½ fat

Nutrition Basics
Brussels sprouts contain a compound, sulforaphane, that is known to have anticancer properties, similar to broccoli.

SAUTÉED GREEN BEANS WITH LEMON ZEST AND PINE NUTS

The traditional high-fat, high-calorie green bean casserole is the way most of us love our green beans. The next time you need a great green bean recipe, try this one; it has an incredible fresh, zingy taste that is just the right balance for a richer entrée. Green beans are only 35 calories a cup and when you have them sautéed in a drop of olive oil with garlic, lemon zest, and pine nuts you won't even miss the old green bean casserole! Use a Meyer lemon or Eureka lemon for the zest—they are sweeter yet still tangy. Lemon zest is best made with a kitchen tool called a zester or microplane, an inexpensive tool you probably already own. It removes only the outermost part of the citrus rind, where the fragrant oils are. This dish can be semi-prepared a day ahead or hours before your dinner. Simply steam the green beans in the microwave, drain, cover, and refrigerate until ready to sauté for 3 minutes just before serving. The green beans will be crisp-tender and full of nutrients, but won't require a long cooking time on your stovetop, freeing up your oven for other dishes.

1 pound trimmed green beans

2 tablespoons water

1 tablespoon olive oil

1 tablespoon minced garlic

¼ teaspoon dried red pepper flakes

Zest of 1 lemon

Sea salt

Freshly ground black pepper

2 tablespoons pine nuts or slivered almonds

1. Place green beans in a large microwavable bowl. Add the water to bowl, cover with plastic wrap, and microwave for 4 minutes, just until par-cooked.

2. Heat the oil in a large sauté pan over medium heat. Add the garlic and red pepper flakes. Sauté until fragrant, about 30 seconds.

3. Thoroughly drain the beans, then add to the pan. Sauté until crisp-tender (al dente), about 3 minutes.

4. Add the lemon zest. Season to taste with salt and pepper.

5. Garnish with the nuts.

SERVES: 6; CALORIES PER SERVING: 65; DIETARY EQUIVALENT: 1 fat, 1 vegetable

Nutrition Basics

Greens beans are widely grown throughout the United States, making them very available in most local markets. (Local produce is always the first choice versus imported produce, which generally has higher pesticide levels than U.S.-grown produce.) If you can't find fresh green beans for some reason, use frozen. Par-cook green beans in microwave (for about half the overall time recommended), drain well, then add to sauté pan with other ingredients. Green beans are high in vitamin K, which plays an integral role in bone health as well as having a high concentration of antioxidants that prevent chronic disease.

CAULIFLOWER PURÉE

David, my kitchen manager, and I get such a kick out of Wellness Kitchen guests who taste this for the first time. Generally they greet the dish with "I do not care for cauliflower," but all we ask is for them to taste it. The look of amazement is priceless and makes us very happy! The best thing about this amazing purée is that most think it tastes better than mashed potatoes, and no guilt whatsoever is called for when eating it. In case you need any more convincing, 1 cup of mashed potatoes made with milk and butter is approximately 300 calories, compared to 1 cup of puréed cauliflower at only 70 calories!

1 cup organic, reduced-sodium, fat-free chicken broth

2 teaspoons chopped garlic

2-pound cauliflower, chopped into florets (discard large stems only)

1 tablespoon no-trans-fat margarine

¼ cup fat-free half-and-half or nonfat milk

½ teaspoon sea salt

½ teaspoon freshly ground black pepper

1. Place broth in steamer, add garlic, and heat to a boil. Add rack; place cauliflower in rack and cover. Reduce heat to a simmer and steam cauliflower for 15–20 minutes or until very tender when pierced with fork.

2. Remove cauliflower from steamer and place in food processor. Process until fairly smooth. Add margarine, fat-free half-and-half, salt, and pepper. Process until very smooth, the consistency of mashed potatoes

SERVES: 4; CALORIES PER SERVING: 70; DIETARY EQUIVALENT: 1 vegetable, ½ fat

Food Tip
Look for cauliflowers in the market that are white with no dark spots, which indicate that the vegetable is not fresh.

CELERY ROOT AND POTATO MASH

Celery root (also called celeriac) may be the ugly duckling of the produce department, but it's definitely the culinary swan of the kitchen. In the Wellness Kitchen, one of the ways we use it is for a "guiltless potato" mash that is half the calories of regular mashed potatoes but definitely not half the flavor! Celery root, along with the horseradish, gives this potato mash a bright, bold, flavor. Try adding peeled, shredded raw celery root to salads for a flavor boost and great crunchy texture.

1 pound (1 large or 2 small) celery root, peeled and cut into 2" cubes

1 pound Yukon Gold or russet potatoes, peeled and cut into 2" cubes

¼ cup fat-free half-and-half

1 tablespoon no-trans-fat margarine

2 teaspoons freshly grated or prepared horseradish

1 teaspoon fresh lemon juice

Sea salt

Freshly ground black pepper

1. In a large pot, add celery root and potatoes. Cover with water by at least 1". Bring to a boil. Reduce the heat to medium, cover partially, and cook until very tender, 20–25 minutes. Drain.

2. Place fat-free half-and-half in small bowl and microwave until very hot but not boiling. Set aside.

3. Mash vegetables by hand, or use a potato ricer or food mill. Stir in the margarine. Add half-and-half to the potatoes, a little at a time, incorporating well after each addition. Stir in the horseradish and lemon juice. Season to taste with salt and pepper.

SERVES: 4; CALORIES PER SERVING: 150; DIETARY EQUIVALENT: 1 carbohydrate, 1 fat, 1 vegetable

Nutrition Basics

Celery root is very high in fiber and very low in carbohydrates, which means it's an excellent choice for those needing to lower their glucose levels. Celery root is highly satiating because of the type of fiber it contains—it keeps you from being hungry for a long period of time.

GRILLED ASPARAGUS WITH SESAME CHILI VINAIGRETTE

❧

In the spring and early summer, when asparagus is in season, I serve platefuls of this dish to my guests. It's delicious at room temperature, so it's perfect for a backyard barbecue or patio party. During the winter months, use this fabulous Asian vinaigrette on steamed broccoli.

Asparagus

1½ pounds asparagus

1 tablespoon olive oil

Sea salt

Freshly ground black pepper

Vinaigrette

1½ tablespoons reduced-sodium soy sauce

¼ cup red wine vinegar

2 tablespoons water

1 tablespoon sesame oil

1 teaspoon chili oil

¾ teaspoon dry mustard

1 teaspoon freshly ground black pepper

1½ tablespoons sugar

1 tablespoon sesame seeds

1. Preheat a clean, well-oiled grill to medium-high heat.

2. Trim ends off asparagus spears. Place in bowl and toss with olive oil. Season lightly with salt and pepper.

3. Place asparagus on grill over medium heat 4–5 minutes, turning once.

4. Meanwhile, mix vinaigrette ingredients in small bowl.

5. Remove asparagus from grill and place on serving platter. Drizzle with vinaigrette while still hot. Serve warm or at room temperature.

SERVES: 6; CALORIES PER SERVING: 85; DIETARY EQUIVALENT: 1 vegetable, 1 fat

Nutrition Basics

The small amount of sesame oil in this vinaigrette adds so much flavor yet barely any calories to plain vegetables. Asparagus is 6 calories a stalk, so there's no limit on the amount you can eat!

GRILLED VEGETABLES WITH FETA VINAIGRETTE

I always make a large platter of these for summer barbecues or dinner parties. When vegetables taste and look this fantastic, guests actually want to eat them. The balsamic vinegar gives the grilled vegetables a tasty glaze, and the last sprinkling of feta adds just the right amount of salt for the vegetables. You can make these a few hours ahead, plate on a beautiful platter, and leave them at room temperature. Just drizzle with vinaigrette right before serving.

Grilled Vegetables

2 small zucchini, cut lengthwise

2 yellow summer squashes, cut lengthwise

1 red onion, cut into ¼" slices

2 firm, ripe tomatoes, cut into ¼" slices

½ pound asparagus spears, trimmed

2 portobello mushrooms, sliced into ½" pieces

2 red or yellow peppers, thinly sliced

1 tablespoon olive oil

2 tablespoons balsamic vinegar

1 tablespoon garlic, chopped

1 teaspoon sea salt

1 teaspoon freshly ground black pepper

Feta Vinaigrette

1 tablespoon olive oil

2 tablespoons red wine vinegar

1 tablespoon water

½ teaspoon dried oregano

½ teaspoon salt

½ teaspoon black pepper

⅓ cup crumbled feta

1 tablespoon finely chopped basil

1. Preheat a clean lightly oiled grill to medium-high heat.

2. Place all vegetables in large bowl and toss with olive oil, vinegar, garlic, salt, and pepper.

3. Grill vegetables for 10 minutes, turning frequently until lightly charred. Transfer vegetables to serving platter.

4. In small bowl, whisk together all ingredients for vinaigrette except the feta cheese and fresh chopped basil.

5. To serve, drizzle vinaigrette over grilled vegetables, sprinkle with feta, and garnish with chopped basil.

SERVES: 8; CALORIES PER SERVING: 80; DIETARY EQUIVALENT: 2 vegetables

Nutrition Basics
Let your vegetables get a little charred for a smoky flavor. Unlike meat (animal protein), slight charring on vegetables is not unhealthy and does not increase risk of cancer. If you have leftover veggies, make a grilled veggie sandwich, add to a salad, or toss in a summer pasta dish.

Chapter 7

Pasta, Grains, and Pizza

If one food group needs a do-over, it's the grains that we consume in this country. Our refined "white" grains have detrimental effects on health by producing a high glycemic load (a rise in blood sugar), plus we tend to eat portions that are way too large. Now, I did say a do-over, not elimination, of grains. Whole grains consumed in controlled amounts can be very beneficial. "Good carbs" are those that are whole grain, with a high fiber content that is metabolized slowly, which means your blood sugar does not spike. If your blood sugar does not spike, you produce less insulin, and therefore have less of the inflammation that causes chronic disease. You also have the benefit of less fat-cell formation, and you are full for a longer time period. Consuming some high-fiber carbs allows you to eat less animal protein, which helps lower your cholesterol and blood pressure; the fiber in these carbs acts as a broom in the gastrointestinal tract, helping the body sweep out contaminants.

I have included a variety of whole-grain recipes that are sure to entice carb lovers. You can easily find a variety of whole grains such as farro, wheat berries, barley, quinoa, spelt, bulgur, and high-protein and whole-grain pastas in just about every market. We use them in a variety of ways in the Wellness Kitchen, such as:

- Adding cooked whole grains to favorite salads and soups
- Making barley risottos
- Whipping up quick pasta stir-fries with plenty of vegetables
- Combining them with large amounts of herbs for delicious side dishes

We even add half whole-grain flour to our pizza dough, making the carbs in these dishes much healthier.

Be sure to not overcook whole grains; it's best if they are a little al dente, so the fiber stays intact. Keep an eye on proper portion sizes, and always look to team up whole grains with plenty of vegetables and low-fat, highly flavorful sauces. In most of our whole-grain recipes, one whole grain can be substituted for another—for example, you could use farro in the Barley with Herbs recipe. Be adventuresome and make the change with this food group; your body and taste buds will thank you!

"HURRY UP" SPAGHETTI

I first sampled this dish for breakfast at a local restaurant. I loved the flavors so much that I modified it into a healthy, easy, vegetarian dinner that has turned into one of my family's favorites. Definitely comfort food! I use high-protein pasta, fresh spinach, vine-ripened tomatoes, garlic, a combination of whole eggs and egg whites, and aged Parmesan cheese to create a seemingly decadent dish that gives all the satisfaction of eating rich pasta in cream sauce without the calories. I call it "Hurry Up" because it's so quick to prepare and is exactly what you're craving when you are hungry right now!

8 ounces high-protein or whole-grain spaghetti

1 tablespoon olive oil

¼ teaspoon dried red pepper flakes

1 (5–6-ounce) bag baby spinach

2 teaspoons chopped garlic

2 medium vine-ripe tomatoes, cut into ¼" dice

½ teaspoon sea salt

½ teaspoon freshly ground black pepper

2 whole eggs plus 4 egg whites, well beaten

⅓ cup grated Parmesan cheese

2 tablespoons chopped fresh basil plus extra for garnish

1. Bring a large pot of plenty of lightly salted water to boil. Cook pasta until al dente (pasta should be tender, but still firm to the bite). Drain (reserving 1 cup of the pasta water) and keep hot.

2. In a sauté pan over medium heat, add olive oil. Add red pepper flakes and spinach; sauté for 2 minutes or until spinach is just wilted.

3. Add garlic, tomato, salt, and pepper; sauté for 1 more minute.

4. Add drained spaghetti and stir until heated through. Make sure the pasta is very hot when adding it to the sautéed spinach.

5. Immediately add beaten eggs to the hot pasta and toss until set. If pasta is dry, add a little of the pasta water until desired consistency is reached.

6. Add Parmesan cheese and basil, tossing well.

7. To serve, divide pasta between four pasta bowls and top with more fresh basil.

SERVES: 4; CALORIES PER SERVING: 395; DIETARY EQUIVALENT: 2 oz. lean protein, 2 carbohydrates, 1 vegetable

Nutrition Basics
To be calorie- and carb-wise, we have portioned 2 ounces of pasta per person with a larger quantity of vegetables. However, if you or a family member needs more calories, you can increase the amount of pasta.

PASTA SAUTÉS

Everyone is excited in the Wellness Kitchen when they learn that not all pasta is unhealthy! We use high-protein pasta (made by substituting some of the white flour for legume flour, increasing the protein and fiber amounts), or we use whole-grain pasta. We allot 2 ounces of pasta per person, add a lean protein, and use a large portion of vegetables to make delicious, complete meals. Don't forget to save a little of the pasta cooking water for these pasta entrées, an Italian trick that makes the sauce velvety.

LINGUINE WITH SHRIMP AND ASPARAGUS

This is a perfect go-to meal after a long day. I can prepare this nourishing, delicious, restaurant-style dinner and be dining in 30 minutes! Fixing it really is faster than if you went out to dinner.

8 ounces high-protein or whole-grain linguine
1 tablespoon olive oil
½ teaspoon dried red pepper flakes
1 pound asparagus, trimmed and cut into 1" pieces
2 teaspoons minced garlic
1 pound medium or large shrimp, peeled and deveined
½ cup grated Parmesan cheese
¼ cup thinly sliced basil
Zest of 1 lemon

1. Bring a large pot of plenty of lightly salted water to boil. Cook pasta until al dente (pasta should be tender, but still firm to the bite). Drain (reserving 1 cup of the pasta water) and keep hot.

2. In large sauté pan over medium heat, add olive oil. Add red pepper flakes and heat for 1 minute.

3. Add asparagus pieces and cook for 3–4 minutes. Add garlic and toss well.

4. Add shrimp and cook for 1–2 minutes until just pink (don't cook through).

5. Add hot pasta and ½ cup pasta water. Cook 1–2 minutes until sauce is slightly thickened. (Add additional pasta water if too dry.)

6. Add Parmesan, basil, and lemon zest. Toss to combine and serve immediately.

SERVES: 4; CALORIES PER SERVING: 370; DIETARY EQUIVALENT: 4 oz. protein, 2 carbohydrates, 1 vegetable

Food Tip
Frozen, peeled, and deveined wild shrimp is a staple that I keep in my freezer. It's always there whenever I've forgotten to take something out the night before or just didn't have time to run to the market. Simply defrost for 10 minutes in cold water.

VARIATIONS

PENNE WITH CHICKEN, ZUCCHINI, AND RED PEPPERS

Omit linguine and add 8 oz. high-protein penne pasta. Omit asparagus and add 2 medium zucchini, cut lengthwise and sliced thinly, and 1 red pepper, cut into thin strips. Omit shrimp and add 2 8-oz. cooked chicken breasts, cut into bite-sized pieces. (Calories: 365 per serving)

SPAGHETTI WITH BROCCOLI, SUN-DRIED TOMATOES, MUSHROOMS, AND ITALIAN SAUSAGE

Omit linguine and add 8 oz. high-protein spaghetti. Omit asparagus and add 1 pound fresh broccoli florets, ½ cup sun-dried tomatoes cut into slices, and 1 cup sliced mushrooms. Omit raw shrimp and add 8 oz. cooked sliced Italian turkey or chicken sausages (2 sausages). Omit lemon zest. (Calories: 400 per serving)

WHITE LASAGNA WITH TURKEY SAUSAGE

My son calls this dish "the white lasagna" because it's made with a light béchamel sauce instead of a tomato sauce. I've always loved the flavor of sausage in lasagna and had an "Aha!" moment one day when I had a pound of ground turkey in my refrigerator: Why not add the spices that are in sausage to the very low-fat ground turkey? So I added dried red pepper flakes, garlic, and fennel seeds and no one knew the difference! The pre-cooked lasagna noodles are a godsend when time is an issue, which it usually is for most of us.

Organic canola or olive oil cooking spray
2 (5–6-ounce) bags baby spinach
1 tablespoon olive oil
12 ounces cremini mushrooms, cleaned and quartered
1 medium onion, chopped
¼ teaspoon dried red pepper flakes
2 teaspoons sea salt, divided
1 teaspoon freshly ground black pepper, divided
1 pound ground turkey
1½ teaspoons fennel seeds
1 cup fat-free half-and-half, at room temperature
1 cup organic, reduced-sodium, fat-free chicken broth
¼ cup all-purpose flour
¾ cup grated Pecorino Romano cheese
2 tablespoons chopped fresh basil
2 teaspoons minced garlic
1 box no-boil lasagna noodles
6 ounces mozzarella, shredded

1. Preheat the oven to 350°F.
2. Lightly coat a 9" × 13" baking dish with cooking spray.
3. In a large microwavable bowl, cook spinach for 2 minutes. Remove and cool slightly. Place on 3–4 paper towels and squeeze out any moisture. Make sure to squeeze all the water out of the spinach so your sauce does not become runny. (You can also use frozen spinach; again, make sure to give it a good squeeze.) Set aside.
4. In a large nonstick skillet, over medium-high heat, add the oil. Sauté the mushrooms, onion, red pepper flakes, 1 teaspoon salt, and ½ teaspoon pepper. Cook, stirring frequently, until the onions are soft.

5. Add the turkey and fennel seeds to the skillet, breaking it up with a spoon until browned.
6. Add well-drained spinach and mix well. Set aside.
7. For the sauce, in a 5-quart saucepan whisk together the half-and-half, broth, and flour. Bring to a simmer over medium heat and stir constantly for 3 minutes. Reduce the heat to low. Add the Pecorino Romano; whisk until the cheese has melted and the sauce is smooth. Remove the pan from the heat; add the basil, garlic, and remaining salt and pepper. Set aside until slightly cooled.
8. Spread 1 cup of the sauce over the bottom of the prepared baking dish. Arrange the lasagna noodles in a single layer. Next, spread with one third of the turkey-spinach mixture followed by some of the sauce. Repeat building the lasagna by layering the lasagna noodles, turkey-spinach mixture, and sauce.
9. Sprinkle with mozzarella and bake until the filling is bubbling and the top is golden, about 30–35 minutes. Cool for 7–8 minutes to set. Cut into squares and serve.

SERVES: 6; CALORIES PER SERVING: 380; DIETARY EQUIVALENT: 2 carbohydrates, 4 oz. protein, 1 vegetable

Nutrition Basics
Not only is the ground turkey "sausage" much lower in saturated fat than "real" sausage, but has much less in sodium as well. Try using it to top pizza and I promise you will not miss real sausage!

PEANUT SESAME NOODLES

This spicy peanut sauce is a favorite in our Wellness Kitchen. It's served with high-protein pasta with added vegetables for crunch, health, and flavor. Our guests may turn up their noses at tofu, but when it's coated with an enticing sauce they are amazed at how much they really like it! For those watching calories, try serving this on a bed of shredded romaine and Napa cabbage for even more volume.

8 ounces high-protein or whole-grain spaghetti or linguine

⅓ cup natural peanut butter

¼ cup organic, reduced-sodium, fat-free vegetable or chicken broth

2 tablespoons reduced-sodium soy sauce

2 tablespoons hoisin sauce

⅓ cup warm water

2 teaspoons minced garlic

2 teaspoons minced ginger

2 tablespoons seasoned rice vinegar

2 teaspoons sesame oil

1 teaspoon dried red pepper flakes

1 cup shredded carrot

4 green onions, sliced thin

1 red bell pepper, cut into thin strips

1 yellow pepper, cut into thin strips

3 tablespoons sesame seeds, toasted

10 ounces extra-firm tofu, cubed (optional)

2 tablespoons chopped peanuts

2 tablespoons finely chopped cilantro (optional)

SERVES: 4 (entrée portion); CALORIES PER SERVING: 485; DIETARY EQUIVALENT: 3 oz. protein, 2 carbohydrates, 1 fat, 1 vegetable

1. Bring a large pot of lightly salted water, to boil. Cook pasta until al dente (pasta should be tender, but still firm to the bite). Drain and keep warm.

2. Meanwhile, in a medium bowl, whisk peanut butter, broth, soy sauce, hoisin sauce, water, garlic, ginger, vinegar, sesame oil, and red pepper flakes until smooth.

3. In a large bowl, toss pasta, carrot, green onions, red peppers, yellow peppers, and sesame seeds with the dressing. Combine well. Gently mix in tofu.

4. To serve, place noodles on large platter or in shallow serving bowl and garnish top with peanuts and cilantro.

Food Tip

I love this dish with tofu, grilled chicken, or shrimp. Add more or less chili paste according to your taste, but remember that when served cold or at room temperature, noodles and vegetables can stand more heat. I also like to use whole-grain pasta for this dish; the nuttiness of whole-grain pasta pairs very well with the peanut sauce.

QUINOA CHILI RELLENOS

I love chili rellenos and considered myself somewhat of a connoisseur of them. But I had mostly given them up because of the guilt-ridden aftermath of my indulgences. A few years ago when quinoa came on the market, I began to see recipes using it for fillings with peppers. After much trial and error, we have developed a recipe in the Wellness Kitchen that has met both of my criteria: wonderful complex relleno flavor and healthfulness! This pepper is filled with a high-protein, high-fiber filling, baked, not fried, and then topped with a fabulous tomato sauce with a small amount of cheese. I actually do not miss the old rellenos of the past one bit!

Chili Rellenos

8 fresh poblano chilies
1 tablespoon olive oil
1 yellow onion, diced
¾ cup quinoa, uncooked and rinsed well
1½ cups organic, reduced-sodium, fat-free chicken broth
1 cup low-fat Mexican cheese blend (or shredded lite Cheddar or Monterey jack)
4 sprigs fresh thyme, leaves removed
1 whole egg plus 2 egg whites, beaten
½ teaspoon sea salt
¼ teaspoon freshly ground black pepper
Organic canola or olive oil cooking spray
½ cup crumbled Cotija cheese
2 tablespoons finely chopped cilantro

Sauce

1 tablespoon canola oil
½ onion, finely chopped
2 teaspoons finely chopped garlic
1 teaspoon dried Mexican oregano
1 (14½-ounce) can Mexican-style stewed tomatoes
1½ cups organic, reduced-sodium, fat-free chicken broth
1 tablespoon white vinegar

1. Set oven to broil or outdoor grill to medium heat.
2. For the poblano chilies: Place chilies directly on a grill (or under the broiler) and char, turning every few minutes, until blackened on all sides. Place in bowl and cover with plastic wrap. Let steam for 10 minutes.

Gently peel off the charred skin. Be careful not to tear the pepper. Slit open one side of the pepper, from stem to bottom. Remove seeds and discard. Set aside.

3. For the filling: Heat oil in medium saucepan over medium heat. Sauté onion for 3 minutes, until softened. Add quinoa, sauté until golden, then add the broth. Cook until quinoa is tender and broth is absorbed, approximately 15–20 minutes. Transfer to a bowl and let cool slightly. Stir in Mexican cheese, thyme leaves, eggs, salt, and pepper. Carefully stuff each pepper with a generous spoonful of the filling. Close the seam and place in a baking dish lightly coated with cooking spray. Reduce oven temperature to 350°F. Bake for 20 minutes or until quinoa mixture is heated through and set.

4. For the sauce: Heat oil in a medium saucepan over medium heat. Sauté onion for 3 minutes, until softened. Add garlic and oregano; stir until fragrant, about 1 minute. Add tomatoes, broth, and vinegar. Bring to a boil, then reduce heat to simmer. Reduce the sauce by half.

5. To serve, ladle ¼ cup sauce on a plate, making a circle about as long as the pepper. Place stuffed pepper on top of sauce. Top with the Cotija cheese and cilantro. Serve extra sauce on the side if desired.

SERVES: 4 (2 peppers each); CALORIES PER SERVING: 420; DIETARY EQUIVALENT: 2 oz. protein, 2 carbohydrates, 1 vegetable, 1 fat

Nutrition Basics

Quinoa is an ancient food that is considered a superfood due to its nutritional profile. Quinoa is one of the few plant foods that contains a complete protein profile with all essential amino acids present, and is high in antioxidants—especially quercetin and kaempferol, which prevent oxidation, a cause of aging in the body. It is thought of as a grain, but quinoa is actually a seed belonging to a family of plants such as spinach and beets. Mother Nature coated the seeds with saponins, a compound that gives off a soapy, bitter flavor to deter birds from eating it. While most of it is removed in processing, rinse with cold water in a paper towel–lined colander to remove any trace before cooking.

BARLEY WITH HERBS

Barley is one of my all-time favorite ancient grains, and ancient it is! It's one of the first grains ever cultivated by man and it's also one of the most nutritious. It has three times more soluble fiber than brown rice and one-third fewer calories. Barley is the grain of choice for those who want to prevent diabetes or who have diabetes, because of its very low glycemic index. The nutty chewiness of barley is delightful in this recipe with fresh herbs and Parmesan. We had one young man in the Wellness Kitchen ask what he was eating when he sampled this dish; he said he wanted to eat the whole dish! Whole grains, like barley, do take more time to cook than processed grains. But you can cut cooking time considerably if you soak the grains in 3 cups of cold water in a bowl for 2–24 hours. Refrigerate until ready to cook. Make sure to drain the grains and reduce the amount of water or broth used in the recipe by at least half. Taste barley after soaking. If it's already close to al dente, it will cook quickly with only a little water added. I often precook barley and freeze it in 2-cup portions that can easily be added frozen to soups or stews.

2 cups organic, reduced-sodium, fat-free chicken broth (4 cups if barley is not pre-soaked)

2 cups barley, drained if pre-soaked (can use other ancient grains, such as farro)

1 cup parsley

¼ cup basil

1 tablespoon fresh thyme leaves

1 clove garlic

2 teaspoons red wine vinegar

1 tablespoon olive oil

½ teaspoon sea salt

¼ teaspoon freshly ground black pepper

¼ cup grated Parmesan cheese

1. In large pot, over high heat, bring broth to a boil. Add barley, cover, and reduce heat to a simmer for 35 minutes until barley is just tender (al dente).

2. Meanwhile, in food processor, combine parsley, basil, thyme, and garlic. Pulse until coarsely chopped. Add vinegar, oil, salt, and pepper. Pulse until well blended.

3. Just before serving, fold the herb mixture into the barley.

4. To serve, place barley in serving bowl and sprinkle Parmesan over the top.

SERVES: 6; CALORIES PER SERVING: 250; DIETARY EQUIVALENT: 2 carbohydrates, 1 fat

Nutrition Basics

Purchasing barley can be somewhat confusing, since there are variations in the processing of this grain. Out of the field, barley has an inedible outer hull that needs to be removed. With or without its hull, barley is considered a whole grain. When the outer hull is removed, the bran layer remains intact, but it requires more time to soak and cook. Pearl barley, commonly found in most markets, has the hull and some of the bran layer removed. It undergoes various degrees of polishing or "pearling," and requires less cooking time. While pearl barley is not considered a whole grain, it has more fiber than most other refined grains because the fiber is throughout the kernel, just not in the bran. One cup of pearled barley contains 6 grams of fiber and 6 grams of protein. One cup of brown rice has 2 grams of fiber and 3 grams of protein. The more tan in color the barley grain is, the less "pearled" it is, resulting in a higher fiber content. For a delicious fiber-packed breakfast, thaw frozen, precooked barley in a microwave for a few minutes and top with yogurt and fruit.

GREEN RICE

Nutritionally speaking, rice (especially white rice), is not a very healthy food. It's one-third higher in carbohydrates than other ancient grains and has almost no fiber. Even brown rice is much lower in fiber than other ancient grains. We did come up with a way to elevate the nutritional status of rice in the Wellness Kitchen, and it's become an absolute favorite. Cook rice as usual, and then add a "super green" concoction of spinach, parsley, and cilantro whirled up in a food processor or blender. Not only is it beautiful to look at, but it tastes amazing. The subtle cilantro flavor pairs beautifully with Asian or Latin food and adds pop to a plain grilled chicken dinner!

2 cups loosely packed spinach, or 5 ounces frozen spinach, thawed
1 cup loosely packed Italian parsley
1 cup loosely packed cilantro
1 teaspoon sea salt
3¾ cups water, divided
1 tablespoon olive oil
1½ cups brown basmati rice
¼ cup pine nuts

Nutrition Basics

Cilantro is a powerhouse of nutrients, high in potassium, magnesium, iron, and vitamins A and C. It is thought to be a digestive aid and an antibacterial agent, decreasing the incidence of urinary tract infections. The high antioxidant levels in cilantro act as an anti-inflammatory agent, improving liver function and promoting heart health. When it comes to cilantro, it seems that people either love or hate it. Cilantro contains the natural compound aldehyde, which tastes bitter and soapy to some people (genetics may determine who perceives this taste). People who can taste this flavor do not like cilantro. Feel free to substitute basil in this recipe.

1. In food processor, pulse spinach, parsley, cilantro, salt, and ¾ cup water. Process until smooth. Set aside.
2. Heat oil in heavy, lidded saucepan, over medium heat. Add rice and cook 2 minutes, stirring constantly, until well coated and lightly toasted (rice will smell fragrant). Stir in remaining water. Bring to a boil; reduce heat to low, cover, and simmer 20–25 minutes, or until liquid has been absorbed.
3. Meanwhile, place pine nuts in small sauté pan and toast lightly over medium-high heat for 2–3 minutes. Set aside.
4. Remove rice from heat and let rest 5 minutes.
5. Fluff with a fork and add spinach-herb mixture. Top with toasted pine nuts.

SERVES: 6; CALORIES PER SERVING: 150; DIETARY EQUIVALENT: 1 carbohydrate, ½ vegetable, 1 fat

GRILLED MARGHERITA PIZZA WITH ARUGULA

What's not to love about this pizza? The slightly charred crust, topped with ripe, sweet tomatoes, cheese, and fresh basil is a winning flavor combination. The arugula salad adds just the right finishing touch to create a gourmet pizza. The individual servings make portion control easy for those watching their waistlines!

8 ounces fresh or thawed whole-wheat pizza dough

2 tablespoons all-purpose flour, for dusting

2 teaspoons finely chopped garlic

2 tablespoons olive oil, divided

6 ounces fresh buffalo mozzarella cheese, sliced ¼" thick

⅓ cup grated Parmesan cheese

5 Roma tomatoes, sliced ¼" thick

2 cups baby arugula

1 tablespoon fresh lemon juice

½ teaspoon freshly ground black pepper

2 tablespoons chopped fresh basil

Nutrition Basics

Topping pizza with salad is a great way to not only enhance nutritional value but add volume as well. If you're out of fresh tomatoes or it's midwinter and they seem tasteless, substitute with jarred, boxed, or BPA-free canned crushed tomatoes. Simply strain then add minced garlic and dried red pepper flakes to taste.

1. Preheat a clean, lightly oiled grill to medium heat.

2. Let pizza dough stand at room temperature for 30 minutes.

3. Divide dough into quarters, forming 4 (2-oz.) balls.

4. Dust dough and countertop lightly with flour. Roll dough into 4 thin rounds and place on baking sheet.

5. Stir garlic into 1 tablespoon olive oil. Lightly brush dough on both sides with garlic oil.

6. Place pizza rounds onto grill for 3 minutes, until crust starts to rise with light grill marks.

7. Turn crusts over and add mozzarella, Parmesan, and sliced tomatoes.

8. Turn grill off. Close cover and continue to bake for 4–5 minutes or until cheese is melted.

9. Meanwhile, in a medium bowl, toss arugula with remaining olive oil, lemon juice, and pepper.

10. Remove the pizzas from grill, sprinkle with basil, and cut into quarters. Plate and top with arugula salad.

SERVES: 8; CALORIES PER SERVING: 240; DIETARY EQUIVALENT: 1 oz. protein, 2 carbohydrates, 1 fat

HARVEST STUFFING

This is my favorite part of the Thanksgiving meal. I have worked really hard over the years to perfect a lower-calorie version of this time-honored dish. Adding more fruits and vegetables gives this traditional stuffing more volume with fewer calories and carbohydrates, yet it's guaranteed to please even the most discriminating stuffing connoisseurs! I find that if I only eat my most favorite carbs at holidays and forgo the ones that I can have anytime, I don't overdo it. Also, skipping one dish at the main meal and instead eating it for lunch the next day is another way not to overeat. Most stuffing recipes add a stick of butter to make it moist, but we found that adding the egg makes the stuffing light and moist, with much less fat and many fewer calories.

Organic canola or olive oil cooking spray
12 slices of rustic, whole-grain bread, cut into ¾" cubes
2 tablespoons olive oil, divided
1 tablespoon no-trans-fat margarine
1 large onion, cut into small dice
3 stalks celery, cut into small dice
1 teaspoon sea salt, divided
½ teaspoon freshly ground black pepper
3 green apples, peeled, cored, and diced
1 tablespoon finely chopped garlic
8 ounces cremini mushrooms, thinly sliced
¾ cup roughly chopped pecans
¾ cup chopped dried tart cherries
¾ cup finely chopped parsley
3 tablespoons finely chopped fresh sage
1 tablespoon fresh thyme leaves
2–3 cups organic, reduced-sodium, fat-free chicken broth
2 eggs, beaten (or ½ cup egg substitute)

1. Preheat oven to 350°F.
2. Spray a 9" × 13" baking dish with cooking spray.
3. Place bread cubes on baking sheet and coat with cooking spray. Bake until golden brown. Place in a large mixing bowl. Set aside.
4. In a large skillet, over medium-high heat, add 1 tablespoon olive oil and the margarine. Add onions, celery, ½ teaspoon salt, and pepper. Sauté for 8–10 minutes until vegetables are tender.
5. Add apples and reduce heat to medium-low. Cook for 10–12 minutes. Add mixture to the bread cubes.
6. Heat remaining 1 tablespoon olive oil in same skillet over medium heat. Add garlic, mushrooms, and remaining salt. Sauté for 5 minutes.
7. Add mushroom mixture to the bread cubes, along with the pecans, cherries, parsley, sage, and thyme. Gently toss to combine.
8. Pour 1½ cups broth over stuffing and gently toss again. Continue to add ½ cup at a time until bread is moistened (but not soggy).
9. Adjust seasonings if needed.
10. Mix in the eggs.
11. Transfer stuffing to prepared baking dish. Bake for 40–50 minutes until top is crisp.

SERVES: 16; CALORIES PER SERVING: 250; DIETARY EQUIVALENT: 1½ carbohydrate, 1 fruit, ½ vegetable, 1 fat

Food Tip
I highly recommend not stuffing your turkey. In order to safely cook stuffed poultry, the stuffing temperature must reach a minimum of 165°F. Roasting to this temperature usually results in an overcooked, dry bird. An unstuffed turkey will cook more evenly and quickly, reducing oven time and resulting in a juicier, moister turkey.

Chapter 8

A Little Sweet

One of the hardest things I have ever had to do is tame my sweet tooth. I actually did it—but it took a long time, years in fact. My mother loved to bake, so sweets were frequently available when I was a kid. As the years passed, I knew that I would have to start limiting my intake of sweets, and so the journey began.

The first step was to move away from daily treats. Every other day was the best I could do initially, then I progressed to just weekend indulgences. I have pretty much given up on sweets during the week, except on very special occasions (not just a hard workday or when out at a fine restaurant!). What I have found is that the less often I have sugar, the less I crave it. We now know this is a fact; the more frequently you have treats, the more you want them. Sugar can be addictive to many people and frequency is what dictates cravings. Cravings are stronger than willpower. If you're trying to cut down on sugar, try limiting indulgences to one or two times a week, never two days in a row, to minimize the cravings. Since most of us can have sweets now and then—after all, total deprivation can lead to binging later—what we need to do is learn to associate treats with special occasions, not with everyday life.

The following recipes are healthier compared to an average dessert; I like to say "less bad" for you than the real deal when in the Wellness Kitchen. We have decreased the sugar, used more whole-grain flours when possible, eliminated butter for healthier fats, and increased the natural fruit as much as possible . . . but these are still treats. They have all the satisfaction of more decadent choices. You will find our warm Fruit Crisp just as satisfying as a warm berry pie, but with 60 percent fewer calories and much less fat. Because our lighter versions are so good, plan wisely and make sure you limit your intake to just once or twice a week. Some of the recipes can be cut in half, or you can set aside half the prepped recipe in the freezer for later use. Freezing leftover treats can help you tame your sweet tooth, too!

FRUIT CRISP

When this is served, I always hear rave reviews, whether in the Wellness Kitchen or at home . . . no matter what the season! It has all the comfort of a crunchy homemade oatmeal cookie with the filling of warm fruit pie. What makes it even more lovable for guests in the Wellness Kitchen is the fact that it's only about a quarter of the calories of a piece of pie. We use small amounts of healthy fat, real oatmeal, less sugar, and seasonal fruit to make a scrumptious dessert that truly has health benefits. I often add a few tablespoons of flavored liqueurs for an additional layer of flavor. My favorite is amaretto, an almond-flavored liqueur that tastes delicious with peaches or apricots. Try crème de cassis with any of the berry crisps!

Fruit

Organic canola oil cooking spray

2 pounds (about 6 apples) Granny Smith or Pippin, peeled, cored, and sliced

1 tablespoon lemon juice

2 tablespoons white sugar

2 tablespoons all-purpose flour

1¼ teaspoons cinnamon

1 tablespoon orange zest

Topping

1 cup rolled oats

½ cup brown sugar

½ cup all-purpose flour (or ¼ cup whole-wheat flour plus ¼ cup all-purpose flour)

½ cup no-trans-fat margarine

1 teaspoon cinnamon

¼ cup walnuts or pecans, measured then roughly chopped

1. Preheat oven to 350°F.

2. Spray a 9" × 13" baking dish with cooking spray.

3. In the baking dish, toss apple slices with lemon juice, white sugar, flour, cinnamon, and zest. Bake for 15 minutes.

4. Meanwhile, in a small bowl mix all topping ingredients with a fork or fingers until crumbly. Do not overmix.

5. Remove apples from oven and sprinkle topping over apples evenly.

6. Return to oven and bake for another 25 minutes, or until topping is golden and fruit is bubbling.

7. Serve warm with lite whipped topping or lite ice cream.

SERVES: 8; CALORIES PER SERVING: 250–270; DIETARY EQUIVALENT: 1 carbohydrate, 1 fruit, 1.5 fats

VARIATIONS

APPLE BLACKBERRY OR BLUEBERRY

Decrease apples to 5. Add 1 cup fresh or frozen blackberries or blueberries, unthawed. Omit cinnamon in fruit filling.

APPLE CRANBERRY

Add ¼ cup dried cranberries, or add 1 cup fresh cranberries plus 2 tablespoons extra sugar to the filling to balance the tartness of fresh cranberries.

APRICOT

Omit apples and add 4 cups fresh, peeled apricot halves. Add ½ teaspoon almond extract or 2 tablespoons amaretto liqueur, and decrease cinnamon to ½ teaspoon. For the topping, omit walnuts or pecans and add sliced almonds.

MIXED BERRY

Omit apples and use 6 cups mixed berries, fresh or frozen, unthawed. Omit flour and add 3 tablespoons tapioca and ¾ teaspoon cinnamon. Omit orange zest and add 2 tablespoons crème de cassis (optional).

PEACH

Omit apples and use 6 ripe, peeled, and sliced peaches. Omit orange zest and add ½ teaspoon almond extract or 2 tablespoons amaretto liqueur, and decrease cinnamon to ¾ teaspoon. For the topping, omit walnuts and pecans and add sliced almonds.

PEACH BLUEBERRY

Omit apples and add 6 ripe, peeled, and sliced peaches. Add 1 cup fresh or frozen blueberries, unthawed. Omit orange zest; add ½ teaspoon almond extract or 2 tablespoons amaretto liqueur, and decrease cinnamon to ¾ teaspoon. For the topping, omit walnuts or pecans and add sliced almonds.

PEAR RASPBERRY OR BLACKBERRY

Omit apples and add 5 ripe peeled pears, sliced. Add 1 cup fresh or frozen raspberries or blackberries, unthawed. Omit orange zest and cinnamon and add ¼ teaspoon ground nutmeg. For the topping, omit walnuts or pecans and add sliced almonds.

Food Tip

Use a variety of frozen berries when out of season; they're great mixed with fall and winter fruits such as apples or pears. When using frozen berries, be sure to add them to the dish frozen; thawing will drain the juice from the berries.

DEEP-DISH APPLE COBBLER

Who does not want to eat a warm, deliciously fruity dessert topped with a light, flakey biscuit that is crunchy on the outside but fluffy inside? I certainly do, but the guilt over the stick of butter made it a rare occasion for me! I tried for ages to find a great lower-fat biscuit topping that did not use a stick of butter, but to no avail. All of my attempts produced a topping that was hard and tough. I even tried a low-fat biscuit mix, but the flavor was too bland. I finally got it! This biscuit topping is tender, delicious, and contains no unhealthy fat. I now make this dessert all year, using whatever fruits are in season: berries, peaches, nectarines, apricots, cherries, and plums in the summer months and apples and pears, sometimes teamed with frozen berries, in the winter months. To make this ahead of time, prepare the fruit and place in baking dish, cover, and refrigerate. Make the topping but do not add the boiling water until right before topping the fruit. (For guidelines on combinations of fruit and spices, check out the variations of Fruit Crisp, earlier in the chapter.)

8 fresh apples, peeled, cored, and sliced into thin wedges
¼ cup plus 3½ tablespoons white sugar, divided
¼ cup plus 2 tablespoons brown sugar, divided
1¼ teaspoons cinnamon, divided
⅛ teaspoon nutmeg
1 teaspoon fresh lemon juice
1 tablespoon cornstarch
½ cup all-purpose flour
½ cup whole-wheat pastry flour
1 teaspoon baking powder
½ teaspoon salt
⅓ cup no-trans-fat margarine
¼ cup boiling water

1. Preheat oven to 375°F.
2. In a large mixing bowl, combine apples, 2 tablespoons white sugar, 2 tablespoons brown sugar, ¼ teaspoon cinnamon, nutmeg, lemon juice, and cornstarch. Toss to coat evenly and pour into a 2-quart baking dish. Bake for 10 minutes.
3. Meanwhile, to make the topping, in a large bowl, combine flours, ¼ cup white sugar, ¼ cup brown sugar, baking powder, and salt. Blend in margarine with fingertips until mixture resembles coarse meal. Stir in boiling water just until combined.
4. Remove apples from oven and drop spoonfuls of topping over them.
5. Mix remaining 1½ tablespoons white sugar with remaining 1 teaspoon cinnamon. Sprinkle over the cobbler. Bake until topping is golden, about 30 minutes.

SERVES: 8; CALORIES PER SERVING: 250; DIETARY EQUIVALENT: 1½ carbohydrate, 1 fruit, ½ fat

Nutrition Basics
Make sure to use enough fruit in your fruit cobblers. I spoon the topping on in 8 even spoonfuls so each serving has controlled amounts of topping and calories. The idea here is more fruit volume than biscuit!

APPLE-RASPBERRY BARS

❧

I love fruit bar cookies. They taste almost like fruit pie, especially when you find a bar that really tastes like fruit, not jam. It's really a very easy dessert to make—it uses common ingredients, doesn't have any pastry dough to roll out, and I do not even peel the apple (which adds more fiber). These bars are low in unhealthy fat, made with some whole-wheat flour, and have much less sugar than traditionally used. They also freeze nicely—that is, if there are any left!

Organic canola oil cooking spray

1½ cups whole-wheat pastry flour, divided

½ teaspoon baking powder

½ teaspoon baking soda

½ teaspoon plus ⅛ teaspoon sea salt, divided

¾ cup brown sugar, packed

3 tablespoons no-trans-fat margarine, softened

1 large egg, beaten

1 teaspoon vanilla

¼ cup chopped walnuts

3 cups fresh raspberries (may substitute frozen raspberries; do not thaw)

2 red apples, cut into small dice (leave peel on for higher antioxidant and fiber intake)

⅓ cup white sugar

2 tablespoons all-purpose flour

2 tablespoons confectioners' sugar for dusting (optional)

1. Preheat oven to 350°F.

2. Line an 8" × 8" baking dish with parchment paper, leaving a 2" overhang on each end. Spray with cooking spray.

3. In a medium bowl, whisk together 1¼ cups whole-wheat pastry flour, baking powder, baking soda, and ½ teaspoon salt.

4. In a large bowl, beat together brown sugar, margarine, egg, and vanilla.

5. Add dry ingredients to wet ingredients and stir until well blended. Remove ⅓ of mixture to another bowl and set aside to make crumb topping.

6. Place remaining dough into baking dish. With your fingertips, press down in an even layer. Bake for 12 minutes, until edges are lightly golden. Remove from oven.

7. Meanwhile, add remaining whole-wheat pastry flour and walnuts to reserved ⅓ dough. Crumble lightly with fingers, set aside.

8. In a saucepan combine raspberries, diced apples, sugar, all-purpose flour, and ⅛ teaspoon salt over medium heat. Cook, stirring, until boiling, then simmer for 5–6 minutes until thickened.

9. Pour hot apple-raspberry filling over baked crust in even layer. Sprinkle with crumb topping.

10. Return to oven and bake 20 minutes until top is golden. Remove from oven and let cool for 45 minutes. Carefully lift bars from pan using the parchment overhang. Peel back parchment on edges and cool completely on wire rack. Cut into 16 bars and dust lightly with confectioners' sugar.

YIELDS: 16 bars; CALORIES PER BAR: 155; DIETARY EQUIVALENT: 1 carbohydrate, 1 fruit

Food Tip

Try wetting your fingertips with water when spreading the dough on the bottom of the baking pan; it makes it less sticky and easier to work with. Make sure you cool these bars before cutting so they have time to really set and not fall apart.

CHOCOLATE WALNUT COOKIES

If you love brownies, you will love these cookies. They're crisp on the outside and fudgy inside with a rich, deep chocolate flavor. We had a Mexican Fiesta in the Wellness Kitchen one day and we added a pinch of cayenne pepper and ½ teaspoon of cinnamon for a tasty twist. This is still a cookie with sugar, but it does not contain any unhealthy fat. There's no butter, no hydrogenated shortening, no white flour. The walnuts are a healthy fat that is high in omega-3s and the dark cocoa used provides a high level of antioxidants that improve heart health.

Organic canola oil cooking spray

6 ounces walnut pieces

4 large egg whites, room temperature

1 tablespoon vanilla extract

3 cups confectioners' sugar

½ cup plus 3 tablespoons unsweetened Dutch processed cocoa powder

¼ teaspoon salt

1. Preheat oven to 350°F.

2. Line sheet pan with parchment paper and lightly spray with cooking spray.

3. Spread walnuts on separate baking sheet and toast in oven for 10 minutes. Let cool.

4. Meanwhile, beat egg whites in mixer using whisk attachment until foamy. Add the vanilla; beat until soft peaks form, about 5–8 minutes.

5. In separate large mixing bowl, whisk confectioners' sugar, cocoa powder, toasted walnuts, and salt together. Gently fold in half of the egg whites; do not overmix. Incorporate other half of egg whites.

6. Spoon batter on prepared sheet pan to make 16 cookies.

7. Bake for 10 minutes; rotate baking sheets once and bake for 10 more minutes or until tops are glossy and slightly cracked. Remove from oven and slide parchment off baking sheet onto counter. Cool for 10 minutes and remove cookies to rack to complete cooling.

8. Store in airtight container for up to 3 days.

SERVES: 16; CALORIES PER SERVING: 170; DIETARY EQUIVALENT: 1 carbohydrate, 1 fat

Food Tip

It's best to use a really good-quality 70 percent dark Dutch processed cocoa powder—it's usually more expensive but worth it. The darker the cocoa powder, the more intense the chocolate taste, and it does not contain any more calories than less expensive cocoa powder.

A Dutch cocoa powder will be darker with a more intense flavor due to its having been washed with potassium, which neutralizes the acid in the natural cocoa bean.

ORANGE CARDAMOM COOKIES WITH DARK CHOCOLATE DRIZZLE

With a shortbread-like texture, these delicious cookies are best right out of the oven, warm and soft. We serve one cookie with a cup of fresh berries for an elegant but healthy dessert in the Wellness Kitchen.

Organic canola oil cooking spray

⅔ cup olive oil, chilled (place in freezer 15–20 minutes until semi-solid but not hard)

1 cup sugar

1 egg

2½ teaspoons vanilla

2 tablespoons orange zest

2 tablespoons orange juice

1¼ cups all-purpose flour

1 cup whole-wheat pastry flour

1 teaspoon cardamom

1 teaspoon baking powder

½ teaspoon baking soda

½ teaspoon salt

2 ounces 70% dark chocolate

1. Preheat oven to 375°F.

2. Spray 2 baking sheets with cooking spray.

3. In large bowl combine oil, sugar, egg, vanilla, orange zest, and orange juice. Mix with hand mixer until smooth.

4. In a separate medium bowl, thoroughly whisk the flours, cardamom, baking powder, baking soda, and salt.

5. Slowly add dry ingredients to wet ingredients until combined.

6. Using a spoon, form mixture into even balls (heaping tablespoon size). Place onto baking sheet and bake for 8 minutes. Transfer cookies to wire rack to cool.

7. Place chocolate in microwavable bowl; heat for 30-second intervals, stirring each time, until chocolate is melted. Drizzle cookies with melted chocolate.

YIELDS: 20–25 cookies; CALORIES PER COOKIE: 125; DIETARY EQUIVALENT: 1 carbohydrate, 1 fat

Nutrition Basics
Using olive oil instead of butter or shortening makes this cookie so much healthier. Be sure to bake desserts with a light, fruity-flavored olive oil versus a heavier, peppery tasting one that is best used with meats, salads, etc. I only bake the number of cookies I need and freeze the remaining dough to use at a later time—that way I am not tempted to eat too many of these delicious cookies!

VARIATION

For lemon olive oil cookies, omit orange zest and juice and substitute the same amount of lemon zest and juice. Omit drizzling chocolate on cookies. (Calories: 115 per serving)

CHOCOLATE CUPCAKES WITH PEANUT BUTTER ICING

Who can resist the combination of dark chocolate and creamy peanut butter? Use high-quality cocoa powder such as Scharffen Berger or Valrhona for a dark, rich, more complex chocolate taste. What we say in the Wellness Kitchen is that these moist cupcakes are not exactly good for you, but they are certainly less bad for you than their high-fat, high-calorie counterparts!

Cupcakes

1¾ cups all-purpose flour
1 cup white sugar
¾ cup cocoa powder
1½ teaspoons baking soda
¾ teaspoon baking powder
1 teaspoon salt
1¼ cups low-fat buttermilk
1 cup brown sugar, lightly packed
2 eggs, beaten
¼ cup canola oil
2 teaspoons vanilla extract
1 cup black coffee, cooled

Peanut Butter Icing

¼ cup natural peanut butter
¼ cup reduced-fat cream cheese
1 cup confectioners' sugar
½ teaspoon vanilla
2 tablespoons chopped salted, dry-roasted peanuts

1. Preheat oven to 350°F.
2. Line a cupcake pan with paper liners.
3. In large bowl, whisk together flour, white sugar, cocoa powder, baking soda, baking powder, and salt. Set aside.
4. In a medium bowl, beat together buttermilk, brown sugar, eggs, oil, and vanilla. Whisk in coffee just until combined.
5. Pour wet ingredients into dry. Combine well; do not overmix.

6. Pour batter into cupcake liners until ⅔ full and bake for 20–25 minutes or until a cake tester comes out clean.
7. Cool in the pan for 10 minutes, then remove to a rack and let cool completely.
8. Meanwhile, mix together all icing ingredients except peanuts.
9. Frost cooled cupcakes and sprinkle with peanuts.

SERVES: 16; CALORIES PER SERVING: 255; DIETARY EQUIVALENT: 2 carbohydrates, 1½ fats

Nutrition Basics

Omitting butter and adding canola oil to these cupcakes gives them less saturated fat. A natural peanut butter icing helps to reduce unhealthy fat typically associated with a traditional butter-cream icing.

GINGER PEAR SPICE CAKE

Everyone is so impressed with this lovely fall and winter dessert. Similar to a pineapple upside-down cake, the pears and small amount of brown sugar caramelize on the bottom so when you invert the cake, you can see the pears in the spicy ginger cake. I just dust the top with a little powdered sugar right before serving; it looks like you went to a French bakery!

Organic canola oil cooking spray
3 ripe pears (preferably Bosc)
1 tablespoon no-trans-fat margarine, melted
2 tablespoons brown sugar
3 teaspoons cinnamon, divided
½ teaspoon nutmeg
2 tablespoons lemon juice
1¼ cups all-purpose flour
1 teaspoon ground ginger
½ teaspoon baking soda
½ cup white sugar
½ cup buttermilk
¼ cup canola oil
½ cup molasses
¼ cup egg substitute (or 2 egg whites, beaten)

1. Preheat oven to 350°F.
2. Line the bottom of 9" round cake pan with parchment paper and coat with cooking spray.
3. Peel pears and cut in half; scoop out core with spoon. Place in microwavable bowl, cover with clean towel, and microwave for 3–4 minutes to soften slightly.
4. In a small bowl, combine melted margarine, brown sugar, 2 teaspoons cinnamon, nutmeg, and lemon juice. Pour into bottom of prepared cake pan. Arrange pear halves on top of sauce in a circle, with cut sides up.
5. In another small bowl, whisk together flour, ginger, baking soda, and remaining cinnamon.
6. In a large bowl, thoroughly combine white sugar, buttermilk, oil, molasses, and eggs.

7. Add dry mixture to wet ingredients, mixing just enough to combine. Pour batter over pears and bake for 25–30 minutes.
8. Serve with lite ice cream or fat-free topping.

SERVES: 6; CALORIES PER SERVING: 150; DIETARY EQUIVALENT: 1 fruit, 1 carbohydrate

Nutrition Basics

This is a dense, moist cake that has a small amount of healthier canola oil versus butter, which is a saturated fat. Also, since there is no need for icing, it is much lower in sugar compared to most cakes. This cake is delicious slightly warm, so you can prepare it ahead, refrigerate, and bring to room temperature for 20 minutes before baking. Pop it into the oven about an hour before serving.

MEYER LEMON AND ROSEMARY OLIVE OIL CAKE

Moist, dense, and intense in lemon flavor, this cake is always a hit in the Wellness Kitchen. Make sure you use Meyer lemons if possible. This orange-colored lemon really is different than standard lemons—fragrant, slightly sweet yet still tangy. You will want to use them for everything lemon! If you are lucky enough to have a large supply of Meyer lemons, juice and zest them and store in ½-cup containers in the freezer for use in later months when they are not available. The addition of the rosemary gives a subtle herbal essence that is delightful with the lemon flavor.

Organic olive oil cooking spray

1½ cups all-purpose unbleached flour

2 teaspoons baking powder

⅛ teaspoon sea salt

5 teaspoons Meyer lemon zest, divided

3 eggs (or ½ cup egg substitute plus one whole egg)

½ cup olive oil

1 cup granulated sugar

½ cup buttermilk

1 teaspoon minced fresh rosemary

1 cup confectioners' sugar, divided

¼ cup plus 2½ teaspoons Meyer lemon juice, divided

Fresh berries

1. Preheat oven to 350°F.
2. Line the bottom of a 9" round cake pan with parchment and coat with cooking spray.
3. In a medium bowl, combine the flour, baking powder, salt, and 4 teaspoons of the zest.
4. In a large bowl, thoroughly whisk together the eggs, olive oil, sugar, buttermilk, and rosemary.
5. Combine the dry ingredients with the wet and whisk together. Pour into the prepared pan. Bake for 25–30 minutes or until a toothpick inserted into the center of the cake comes out clean. Take cake out of oven and place on a rack to cool for 10 minutes, then invert onto serving plate.
6. After another 10 minutes, poke the cake all over with a heavy fork. Mix together ¼ cup confectioners' sugar with ¼ cup Meyer lemon juice. Spoon the syrup over the top of the cake a little at a time, letting the syrup fill all the holes and spreading it around with the back of the spoon.
7. Let the cake completely cool. Just before serving combine the remaining confectioners' sugar with 2½ teaspoons Meyer lemon juice. Coat the top of the cake with the glaze and sprinkle the remaining zest on top.
8. To serve, cut into wedges and garnish with fresh berries.

SERVES: 8; CALORIES PER SERVINGS: 295; DIETARY EQUIVALENT: 1½ carbohydrates, 3 fats

Nutrition Basics

Using olive oil instead of traditional butter in this cake makes it healthier because of the higher omega-3 fat content and much less saturated fat.

BUTTERMILK CAKE WITH SUMMER FRUIT

This is one of those recipes that make you wonder how something can taste so good yet be so easy and quick to bake. I love to make this with all kinds of summer berries or stone fruits, such as peaches, nectarines, apricots, plums, or any combination of them. The moist cake cooks around the fruit and the single tablespoon of sugar over the top gives this delectable cake a little crunch. And the best part: it's about two-thirds fewer calories than a regular piece of cake! Try serving it warm with a small scoop of lite ice cream or frozen yogurt.

Organic canola oil cooking spray

1 cup all-purpose flour

½ teaspoon baking soda

½ teaspoon baking powder

¼ teaspoon salt

½ cup plus 1 tablespoon sugar, divided

¼ cup no-trans-fat margarine, softened

1 egg

1 teaspoon vanilla

½ cup buttermilk

2 cups strawberries, hulled and halved (may substitute other berries or sliced peaches, nectarines, or apricots)

1 tablespoon confectioners' sugar

Fat-free whipped topping or lite ice cream

1. Preheat oven to 350°F.

2. Spray a 9" × 9" square cake pan or a 9" round cake pan with cooking spray.

3. In large bowl, combine flour, baking soda, baking powder, and salt. Set aside.

4. In a medium mixing bowl, with a hand mixer beat ½ cup sugar with margarine until light and fluffy.

5. Add egg and vanilla, and continue to whip until light and fluffy.

6. Add wet mixture to dry ingredients.

7. Slowly add buttermilk, combining until just incorporated. Do not overmix.

8. Pour batter in prepared cake pan and arrange fruit on top of batter.

9. Sprinkle fruit with remaining sugar and bake for 20 minutes or until cake is golden.

10. Cool for 10 minutes and invert cake onto plate. Lightly dust with confectioners' sugar just before serving.

11. Cut into 8 squares or wedges. Serve warm with fat-free whipped topping or lite ice cream.

SERVES: 8; CALORIES PER SERVING: 200 (cake only); DIETARY EQUIVALENT: 1 carbohydrate, 1 fruit, 1 fat

Food Tip

This cake is best served warm right out of the oven, so I often prepare the dry portion of ingredients ahead of time and mix with wet ingredients an hour or so before serving. You can just use a whisk and two bowls—no dragging out the mixer!

BANANA CHOCOLATE CREAM TART

David, my Wellness Kitchen manager, made this for my last birthday because he knows how much I love this dessert. I made him promise to only let me have one piece, but I shouldn't have worried; with everyone else lined up for it, it was gone in a flash! Make sure you use plenty of sliced bananas for a satisfying portion and the healthful benefits of high potassium, which your body needs to regulate blood pressure.

Organic canola oil cooking spray
1 cup rolled oats (raw oatmeal)
2 tablespoons whole-wheat flour
¼ cup brown sugar
3 tablespoons finely chopped almonds
¼ cup plus 1 tablespoon no-trans-fat margarine, divided
1 teaspoon vanilla
5 tablespoons white sugar, divided
1 egg yolk
⅛ teaspoon sea salt
1 tablespoon amaretto liqueur or ½ teaspoon almond extract
2 tablespoons all-purpose flour
1 cup of fat-free half-and-half
3 bananas, sliced into ¼" rounds
2 ounces 70% dark chocolate
1 tablespoon almond slivers

1. Preheat oven to 350°F.
2. Spray a 9" tart pan with cooking spray.
3. In medium bowl, combine oats, whole-wheat flour, brown sugar, almonds, ¼ cup margarine, and vanilla. Mix well with fork or fingers. Press crust evenly on sides and bottom of prepared tart pan. Bake 20 minutes or until crust is lightly browned. Cool completely.
4. In a small bowl, combine 4 tablespoons white sugar, egg yolk, salt, amaretto, and all-purpose flour. Whisk until well blended. Set aside.
5. In a small saucepan over medium heat, bring fat-free half-and-half to a boil. Slowly add sugar/egg mixture, whisking briskly. Continue to cook until pastry cream comes to a boil again. Whisking continuously, cook for 1 minute more or until cream has thickened slightly. Remove from heat; whip in the remaining margarine.
6. Scrape pastry cream into bowl, cover with plastic wrap directly on the surface of the cream, and refrigerate until cooled, about 30 minutes.
7. To assemble tart: Pour cooled pastry cream into tart shell. Arrange banana slices over the cream in a circular pattern working from the outside in. Sprinkle with remaining white sugar. Place under broiler for 30 seconds or just until bananas are lightly browned. Set aside.
8. Place chocolate in microwavable bowl. Microwave on high for 30-second intervals until chocolate is melted, stirring after each interval.
9. Drizzle melted chocolate over tart and sprinkle with slivered almonds. Refrigerate until ready to serve.

SERVES: 8; CALORIES PER SERVING: 245; DIETARY EQUIVALENT: 1 carbohydrate, 1 fruit, 1 fat

Food Tip
Make sure you continuously stir the pastry cream—you won't be able to multitask while making that part. It can easily burn and then you would have to start all over again!

STRAWBERRY HONEY TART

It's hard to believe that this tart is made with Greek yogurt. Draining Greek yogurt gives it an even richer, thicker texture, similar to cream cheese. I love eating a tasty dessert that really has health benefits! Try making this tart with a variety of summer fruits: blueberries, blackberries, raspberries, peeled peaches, nectarines, apricots, or create your favorite mix. One of my favorites is fresh peaches and blueberries. I use a low-sugar peach jam for the glaze.

2 (6-ounce) nonfat vanilla Greek yogurt (Place 2 paper towels over a sieve, add yogurt, place over a small bowl. Refrigerate and let drain for 2 hours.)

Organic canola oil cooking spray

1 cup rolled oats (raw oatmeal)

2 tablespoons wheat flour

¼ cup brown sugar

3 tablespoons finely chopped pecans or almonds

¼ cup no-trans-fat margarine

1 teaspoon vanilla

1 tablespoon orange zest

2 pints strawberries, hulled and sliced in half

1 tablespoon agave syrup or "fruit-only" jam

1. Preheat oven to 350°F.

2. Spray 9" tart pan with cooking spray.

3. In medium bowl, combine oats, flour, sugar, nuts, margarine, and vanilla. Mix well with fork or fingers.

4. Transfer to a tart pan, pressing oat mixture evenly on sides and bottom. Bake 20 minutes or until crust is lightly browned. Cool completely.

5. Add orange zest to drained yogurt and mix well. Spoon over cooled crust, spreading evenly on bottom.

6. Place berry halves in circular pattern, starting on the outside and working in.

7. Warm agave syrup in microwave for 10 seconds. Brush tops of berries with agave syrup.

8. Refrigerate until ready to serve.

SERVES: 6; CALORIES PER SERVING: 265; DIETARY EQUIVALENT: 1 oz. protein, 1 carbohydrate, 1 fruit, 1 fat

Nutrition Basics

In nutrition, there's a saying that berries are "chemopreventive." They are high in antioxidants that protect your body from certain kinds of cancers by inhibiting tumor formation and possibly turning on genes that suppress cancer cells. I suggest a daily serving of this fruit group.

BALSAMIC ROASTED STRAWBERRIES

Simple, easy, and delicious! The acid in the balsamic vinegar acts as a flavor enhancer and brings out the fruitiness of the strawberries. I always hope there is some left over to spoon over Greek yogurt or oatmeal the next morning! One cup of berries is only 60 calories, so the additional small amount of sugar and margarine still makes this an incredible low-calorie treat.

1 tablespoon no-trans-fat margarine
1 teaspoon vanilla
1 tablespoon brown sugar
1 tablespoon balsamic vinegar
3 pints fresh strawberries, hulled

1. Preheat oven to 400°F.
2. In a small, microwavable bowl, melt margarine on low power. Add vanilla, brown sugar, and balsamic vinegar; whisk until smooth.
3. Place berries in 9" × 13" baking dish and coat with balsamic mixture.
4. Roast for 40–45 minutes or until soft and reduced.
5. Serve warm over lite vanilla ice cream as a sundae, or as a topping for plain yogurt, cottage cheese, or oatmeal.

SERVES: 6 (½-cup servings); CALORIES PER SERVING: 80; DIETARY EQUIVALENT: 1 fruit, ½ fat

Food Tip
Do not wash berries until just before serving or using. Leaving damp berries in the refrigerator will cause them to spoil quickly.

GRILLED AMARETTO PEACHES WITH VANILLA ICE CREAM

I make these in midsummer when peaches are at their peak. I love the unique flavor combination of peach and almond. Pair the grilled peach halves with a small scoop of lite vanilla ice cream, dust with cinnamon, and you probably will be serving the best dessert of the summer! You can also grill nectarine halves, mango slices, or apricot halves. No matter what fruit you choose, you'll come out ahead: A slice of peach pie and a scoop of ice cream is approximately 900 calories, but the grilled peach half and a scoop of lite ice cream is 170. That's a major calorie savings, yet it's just as satisfying!

4 large, ripe peaches, blanched, peeled, halved, and pit removed
¼ cup sugar
3 tablespoons amaretto liqueur
Lite vanilla ice cream or frozen yogurt

1. Preheat lightly oiled grill to medium-low heat.
2. To blanch the peaches: Bring large pot of water to a boil. Score the bottom of each peach with an X. Put peaches in boiling water for 2–3 minutes. Use a slotted spoon to remove and place in an ice water bath. Remove skin with a paring knife. Cut peaches in half and remove pits.
3. Place sugar in shallow bowl. Roll peaches in sugar, shaking off any excess.
4. Grill peaches until sugar is melted, about 3–4 minutes. Turn over and continue grilling for 3 more minutes.
5. Brush amaretto on peaches (peaches will flame for a few seconds).
6. Remove peaches from grill and place in serving dishes. Top each with a small scoop of lite vanilla ice cream or nonfat frozen yogurt.

SERVES: 8; CALORIES PER SERVING: 150 (peaches plus 1 serving of nonfat frozen yogurt); DIETARY EQUIVALENT: 1 fruit, 1 carbohydrate

Food Tip
Blanch and peel the peaches a few hours before grilling, then place them in an airtight container and refrigerate until ready to serve. Don't worry if they turn slightly brown; they are going on the grill anyway.

BLUEBERRY COMPOTE

My son has been known to eat the entire compote in one sitting; it tastes just like blueberry pie filling! He spoons it on nonfat Greek yogurt or cottage cheese for a healthy afterschool snack. I love a scoop on a bowl of warm oatmeal topped with nonfat vanilla Greek yogurt. YUM! Blueberries are an excellent source of antioxidants and vitamins A and C. Besides oatmeal and yogurt, you can also cool it and pour over cold cereal or sliced bananas.

16 oz. frozen blueberries

1 tablespoon sugar or honey (can use non-caloric sweetener)

1 tablespoon cornstarch mixed in 2 tablespoons of cold water

1 tablespoon lemon juice

½ teaspoon cinnamon

½ teaspoon vanilla (optional)

1. Combine berries, sugar, cornstarch mixture, and lemon juice in a small saucepan.

2. Place over medium heat, bring to a boil, then reduce to a simmer for 4–5 minutes until thickened.

3. Remove from heat, add cinnamon and vanilla (if using), and stir well.

4. Serve warm or cold.

SERVES: 4; CALORIES PER SERVING: 80; DIETARY EQUIVALENT: 1 fruit

Nutrition Basics

It's true, blueberries are a superfood! They are a very concentrated source of antioxidants that reduce the risk of certain cancers. Studies show they also promote memory and cognitive health associated with aging. Many studies encourage one serving of berries per day. This is easy to do with frozen berries so readily available and economical.

PINEAPPLE WITH GINGER-VANILLA SYRUP

Look for the new hybrid pineapples labeled "gold"—they are so sweet and flavorful. The tangy sweetness of pineapple marries well with the spiciness of the ginger, and the vanilla adds a warmth that is a flavor explosion in your mouth. Addictive!

1 piece fresh ginger (3"), peeled and thinly sliced
1 vanilla bean, split and scraped
¼ cup honey
½ cup water
1 whole pineapple
Candied ginger, thinly sliced for garnish (optional)

1. In small saucepan, combine ginger, vanilla seeds, honey, and water. Bring to a boil and then reduce heat to simmer for 5–7 minutes or until thickened. Remove from heat and let cool.
2. Meanwhile, peel and cut pineapple into quarters; remove the core, and cut into spears.
3. In large plastic bag or bowl, combine pineapple and syrup.
4. Cover and refrigerate for 1 hour or longer, up to 3 days.
5. To serve, place pineapple spears in serving bowl, pour syrup over pineapple, and garnish with candied ginger or mint.

SERVES: 4; CALORIES PER SERVING: 220; DIETARY EQUIVALENT: 1 fruit

Nutrition Basics

Ginger is not only flavorful, but also good for you! Ginger contains potent compounds called gingerols that act as anti-inflammatory agents in the body and improve gastrointestinal health by relaxing the intestinal tract, resulting in less gas and nausea. Use the edge of a teaspoon to peel the ginger; it goes right over the bumps and ridges but does not result in losing as much of the ginger as a regular peeler does.

PEAR-CRANBERRY SAUCE

This cranberry sauce requires less sugar than traditional recipes since the pears add sweetness naturally. The fresh cranberries are bursting with antioxidants that help fight major diseases and promote longevity. Keep an extra bag of cranberries in your freezer to use past the holiday time, when they are hard to find in the market. (Fresh cranberries can be frozen up to 6 months.) Add a tablespoon of this sauce to your turkey sandwiches with just a touch of lite mayonnaise.

1 (12-ounce) package fresh cranberries

1 cup water

⅓ cup sugar

2 ripe pears, peeled, halved, cored, and diced into bite-sized pieces

1 teaspoon vanilla

½ teaspoon cinnamon

1. In medium saucepan, add cranberries, water, sugar, and pears.
2. Cook over medium heat until boiling, turn to medium-low heat, and continue cooking until berries pop, about 10 minutes.
3. Remove from heat; add vanilla and cinnamon.
4. Refrigerate and cover until serving time.

SERVES: 8–10 (⅓-cup servings); CALORIES PER SERVING: 65; DIETARY EQUIVALENT: 1 fruit

Nutrition Basics

If you need to decrease your sugar intake even further, reduce the sugar in this recipe to 2 tablespoons and add 1 tablespoon of stevia when removed from heat.

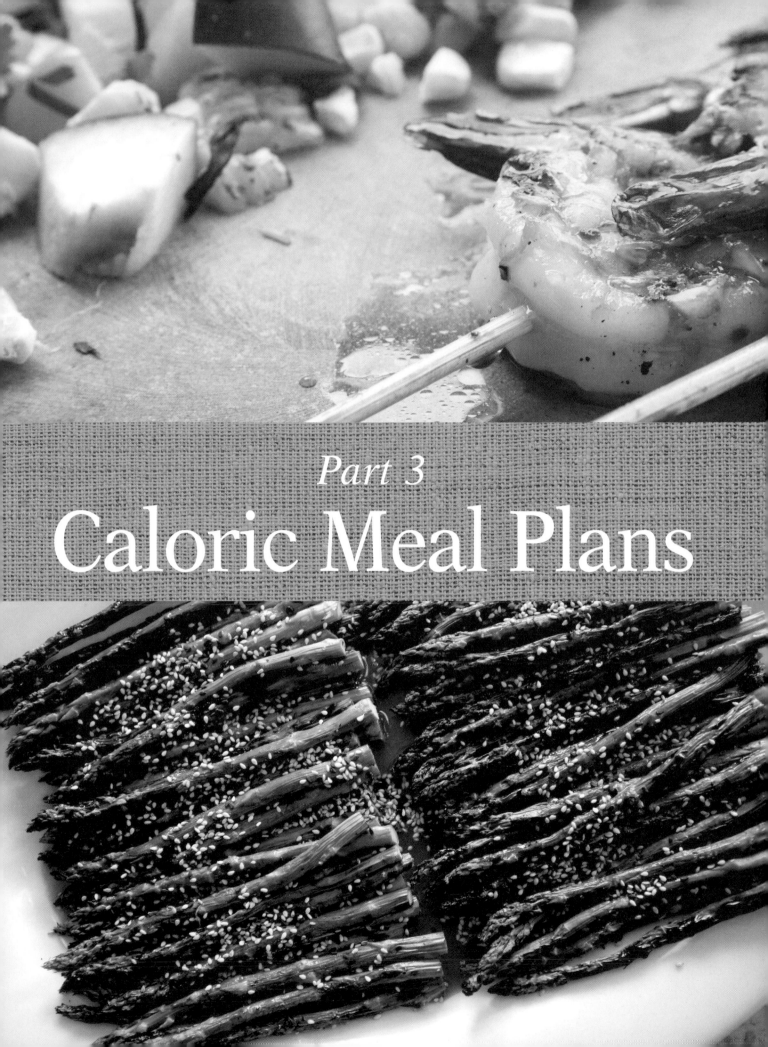

Part 3
Caloric Meal Plans

1300-Calorie Menu

DAILY TOTALS

- 8 oz. lean protein
- 4 carbohydrate servings
- 3 fruits
- Vegetables—unlimited
- 2 fats

Sample Breakfast Menus

BREAKFAST TOTALS

- 1 oz. protein
- 1 carbohydrate
- 1 fruit
- 250 calories

Breakfast Menu, Option 1

Food	Dietary Equivalent
3 oz. nonfat Greek yogurt	1 oz. protein
½ cup high-fiber cereal	1 carbohydrate
1 cup mixed berries	1 fruit

Breakfast Menu, Option 2

Food	Dietary Equivalent
1 tablespoon natural peanut butter, soy-nut butter, or almond butter	1 protein
1 slice whole-grain toast	1 carbohydrate
½ banana	1 fruit

Breakfast Menu, Option 3

Food	Dietary Equivalent
APPLE-CINNAMON OATMEAL— ⅓ cup dried oatmeal plus ⅔ cup water	1 carbohydrate, 1 fruit
3 oz. nonfat Greek yogurt	1 oz. protein

Sample Lunch Menus

LUNCH TOTALS

- 2 oz. lean protein
- 1 carbohydrate
- 1 fruit
- Vegetables—unlimited
- 1 fat
- 350–400 calories

Lunch Menu, Option 1

Food	Dietary Equivalent
½ cup tuna with 1 tablespoon lite mayonnaise	2 oz. protein, 1 fat
1 slice whole-grain bread	1 carbohydrate
15 grapes	1 fruit
Large salad with lettuce, tomato, cucumber, mushrooms, etc.	Vegetable
2 tablespoons lite dressing	1 fat

Lunch Menu, Option 2

Food	Dietary Equivalent
1 oz. turkey, 1 oz. low-fat cheese	2 oz. protein
1 slice whole-grain bread	1 carbohydrate
1 apple	1 fruit
Lettuce, tomato, mustard	Vegetable

Lunch Menu, Option 3

Food	Dietary Equivalent
2 6" soft tacos with grilled chicken or fish	2 oz. protein, 1 carbohydrate
Salsa	Vegetable

Sample Snacks

SNACK TOTALS

- 1 oz. protein
- 1 fruit
- Vegetables—unlimited
- 150 calories

Snack options

Food	Dietary Equivalent
3 oz. nonfat Greek yogurt with 1 cup fruit added	1 protein, 1 fruit
12 almonds, 1 fruit	1 fruit
1 oz. low-fat cheese, 1 fruit	1 protein, 1 fruit

Sample Dinner Menus

DINNER TOTALS

- 4 oz. lean protein
- 2 carbohydrates
- Vegetables—unlimited

- 1 fat
- 500 calories

Dinner Menu, Option 1

Food	Dietary Equivalent
4 oz. CHICKEN PICCATA	4 oz. protein
1 cup BARLEY WITH HERBS	2 carbohydrates
1–2 cups green beans or other vegetable	Vegetable
Garden salad with 2 tablespoons lite dressing	Vegetable, 1 fat

Dinner Menu, Option 2

Food	Dietary Equivalent
4 oz. SPINACH-STUFFED TURKEY MEATLOAF	4 oz. protein
1 cup garlic roasted potatoes	2 carbohydrates
1 cup roasted green beans	Vegetable
Garden salad with 2 tablespoons lite dressing	Vegetable, 1 fat

Dinner Menu, Option 3

Food	Dietary Equivalent
2 QUINOA CHILI RELLENOS	2 carbohydrates, 4 oz. protein
Caesar salad with 2 tablespoons lite dressing	Vegetable, 1 fat

1500-Calorie Menu

DAILY TOTALS

- 8 oz. lean protein
- 5 carbohydrate servings
- 3 fruits
- Vegetables—unlimited
- 2 fats

Sample Breakfast Menus

BREAKFAST TOTALS

- 1 oz. protein
- 1 carbohydrate
- 1 fruit
- 250 calories

Menu 1	
Food	**Dietary Equivalent**
3 oz. nonfat Greek yogurt	1 protein
½ cup high-fiber cereal	1 carbohydrate
1 cup mixed berries	1 fruit

Menu 2	
Food	**Dietary Equivalent**
1 tablespoon natural peanut butter, soy-nut butter, or almond butter	1 protein
1 slice whole-grain toast	1 carbohydrate
½ banana	1 fruit

Menu 3	
Food	**Dietary Equivalent**
APPLE-CINNAMON OATMEAL— ⅓ dried oatmeal plus ⅔ cup water	1 carbohydrate, 1 fruit
3 oz. nonfat Greek yogurt	1 protein

Sample Lunch Menus

LUNCH TOTALS

- 2 oz. lean protein
- 2 carbohydrates
- 1 fruit
- Vegetables—unlimited
- 1 fat
- 450 calories

Menu 1

Food	Dietary Equivalent
½ cup tuna with 1 tablespoon lite mayonnaise	2 oz. protein, 1 fat
2 slices whole-grain bread	2 carbohydrates
Large salad with lettuce, tomato, cucumber, mushrooms, etc. and 2 tablespoons lite dressing	Vegetable, 1 fat
15 grapes	1 fruit

Menu 2

Food	Dietary Equivalent
1 oz. turkey and 1 oz. low-fat cheese	2 oz. protein
1 slice whole-grain bread	1 carbohydrate
1 cup chicken noodle or other broth-based soup	1 carbohydrate
1 apple	1 fruit
Lettuce, tomato, mustard	Vegetable
1 tablespoon lite mayonnaise	1 fat

Menu 3

Food	Dietary Equivalent
2 soft tacos with grilled chicken or fish	2 oz. protein, 1 carbohydrate if single corn tortilla
½ cup beans	1 carbohydrate
Salsa	Vegetable
1 cup melon or ½ cup pineapple	1 fruit

Sample Snacks

SNACK TOTALS

- 1 protein
- 1 fruit
- Vegetables—unlimited
- 200 calories

Snack options	
Food	**Dietary Equivalent**
6 oz. nonfat Greek yogurt, less than 120 calories	1 protein
1 tablespoon natural nut butter	1 protein
12 almonds, 4 pieces dried fruit	1 fruit and 1 oz. protein
1 oz. low-fat cheese, 1 fruit	1 oz. protein and 1 fruit

Sample Dinner Menus

DINNER TOTALS

- 4 oz. lean protein
- 2 carbohydrates
- Vegetables—unlimited
- 1 fat
- 550 calories

Menu 1	
Food	**Dietary Equivalent**
4 oz. CHICKEN PICCATA	4 oz. protein
1 cup BARLEY WITH HERBS	2 carbohydrates
1 cup ORANGE-GLAZED CARROTS	Vegetable
Garden salad with 2 tablespoons lite dressing	1 fat

Menu 2	
Food	**Dietary Equivalent**
4 oz. SPINACH-STUFFED TURKEY MEATLOAF	4 oz. protein
1 cup garlic roasted potatoes	2 carbohydrates
1 cup roasted green beans	Vegetable
Garden salad with 2 tablespoons lite dressing	1 fat

Menu 3	
Food	**Dietary Equivalent**
2 QUINOA CHILI RELLENOS	2 carbohydrates, 4 oz. protein
Caesar salad with 2 tablespoons lite dressing	1 fat

1800-Calorie Menu

DAILY TOTALS

- 10 oz. lean protein
- 6 carbohydrate servings
- 3 fruits
- Vegetables—unlimited
- 3 fats

Sample Breakfast Menus

BREAKFAST TOTALS

- 1 oz. protein
- 2 carbohydrates
- 1 fruit
- Vegetables—unlimited
- 1 fat
- 400 calories

Menu 1

Food	Dietary Equivalent
1 whole egg or 3 egg whites	1 protein
2 pieces whole-grain toast	2 carbohydrates
1 cup mixed berries	1 fruit
Vegetables: peppers, mushrooms, onions, spinach, tomato, etc.	Vegetable
1 teaspoon margarine	1 fat

Menu 2

Food	Dietary Equivalent
1 tablespoon natural peanut butter, soy-nut butter, or almond butter	1 protein
2 slices whole-grain toast	2 carbohydrates
½ banana	1 fruit

Menu 3

Food	Dietary Equivalent
6 oz. nonfat Greek yogurt, less than 120 calories	1 protein
APPLE-CINNAMON OATMEAL—⅔ cup dried oatmeal plus 1⅓ cups water	2 carbohydrates, 1 fruit

Sample Lunch Menus

LUNCH TOTALS

- 3 oz. lean protein
- 2 carbohydrates
- 1 fruit
- Vegetables—unlimited
- 1 fat
- 500 calories

Menu 1

Food	Dietary Equivalent
3 oz. turkey	3 oz. protein
2 slices whole-grain bread	2 carbohydrates
1 apple	1 fruit
Lettuce, tomato, mustard	Vegetable
Garden salad with 2 tablespoons lite dressing	Vegetable, 1 fat

Menu 2

Food	Dietary Equivalent
3 soft tacos with grilled chicken, fish, or steak	3 oz. protein
3 single 6" corn tortillas	2 carbohydrates
Salsa	Vegetable
1 cup melon or ½ cup pineapple	1 fruit

Menu 3

Food	Dietary Equivalent
6" Subway turkey or chicken sandwich, double the vegetables	3 oz. protein, 2 carbohydrates
15 grapes	1 fruit
Garden salad with 2 tablespoons lite dressing	Vegetables, 1 fat

Sample Snacks

SNACK TOTALS

- 1 oz. protein
- 1 carbohydrate
- Vegetables—unlimited
- 200 calories

Snack options

Food	Dietary Equivalent
12 almonds, 6 high-fiber crackers	1 carbohydrate, 1 oz. protein
6 oz. nonfat Greek yogurt, less than 120 calories, 1 low-fat granola bar	1 protein, 1 carbohydrate
1 oz. low-fat cheese, 1 mini bag of lite popcorn	1 protein, 1 carbohydrate

Sample Dinner Menus

DINNER TOTALS

- 5 oz. lean protein
- 2 carbohydrates
- 1 fruit
- Vegetables—unlimited
- 1 fat
- 650–700 calories

Menu 1	
Food	**Dietary Equivalent**
5 oz. CHICKEN PICCATA	5 oz. protein
1 cup BARLEY WITH HERBS	2 carbohydrates
1 cup SAUTÉED GREEN BEANS WITH LEMON ZEST AND PINE NUTS	Vegetable
Garden salad with 2 tablespoons lite dressing	Vegetable, 1 fat
1 cup melon	1 fruit

Menu 2	
Food	**Dietary Equivalent**
5 oz. SPINACH-STUFFED TURKEY MEATLOAF	5 oz. protein
1 cup garlic roasted potatoes	2 carbohydrates
1 cup ROASTED GREEN BEANS WITH PINE NUTS	Vegetable
Salad with 2 tablespoons lite dressing	Vegetable, 1 fat
1 cup mixed berries	1 fruit

Menu 3	
Food	**Dietary Equivalent**
3 QUINOA CHILI RELLENOS	2 carbohydrates, 4 oz. protein
Caesar salad with 2 tablespoons lite Caesar dressing and 2 tablespoons Parmesan cheese	Vegetable, 1 fat, 1 oz. protein
1 cup pineapple	1 fruit

2000-Calorie Menu

DAILY TOTALS

- 11 oz. lean protein
- 7 carbohydrate servings
- 3 fruits
- Vegetables—unlimited
- 3 fats

Sample Breakfast Menus

BREAKFAST TOTALS

- 1 oz. protein
- 2 carbohydrates
- 1 fruit
- Vegetables—unlimited
- 1 fat
- 450–500 calories

Menu 1

Food	Dietary Equivalent
1 whole egg or 3 egg whites	1 oz. protein
2 pieces whole-grain toast	2 carbohydrates
1 orange	1 fruit
Vegetables: peppers, mushrooms, onions, spinach, tomato, etc.	Vegetable
1 teaspoon margarine	1 fat

Menu 2

Food	Dietary Equivalent
1 tablespoon natural peanut butter, soy-nut butter, or almond butter	1oz. protein
2 slices whole-grain toast	2 carbohydrates
½ banana	1 fruit

Menu 3

Food	Dietary Equivalent
6 oz. nonfat Greek yogurt, less than 120 calories	2 protein
APPLE-CINNAMON OATMEAL, ⅔ cup dried oatmeal plus 1⅓ cups water	2 carbohydrates, 1 fruit

Sample Lunch Menus

LUNCH TOTALS

- 3 oz. lean protein
- 2 carbohydrates
- 1 fruit
- Vegetables—unlimited
- 1 fat
- 550–600 calories

Menu 1

Food	Dietary Equivalent
3 oz. turkey	3 oz. protein
2 slices whole-grain bread	2 carbohydrates
1 apple	1 fruit
Lettuce, tomato, mustard	Vegetable
Garden salad with 2 tablespoons lite dressing	Vegetable, 1 fat

Menu 2

Food	Dietary Equivalent
3 soft tacos or 2 large 10" with grilled chicken, fish, or steak	3 oz. protein
3 single 6" corn tortillas	1½ carbohydrates
1 cup melon	1 fruit
Salsa	Vegetable

Menu 3

Food	Dietary Equivalent
6" Subway turkey or chicken sandwich, double the vegetables, mustard	3 oz. protein, 2 carbohydrates
15 grapes	1 fruit
Garden salad with 2 tablespoons lite dressing	Vegetable, 1 fat

Sample Snacks

SNACK TOTALS

- 1 oz. protein
- 1 carbohydrate
- Vegetables—unlimited
- 200 calories

Snack Options

Food	Dietary Equivalent
12 almonds, 6 high-fiber crackers, raw carrots	1 carbohydrate, 1 vegetable, 1 oz. protein
8 walnuts, 1 mini bag of lite popcorn	1 protein, 1 carbohydrate
6 oz. nonfat Greek yogurt, less than 120 calories, ½ cup high-fiber cereal	1 protein, 1 carbohydrate

Sample Dinner Menus

DINNER TOTALS

- 6 oz. lean protein
- 2 carbohydrates
- 1 fruit
- Vegetables—unlimited
- 1 fat
- 700–750 calories

Menu 1

Food	Dietary Equivalent
6 oz. CHICKEN PICCATA	6 oz. protein
1 cup BARLEY WITH HERBS	2 carbohydrates
1 cup ROASTED SPAGHETTI SQUASH WITH PARMESAN	Vegetable
Garden salad with 2 tablespoons lite dressing	Vegetable, 1 fat
1 cup melon	1 fruit

Menu 2

Food	Dietary Equivalent
6. oz. SPINACH-STUFFED TURKEY MEATLOAF	6 oz. protein
1 cup garlic roasted potatoes	2 carbohydrates
1 cup SAUTÉED GREEN BEANS WITH LEMON ZEST AND PINE NUTS	Vegetable
Salad with 2 tablespoons lite dressing	Vegetable, 1 fat
1 cup mixed berries	1 fruit

Menu 3

Food	Dietary Equivalent
2 QUINOA CHILI RELLENOS	2 carbohydrates, 4 oz. protein
Caesar salad with 2 tablespoons lite Caesar dressing and 4 tablespoons Parmesan cheese	1 fat, 2 oz. protein
1 cup pineapple	1 fruit

Seasonal Special Occasion Menus

I know that many in the field of nutrition and medicine promote the concept of "eat to live," and of course I completely agree that we need to focus on health in our daily lives. But I also truly believe that good food is one of the most inevitable and accessible pleasures, a real necessity of life. I believe that one can "eat to live" but there is no reason that it can't consist of food that is wonderful in flavor and totally satisfying, physically and psychologically. Special occasions mean special food to most of us. A gathering of friends and family around a table with "celebration" food allows us to reconnect and recharge, giving us a sense of who we are. Celebrations allow us to recognize the importance of an event or person and just how powerful our close relationships are. Throughout our lives we have learned to associate celebrations with foods that are not generally part of daily intake. While I cannot say we should have stuffing daily, I cannot imagine a Thanksgiving without stuffing; it would not seem like Thanksgiving at all to me!

Really good food is made with wholesome, fresh ingredients cooked in a simple, interesting way. Since many of us have "celebration association" with certain foods, I have tried to include them here, but tweaked them to be more healthy and flavorful. Your guests will not know that the Pear-Cranberry Sauce (Chapter 8) is not the usual high-sugar sauce; they will just think "Yum!" Nor will they think that the Chocolate Cupcakes with Peanut Butter Icing (Chapter 8) for a birthday celebration are anything but the real deal!

I have planned more special occasion menus than I can count for my friends, family, and the Wellness Kitchen. I often get panicked calls from those desperate for a menu that works—appealing, fantastic foods that go together, are easy to make, and can be done in minimal time. I often thought this would make a great business: just provide an easy menu and recipes so anyone can pull off entertaining in style! Since it is my goal that you use this book for almost all your cooking, including special occasions, I have pulled together menus and recipes to guide you in making your celebrations fantastic, and I guarantee you rave reviews. Menus are seasonal, which means the freshest and most flavorful food. Many of the recipes can be made ahead of time so you too can enjoy the celebration!

Spring

- Couscous and Arugula Salad with Fresh Basil Dressing (Chapter 3)
- Asparagus Soup (Chapter 4)
- Chicken Marsala (Chapter 5)
- Barley with Herbs (Chapter 7)
- Orange-Glazed Carrots (Chapter 6)
- Balsamic Roasted Strawberries with Vanilla Ice Cream (Chapter 8)
- Curried Coconut Carrot Soup (Chapter 4)
- Thai Kale Salad (Chapter 3)
- Asian Flank Steak with Sweet Slaw (Chapter 5)
- Grilled Asparagus with Sesame Chili Vinaigrette (Chapter 6)
- Pineapple with Ginger-Vanilla Syrup (Chapter 8)

Summer

- Fire-Roasted Peppers Stuffed with Feta (Chapter 2)
- Mixed greens with Lite Lemon Vinaigrette (Chapter 3)
- Puréed Zucchini Basil Soup (Chapter 4)
- Texas BBQ Chicken (Chapter 5)
- Tabouleh Salad with Grilled Vegetables (Chapter 3)
- Grilled Amaretto Peaches with Vanilla Ice Cream (Chapter 8)
- Roasted Tomato Soup with Parmesan Crostini (Chapter 4)
- Grilled Naan with Herbs and Feta (Chapter 4)
- Spinach Salad with Wheat Berries and Feta (Chapter 3)
- Cedar-Grilled Salmon with Fresh Herbs (Chapter 5)
- Roasted Green Beans with Pine Nuts (Chapter 6)
- Buttermilk Cake with Summer Fruit (Chapter 8)

Fall

- Hummus with Baked Pita Chips, crudités (Chapter 2)
- Puréed Broccoli Cheese Soup (Chapter 4)
- Pulled Turkey Sandwiches with Cranberry BBQ Sauce (Chapter 5)
- Chipotle Cilantro Slaw (Chapter 3)
- Chocolate Cupcakes with Peanut Butter Icing (Chapter 8)

Thanksgiving

- Ginger Carrot Soup (Chapter 4)
- Farmers' Market Salad with Roasted Butternut Squash (Chapter 3)
- Perfect Roasted Turkey (Chapter 5)
- Cauliflower Purée (Chapter 6)
- Lime-Glazed Roasted Yams (Chapter 6)
- Honey-Roasted Root Vegetables (Chapter 6)
- Harvest Stuffing (Chapter 7)
- Pear-Cranberry Sauce (Chapter 8)
- Apple Cranberry Crisp (Chapter 8)

Winter

- Red Carrot Soup (Chapter 4)
- Date, Pear, and Goat Cheese Salad with Pomegranate Vinaigrette (Chapter 3)
- Perfect Roasted Chicken with Broccoli Rabe and Potatoes (Chapter 5)
- Chocolate Walnut Cookies (Chapter 8)

Holiday

- Crab Cakes (Chapter 2)
- Sherried Mushroom Soup (Chapter 4)
- Arugula Salad with Apples and Mint (Chapter 3)
- Salmon Wellington (Chapter 5)
- Sautéed Balsamic Brussels Sprouts (Chapter 6)
- Ginger Pear Spice Cake (Chapter 8)

Kitchen Conversion Tables

These equivalents have been slightly rounded to make measuring easier.

Liquid Volume Conversions			
1 teaspoon	-	⅓ tablespoon	5 ml.
1 tablespoon	½ fl. oz.	3 teaspoons	15 ml.
2 tablespoons	1 fl. oz.	⅛ cup, 6 teaspoons	30 ml.
¼ cup	2 fl. oz.	4 tablespoons	60 ml.
⅓ cup	2⅔ fl. oz.	5 tablespoons + 1 teaspoon	80 ml.
½ cup	4 fl. oz.	8 tablespoons	120 ml.
⅔ cup	5⅓ fl. oz.	10 tablespoons + 2 teaspoons	160 ml.
¾ cup	6 fl. oz.	12 tablespoons	180 ml.
1 cup	8 fl. oz., ½ pint	16 tablespoons	240 ml.
2 cups	16 fl. oz., 1 pint	32 tablespoons	480 ml.
4 cups	32 fl. oz.	1 quart	946 ml.
1 pint	16 fl. oz.	32 tablespoons	480 ml.
2 pints	32 fl. oz.	1 quart	946 ml.
8 pints	1 gallon, 128 fl. oz.	4 quarts	3785 ml/3.78 liters
4 quarts	1 gallon, 128 fl. oz.	1 gallon	3785 ml/3.78 liters
1 liter	1.057 quarts	34 fl. oz.	1000 ml.
1 gallon	4 quarts	128 fl. oz.	3785 ml. / 3.78 ml.

Dry Weight Conversions		
1 oz.	-	30 grams
2 oz.	-	55 grams
3 oz.	-	85 grams
4 oz.	¼ lb.	125 grams
8 oz.	½ lb.	240 grams
12 oz.	¾ lb.	375 grams
16 oz.	1 lb.	454 grams
32 oz.	2 lbs.	907 grams
¼ lb.	4 oz.	125 grams
½ lb.	8 oz.	240 grams
¾ lb.	12 oz.	375 grams
1 lb.	16 oz.	454 grams
2 lbs.	32 oz.	907 grams
1 kilogram	2.2 lbs., 35.2 oz.	1000 grams

Index